*Philosophy through
the Looking-Glass*

Philosophy through the Looking-Glass

Language, nonsense, desire

JEAN-JACQUES LECERCLE

Professor of English Language and Literature, University of Nanterre

OPEN COURT

La Salle, Illinois

OPEN COURT and the above logo are registered
in the U.S. patent and trademark office.

OC 877   10 9 8 7 6 5 4 3 2 1

ISBN 0-8126-9004-4

First published 1985

© 1985 Jean-Jacques Lecercle

Set in 11/12 Baskerville II

Printed and bound in Great Britain by
Anchor Brendon Ltd,
Tiptree, Essex

Library of Congress Cataloging in Publication Data

Lecercle, Jean-Jacques
Philosophy through the looking-glass.

(Problems of modern European thought)
Includes bibliographies and index.
1. Languages – Philosophy.   2. Meaning (Philosophy)
I. Title   II. Series
P106.L33   1985   149'.94   85–15283

ISBN 0-8126-9004-4

Contents

Acknowledgements

I would like to thank the editors of this series, Alan Montefiore and Jonathan Rée, for their untiring encouragement and help, without which this book would never have been written. Alan Montefiore has finally convinced me that meaning what one says and saying what one means are not quite the same thing. Jonathan Rée's objections to one chapter have often induced me to write the next; he has also suggested innumerable improvements to the text. Neither of them is, of course, responsible for the mistakes that may remain.

Claire L'Enfant of Hutchinson has, with quiet efficiency and constant courtesy, more or less kept me to my schedule.

My wife, Ann Lecercle-Sweet, has read, discussed, and often corrected the first draft of each chapter.

My gratitude also goes to Sally Sweet and Noreen Vivian, who have welcomed me in their houses and patiently answered my countless philological questions.

Lastly, I wish to thank the generations of Nanterre students on whom I have imposed the contents of Chapter 2.

Jean-Jacques Lecercle
Paris

Introduction

Freud's unwitting but notorious patient, Schreber, was convinced that God had chosen him to bring the new Messiah into the world, and that his body was therefore being turned into that of a woman. He also believed that everyone he met had died, that what he saw and heard was only fleeting images of people, ghostly apparitions sent by God to taunt and tempt. When he could no longer bear the ceaseless teasing of aggressive voices, he screamed as loud as he could, which annoyed the neighbours, especially at night, and meant that he had to be restrained.

The case is clear: he suffered from acute paranoia, the main symptom of which is delirium. But not all the ideas suggested by the word 'delirium' fit his condition: there was excitement, sometimes to the point of frenzy; hallucinations were plentiful and long-lasting; but there was no mental confusion or wildly absurd language. Or at least, these symptoms disappeared when, without in any way renouncing his delirious convictions, he started writing his memoirs, in order to convince those who had committed him to an institution of his sanity, and to present his convictions to a wider audience. If Schreber's fits of incoherent shouting were a case of 'delirium', perhaps another word should be found to describe the *reflexive* phase, in which he writes down his peculiar ideas, but also attempts to analyse them.

One form of 'delirium', therefore, is of particular interest not only to the psychiatrist, but also the philosopher: the kind of reflexive 'delirium' in which the patient expounds his system, attempts to go beyond the limits of his madness, to introduce method into it, in which also he hesitates between science, after which he strives and for which he longs, and the wildest fiction. Mere delirium is poor and repetitive: this other type, which I shall call, for reasons soon to be explained, *délire*, is rich and imaginative; it calls for the respect and attention of the man of science, of the psychologist and the philosopher. Helen Smith, the Geneva medium in whom Saussure was briefly interested, talked in an imaginary tongue which she sometimes claimed was Martian and sometimes Sanskrit. Saussure quickly saw through this delirious production,[1]* recognizing ill-disguised French sentences in it. On the other hand, Perceval, the Victorian schizophrenic rediscovered by Bateson, or Wolfson, 'l'étudiant en idiomes dément', either anticipate the psychiatrist's discoveries (in the case of Perceval, Freud's analyses of the psychopathology of everyday life) or open up new vistas for him: their wildest fictions contain an element of truth, their *délire* an element of science.

Let us go one step further, from method in madness to madness in method. There are privileged moments in the history of thought when the clouds of unknowing seem to dissolve, when a fundamental break is made, a Copernician revolution overturns the old pre-scientific order, a new continent opens up for science. Or so the rationalist tradition in epistemology, from which some of the preceding metaphors are borrowed, tells us. It is of course debatable whether sciences advance in this fashion, whether there is such a thing as an 'epistemological break'. But if there ever was one in linguistics, the name of Saussure should be associated with it. Before Saussure, there was only an estimable field of study, philology, within which, no doubt, some notable results, like the reconstruction of Indo-European, had been achieved; after Saussure, there was the alluring glamour and rapid development of a new science, linguistics.

This picture is unjust and erroneous – not only because Saussure was first (and, to himself, foremost) a philologist, whose masterpiece was the *Mémoire sur le système des voyelles dans les langues indo-européennes* (1878), but because we have come to realize that there are two Saussures, or rather that, behind (or beneath) the founder of a new science and the author of the celebrated *Cours*, there is another, Hyde-like, character, the demented seeker of anagrams. The rather staid scientist confided to his notebooks the (never published) results of his research into archaic Latin verse; he thought that, beneath the lines of a Latin hymn, he could find an anagram of the name of the God to whom the text was dedicated. Since it can be plainly shown (as he himself came to realize) that this is not the case, we are back with a form of delirious conviction. But not with delirium, for Saussure always treated his idea as a hypothesis: he attempted to prove it, and when he realised he could not do so, he

* Superior figures refer to the Notes at the end of each chapter.

2

abandoned it. Madness there was to a certain extent, but he remained firmly within the boundaries of method.

Thus, I find myself with a threefold distinction: first, unreflexive delirium, the repetitive and unimaginative discourse of paranoiacs; then a reflexive delirium which I am calling *délire*, created by talented patients who write down their experience and devote their time to argument and what they take to be science; and finally, the shady activities of a scientist who yields to a mild form of mania, '*une idée fixe*'.

The object of the present book is the *délire* which is not merely delirium: both a concept, widely used in contemporary French philosophy (we shall have to ask ourselves how a psychiatric term can become a philosophical concept), and a tradition, a corpus of delirious texts (not produced only by mental patients, but also by poets, novelists or linguists) and of analyses of *délire* (in linguistics, in psychoanalysis, in philosophy). It will soon appear that *délire* provides a new approach to the classic philosophical problem of sense and nonsense, that it is the discursive locus where philosophy consorts with the March Hare: as we shall see, the peculiarity of *délire* does not reside in its lack of meaning (the confusion of words involves the meaninglessness of the propositions uttered), but in its surfeit of it.

In the years 1906–10, when he was giving the series of lectures which became the posthumous *Cours*, Ferdinand de Saussure was engaged in private research on a variety of texts, ranging from the archaic Latin poetry of the Saturnian verse to the Rig Veda and the Niebelungen. To his own amazement, he discovered that they all conformed to similar rules of composition, which went far beyond the well-known practice of alliteration and rhyme. At first, he thought that a law of compensation was at work, ensuring that each sound in a given line had its equivalent in the next. But as he pursued his research, the discovery became more specific: the composition of a poetic text in that tradition was based on a pre-text, a word which provided the text with its main theme, but did not necessarily appear on the surface. Behind the text, there lay the anagram which accounted for its origin and at least part of its meaning: a hymn was phonetically built with the syllables that form the god's name. An oracle, mentioned by Livy, not only contained the names of the Pythia who uttered it and of Apollo who spoke through it: to the inquisitive eye, in the shape of an anagram, it revealed the secret message that Apollo the devious could not express clearly.

A poetic text, therefore, was a cryptogram concealing a pretext. The presence of theme-words could be ascertained by the discovery of a *locus princeps*, usually part of a line situated at the beginning of a text or passage, in which the anagram was particularly systematic or obvious, and which began and ended with the same sounds as the concealed word. Thus, Lucretius's *De Natura Rerum* begins with a hymn to Venus. In the following lines (10–13) Saussure found an anagram of Aphrodite:

> *Nam simul ac species patefactast verna diei,*
> *et reserata viget genitabilis aura favoni,*
> *aeriae primum volucres te, diva, tuumque*
> *significant initum perculsae corda tua vi.*[2]

What Saussure calls the 'mannequin', i.e. the *locus princeps* occurs in line 12: 'Aeriae primum volucres tE'. In the four lines Saussure also found the requisite syllables: 'af' in 'aurAFavoni', 'rod' (inverted into 'ord') in 'perculsae cORDa', 'di' in 'te DIva', 'it' in 'inITum' and 'te' at the end of the 'mannequin'.

I have quoted one of Saussure's more convincing examples. Yet even here there is no doubt that he stretches the bounds of plausibility. At least one objection immediately comes to mind: if the rules are lax enough and the context sufficient, almost any word could be found in any text. Indeed, Saussure himself soon became aware of this proliferation of anagrams: not only did he find several in the same passage, but he started finding them even in Caesar's *Commentaries* and Cicero's letters. The device was not confined to poetry, not even to formally written prose: even in his most relaxed moments, Cicero could not help using anagrams. Saussure's conviction began to fade.

But Saussure's main reason for stopping his research and keeping the results unpublished, was that he had failed to find objective proof. He realized that there was no historical evidence whatsoever for what, from the extent of his discoveries, must have been one of the most common techniques of literary composition. Imagine someone suddenly noticing that in many poems the lines rhyme, and that no one has ever mentioned it before, even in treatises on poetic composition. The question of interpretative madness immediately arises: unless proof is produced, there is little difference between this kind of discovery and a mental patient's illuminations. Saussure, who was finding anagrams everywhere, looked for such proof. He tried to reinterpret cryptic hints in ancient writers. He wrote to the headmaster of Eton to inquire about one Thomas Johnson, a seventeenth-century author of Latin verse whose poems had been used for teaching in the college. Eventually, he approached one

4

of his contemporaries, an Italian professor who also wrote in Latin. The answer must have been negative, for Saussure abandoned the whole project shortly afterwards.

Saussure's scientific sanity is shown by the fact that he was able to treat his discovery as a hypothesis, and to discard it when it proved untenable. Yet there is no doubt that an element of *délire* intrudes in the attempt: the length and scope of the search, the enthusiasm and energy that Saussure devoted to it are ample indication of this. Saussure saw through the linguistic inventions of Helen Smith, but he had one thing in common with her: a sense of illumination and certainty. And this is one of the characteristics of the tradition I am going to explore. The delirious patient and the inspired linguist, driven by conviction, both go beyond the bounds of common sense. Another characteristic, again common to the medium and the linguist, is the proliferation of discoveries: once the key has been found, the inquirer realizes that it opens all doors. Helen Smith's mediumnic 'novels' multiplied: not being content with her incarnation as a Martian lady, she also, in her trances, became the favourite wife of a fifteenth century Indian prince (and she duly spoke a meaningless jargon interspersed with a few words of Sanskrit) and a reincarnation of Marie-Antoinette. As we have seen, Saussure's discovery soon became the key to all texts, and anagrams in a single text tended to multiply.

But even if we take Helen Smith's experience of possession seriously, it differs in one essential respect from Saussure's research. As Saussure himself noted, Helen Smith's linguistic productions in Martian and Sanskrit were poor. She was not interested in language, which for her was a tiresome instrument which she was compelled to use to communicate her visions. Not so Saussure, of course: a love for language and its workings is discernible in all his endeavours. He never forgets the *reality* of language, the materiality of its sounds, the ways in which the words are organized by syntax. In other words, the key which he discovers is a linguistic device, which operates both in and on language and only generalizes perfectly acceptable procedures. As Starobinski notes,[3] poets often compose their texts, consciously or unconsciously, by using the same phonetic material, the same syllables over and over again. The discovery of anagrams as a technique of poetic composition is but one step further in the same direction. It is true that by taking that step Saussure crosses the border of common sense. But he does this because he is impelled by his love of language, and in a direction which language itself indicates, so that it is by no means certain that his discoveries are mere delusions (perhaps this is what he himself decided when he abandoned his research) rather than the unveiling of the deepest workings of language. The posterity of the 'other' Saussure suggests that the second solution might be the right one.

This insistence on the reality of language, this respect for the system of *langue*, is what prevents Saussure's *parole* from dissolving into delirium. But his elaborate construction of a fantastic key to all texts took him away from the arid solidity of science. He dwelt on the frontier between science and unreason, in that no man's land where the madman, the poet and the scientist meet, where the philosopher sits down to tea with the March Hare: the fine distinction between madness and good sense has, on that borderline which I have called *délire*, no importance, for, as the Cheshire Cat says, in a world where everyone is mad, nobody is.

It is the aim of this book to explore the delirious borderline between sense and nonsense. *Délire* as I shall now use the word is a form of discourse, which questions our most common conceptions of *language* (whether expressed by linguists or by philosophers), where the old philosophical question of the emergence of sense out of *nonsense* receives a new formulation, where the material side of language, its origin in the human body and *desire*, are no longer eclipsed by its abstract aspect (as an instrument of communication or expression). Language, nonsense, desire: *délire* accounts for the relations between these three terms.

The dominant tradition in the conception of language regards it as an instrument for communication – although natural languages are imperfect instruments which have to be purified or translated into logical language. Language enables us to live in society, it is the vector of our everyday intercourse with our fellow men; it also enables us to phrase our attempts to express truth. In other words, language makes sense; in spite of its shortcomings, it conveys our search for truth and notes down the rules of our method. It can do all this – which allows, among other things, the writing of books – because of its abstract character: an intellectual faculty (language), realized through ideal systems (natural languages as *langues*.) But this characterization of language, vague and unsatisfactory as it is, is itself an abstraction. It deliberately ignores various experiences of language which are the daily lot of every speaker: words often fail us, that is, fail to express what we mean; or, conversely, they express too much, more than we mean: they utter what we refuse to recognize, what we would rather have left unsaid. In other words, language becomes tainted by desire, by the actions and passions of our body, by its instinctual drives. Language loses its capacity to communicate. But it can also, at the same time, increase its power: it ceases to be controlled by the subject but on the contrary rules over him. Instead of truth, we have fiction; instead of sense, nonsense or absurdity; instead of abstraction, desire. Instead of method, we have the madness of *délire*.

Another tradition emerges, suppressed but persistent, in which language is both 'liberated' (from the systematic rules of its structure: a doubtful benefit) and dominant (it imposes its workings on the subject, who loses mastery). Mad linguists and 'fous littéraires' make up this tradition. This is the age-old tradition of 'speaking in tongues' (which goes back to the ancient religious practices mentioned in Paul's *Epistle to the Corinthians*), of possessed visionaries, like the nineteenth-century Irvingite sect which Perceval joined before he was locked up. It is also the tradition of linguistic cranks, inspired by a love of language which knows no bounds, who kept going back to the insoluble problems of the origin of language (Brisset, as we shall see, discovered it in the croaking of frogs) or of the universal language spoken before Babel. Raymond Queneau called these eccentrics (together with those who squared the circle and proved that the earth did not move) 'fous littéraires': he started writing a thesis on the subject, and ended up including the material in one of his novels, *Les Enfants du Limon*. And the term 'literary' is apt. The tradition is rife with eccentric poets and novelists, whose devices for literary composition defy the sanest rules of poetic method: Roussel is the best known of these.

The suppressed tradition of *délire* is not autonomous: it depends on the dominant tradition of controlled and instrumental language. When it is mentioned by St Paul, the act of speaking in tongues is, if not condemned, confined to definite circumstances: when the spirit impels you; but speaking ordinary language is a much better way of preaching the gospel. As in the dialectic of master and slave, the relation of dependence is reciprocal: the dominated haunts the dominant, and 'returns' within it. This accounts for the fascination which the tradition of *délire* has always had for poets; it also accounts for the fact that it has now found its philosophers. Therefore the *philosophical* tradition of *délire* which I shall explore has two aspects: a theory of *délire*, of its liberating value; and a theory of the reduction of *délire*, of *délire* as a symptom of the dereliction of the linguistic order.

7

Even if *délire* is primarily a psychiatric concept, it should not come as a surprise that it has found its philosophers: for the love of language which is the essential characteristic of delirious writers has reflexive value; it produces, almost by spontaneous generation, amateur linguists. Paradoxically, those (i.e. most of us) who *use* language as a tool treat it as if it were transparent, the mere vehicle of thought (as the French proverb has it: 'ce qui se conçoit bien s'exprime clairement' – if the ideas are clear, so is their expression). They leave the inquiries into the nature of workings of language to specialists, linguists or philosophers. On the other hand, the logophiliacs of our tradition[4] do care for language; they are interested in its power, in the way it works: they are 'natural' philosophers of language. And they anticipate the work of the professional who takes them seriously: schizophrenics teach Freud and pave the way for Deleuze; demented linguists go beyond structuralism. Sometimes, as in the case of Saussure, the two roles, and the two aspects of the tradition coincide in a single person.

One thing is still unclear: the choice of the *French* word, '*délire*'. I must justify its untranslatability. First, I cannot find an English equivalent for it. The obvious candidate is 'delirium', which shares the etymology and use in psychiatric contexts. But it is too narrow: there is no delirium outside psychiatry, and wider uses are both rare and explicitly metaphorical (the *Oxford English Dictionary* (*OED*) quotes George Eliot: 'the gorgeous delirium of gladiatorial shows'). The word can describe Schreber's fits of screaming, but not Saussure's search for anagrams.

The other possible translations are equally unsatisfactory. Neither 'delusion' nor 'frenzy', 'mania', 'raving' (or even 'ranting') have the meaning I am looking for. Thus, 'delusion' (the *OED* defines it as 'anything that deceives the mind with a false impression; a deception; a fixed false opinion with regard to objective things, esp. a form of mental derangement') points out an important element in my definition of *délire*: its systematic aspect, the long and painful construction of a system, an '*idée fixe*'. But since it is defined in terms of falsehood or deception, 'delusion' fails to capture the element of truth that is present in *délire*: logophiliacs suffer from a delusion about language, but it is one which is founded on the reality of language. There are no deliberate anagrams where Saussure seeks them, but language does work by organizing phonic material in a similar fashion, which has been called paragrammatic.[5] In other words, the abstraction of language is based on the material expression of oral drives, on shouts and screams.

8

The same goes for the other possible translations. Therefore, I find myself with a cluster of partial equivalents, but no single English word. However, this might be taken to mean that the French word is ambiguous, and that all that is lost in translation is a possibility of confusion. The difficulty here is familiar to translators of philosophical texts: even if we leave aside the puns in Heidegger and Lacan (but they are not really exceptions), there are many cases where the original term had to be preserved, 'en français dans le texte'. The best known examples are perhaps Saussure's *langue* and *parole*. But my reason for not adopting an English equivalent for *délire* is a little stronger: to assign an English name to the concept would assume a conception of language on which the concept of *délire* casts doubt. In order to translate '*délire*', I would have to have Humpty-Dumpty's confidence in the speaking subject's mastery over language, I would have to be prepared to state that 'glory' means 'a nice knock-down argument', if I decide that it does. And Alice's objection to this, based on a conventional theory of naming ('glory' means what it does by convention, and nobody can alter this on his/her own) is inadequate. *Délire*, as an experience of possession, of loss of control by the subject, reverses the relation of mastery. As Humpty-Dumpty says, the question is 'who is master?'. In the case of *délire* the answer is: language.

Of course, it is to be hoped that in writing about *délire* I shall not myself be delirious (although the question of reflexivity is bound to arise at some stage). But we cannot escape the dependence of a concept on the language – and the culture – in which it appears. In other words, the (philosophical) grammar of *délire* is dependent on the function of the word in French sentences. Grammatically speaking, then, the word '*délire*' comes in three forms: as an intransitive verb ('*il délire*'), a present participle ('*délirant*'), sometimes used as a noun ('*le délirant*': he who utters *délire*) and a noun. The verb denotes an action, but can take no object: *délire* is a form of discourse, but not the same sort of speech-act as 'asking' (one asks a question) or 'telling' (one tells a tale). The suggestion is that the act is unintentional, that the subject of *délire* is not in control of his own speech production (we can oppose, for instance, 'il parle', which suggests that I, the listener, do not understand what the speaker says, although I am aware that he is talking, to 'il dit que. . .', a transitive verb with a completive clause as object, where I understand, and am able to repeat, paraphrase, or translate).[6] The present participle, used as a noun, denotes the subject of an action limited in time (as opposed

9

to a lasting state, which is one of the interpretations of the English 'delirious'): *délire* is the present production of delirious discourse, it is not a condition, like paranoia, even if it is chronic. (The relation between '*délirer*' and '*délirant*' is like that between 'rave' and 'raving'.) The noun itself is used to designate either the state of someone who is delirious, or the contents of the delirious act, i.e. a text or corpus of texts. This is where the grammar of *délire* is language-specific: in this shift, which turns *délire* into an object, which can be isolated, divided into parts and studied. Nor is it appropriate to decree that this shift is philosophically unacceptable, that propositions like 'Schreber's *délire* is such and such' need to be translated into others of the form 'Schreber *délires* (verb) in such and such a way'. The lesson of *délire* is that we must take this shift as an irreducible fact. There is a link between this argument and the preceding one; language, after all, is master: such is the lesson of *délire*. In a way, this is a book about the shift which has turned an intransitive verb into a noun denoting an object (in this case, an object of philosophical inquiry).

So far, I have offered three related arguments for my use of the word '*délire*': an argument of convenience (I cannot find a single equivalent for the French word); a reflexive argument (I refuse to choose an English name for the concept, because this would contradict the idea of *délire*); and a grammatical argument (the grammar of *délire* is language-specific). I shall now add a fourth, a historical one: *délire* is not only the name of a concept, it is an indication of a cultural conjuncture, of a tradition. The French word must be preserved because there is no tradition of *délire* in Anglo-Saxon cultures, no way of subsuming such a variety of texts under a single concept. I shall sketch two important aspects of this cultural context – structural linguistics and Lacanian psychoanalysis – in order to account for the appearance of a philosophy of *délire* in the work of Gilles Deleuze (Chapters 3 and 5).

Philosophy is often defined in terms of its relation to science. In French schools, they still say that a philosopher is a specialist in generalities (the real specialist being the scientist, who studies a definite object). The task of philosophy is to justify the practice of scientists. The difficulty is that philosophers often find it irksome to be relegated to an ancillary status, and that, at least in what is sometimes called 'exact' sciences, scientists pay little attention to the precepts that philosophy produces for their benefit. But social scientists are usually more tractable: they are unsure of the scientificity of their subjects, and more willing to accept the help offered by the philosopher, whose task it is to establish whether historical materialism or psychoanalysis, to mention the two most controversial cases, are scientific or not. Contemporary French philosophy has been largely concerned with these problems. It nurtured a distinguished school of rationalist epistemology (Bachelard, Canguilhem), and the status of historical materialism and psychoanalysis was always an important question (one need only mention the role of a critique of epistemology in Althusser's version of Marxism, or his early article on Lacan). In this context, linguistics came to occupy a prominent position on the French philosophic scene. It is a social science, and therefore more open to philosophical influences. But among social sciences, it is undoubtedly the one whose claim to scientificity is least questionable: so much so that it has come to provide a paradigm for other social sciences, from anthropology to psychoanalysis. For philosophers, it has another advantage, in its closeness to one of the traditional sectors of philosophy, the philosophy of language. Even if the two disciplines are kept separate, they presumably have a common frontier. Linguistics therefore became an inspiration not only for other social sciences, but also for philosophy: structural linguistics gave rise to the philosophy of structuralism, which was an important part of French culture in the 1960s and 1970s.

It may sound paradoxical that *délire* should have a place in a tradition dominated by the concepts of structure and system. For is not *délire* that which dissolves linguistic and psychological structures, and which cannot be accounted for in terms of a system? The paradox is only apparent, though, for *délire* is seen by structural analysis of discourse as its *limit*. It is the greatest challenge that can be offered to structuralism: if structuralism can account even for *délire*, then its validity will be proved. *Délire* as a concept is, as Vincent Descombes has noted,[7] a paradoxical product of structuralism. So *délire* is not only (as discourse) the embodiment of a second aspect of language, the shady aspect of the expression of instinctual drives as opposed to the abstraction of language as an instrument of communication and rational argument, it is also (as concept) the main object of a different conception of language, opposed to the structuralist one, and emphasizing the materiality of words and their relation to the subject's desire. There is, therefore, a linguistics of *délire*, both dependent on and opposed to structural linguistics; it takes the literary tradition of *délire* as its text.

But *délire* is not a mere by-product of structuralism. It cannot be easily reduced, for it raises the problem of the relationship between the structure and a subject: a spectre is haunting structuralism, the spectre of the subject. In French linguistics, the spectre appeared in the autochthonous tradition of *énonciation* (the process of *énonciation* involves the uttering subject, in contrast to the utterance, *l'énoncé*, which can – and indeed must – be studied independently of any subject). But the methodical study of shifters and other forms of indication of the uttering subject within his utterance is not sufficient. The tension between structure and subject worked its way into philosophy. In Marxism, probably the dominant school in France in the 1960s, it took the ultimately unsatisfactory form of a separation between a version of Marxism influenced by structuralism (roughly, the early work of Althusser, with its 'theoretical anti-humanism') and 'humanist' Marxism (various versions, from Sartre to Garaudy). So it found its best expression, and a tentative solution, in the Lacanian version of psychoanalysis, sometimes termed 'philosophical', or 'structuralist' or 'linguistic',[8] which was seen as announcing a structural 'science of the subject'. I shall have occasion to return to this both in Chapter 2 (The linguistics of *délire*) and in Chapter 4 (The psychoanalysis of *délire*): the reader will find a critical introduction to Lacan's main themes in David Archard's work on the unconscious.[9] All I wish to do now is to indicate two directions which the Lacanian doctrine takes, for both are relevant to the study of *délire*.

The first concerns linguistics: the characteristic of Lacan, as is now well-known, is that he builds on the work of Saussure and Jakobson, and places language and its workings (analysed in terms of rhetoric) at the centre of his return to Freud. One thing is certain after reading Lacan's interpretation of Freud: Freud is a great linguist. The consequence of this is that desire is inextricably linked to language (in the famous Lacanian formula, of which Archard gives a particularly lucid exposition, desire is defined as a metonymy, 'the metonymy of the want-to-be'). *Délire* then becomes a prime object of interest, and, following Freud, we all have to learn something from President Schreber.

The second direction takes us towards philosophy: from Freud's *ego* (a psychological concept), we go to Lacan's *subject*, a philosophical concept. Language as inhabited by the (desiring) subject, the subject as possessed by language: if the first formulation corresponds to the object of the psychoanalyst's study, the second is a good description of the phenomenon of *délire*. Lacanian psychoanalysis is an obvious point of reference for a study of *délire*: as we shall see, it forms one side of the tradition I am attempting to describe.

12

My path is therefore clear. I shall devote the first chapter to the *literary* corpus of *délire*; the second and fourth to the linguistic-psychoanalytic side of the tradition; and the third and fifth to the philosophy of *délire* proper, the philosophy of Gilles Deleuze.

Notes

1 The application of the term 'delirium' to the Geneva medium is questionable. For in spite of the apparent 'possession' of Helen Smith by her unintelligible discourse, a doubt remains as to the genuineness of her experience. As Lacan insists, the possibility of deception is the surest indication of the presence of a subject. Even if we discard the crude question (was she taking her public for a ride?) some of her attitudes suggest that she was in control of her language: when Flournoy, the psychologist who studied her case, told her, after consulting Saussure, that her Martian or Sanskirt were in fact French, she produced sentences in total gibberish, which she called Uranian. cf. T. Flournoy, *Des Indes à la planète Mars*, Geneva 1900 (Paris: Seuil, 1983).

2 I do not give a translation of these lines, in order to stress the fact that, in this case, the surface meaning of the text is relatively unimportant. cf. J. Starobinski, *Les Mots sous les Mots* (Paris: Gallimard 1971), p. 80.

3 Starobinski, p. 158.

4 The term was coined by Michel Pierssens, who gives a partial account of the tradition.

5 J. Kristeva, 'Pour une sémiologie des paragrammes', in *Sèmeiotikè*, (Paris: Seuil 1969).

6 I am aware that the two verbs differ semantically in that they can be used to answer two different questions: 'what is he doing?' (he is talking. . .), 'what is he talking about?' (he says that. . .). My point is that the intransitive verb is used where there is no object, either because I am not interested in it or cannot grasp it, or because the act precludes the existence of an object: in 'il délire', language is subject of the act ('la langue le délire', cf. Chapter 2) rather than object (in his act he uses language and produces discourse).

7 V. Descombes, *Le Même et l'Autre* (Paris: Minuit 1979), p. 125 (English translation: *Modern French Philosophy* (Cambridge University Press 1980)).

8 It is difficult to imagine someone writing a book entitled 'the philosophy of Melanie Klein'. Yet, Alain Juranville's *Lacan et la philosophie* was published in 1984 (Paris: PUF).

9 David Archard, *Consciousness and the Unconscious* (Hutchinson 1984), especially ch. 3.

Further reading

Excerpts from Saussure's anagrams notebooks are published in Starobinski's book, *Les Mots sous les Mots* (Paris 1971) (English translation, *Words upon words* (New Haven, Yale University Press 1979)). The best short introduction to Saussure is Jonathan Culler, *Saussure* (London 1976). The journal *Semiotext* has published two issues on 'the other Saussure', **I** no. 2 (1974) and **II** no. 1 (1975); cf. also Louis Jean Calvet, *Pour et contre Saussure* (Paris: Payot 1975).

For Schreber's text and Freud and Lacan's analyses, cf. Chapter 4. Helen Smith's case was studied by Theodore Flournoy, *Des Indes à la planète Mars* (Paris: Seuil 1983 and Geneva: Slatkine

1983 (first published 1900)) cf. also *Perceval's Narrative*, edited by Gregory Bateson (Stanford: Stanford University Press 1961).

The tradition of logophiliacs is studied in Michel Pierssens, *La Tour de Babil* (Paris: Minuit 1976) (English translation: *The Power of Babel* (Routledge & Kegan Paul 1980)). *Les Fous du Langage* is the title of Marina Yaguello's book on linguistic eccentrics (Paris: Seuil 1984). In *Mimologiques* (Paris: Seuil 1976), Gerard Genette studies the linguistic tradition of Cratylism. Raymond Queneau's novel, *Les Enfants du Limon* was published in 1938.

On Lacan, cf. David Archard's book in this series, *Consciousness and the Unconscious* (Hutchinson 1984), especially ch. 3. On humanism and anti-humanism in French Marxism, cf. Kate Soper's forthcoming book on *Humanism and Anti-Humanism*, also in this series.

The French tradition of '*énonciation*' linguistics is associated with the names of Emile Benveniste (*Problèmes de Linguistique Générale*, vol. 1 (Paris: Gallimard 1966) – translation, *Problems in General Linguistics* (University of Miami Press 1971) – and vol. 2 (Paris: Gallimard 1974)) and Antoine Culioli (cf., for instance, 'La formalisation en linguistique', *Cahiers pour l'Analyse*, **9**, (Paris, 1968)).

1
The literature of délire

Introduction

A novel where the most extraordinary and absurd adventures merely serve to bridge the gap between the two words involved in a pun; a book of grammar in which it is revealed, by strictly philological means, that Man's ancestor is not the banal ape, but the frog; a partial translation of *Through the Looking-Glass* that promptly turns into gibberish, and a commentary in which the poet, eighty years afterwards, accuses Lewis Carroll of having plagiarized him; the story of an American schizophrenic's life, written in French because the words of his mother tongue cause him physical pain. Roussel, Brisset, Artaud, Wolfson: such is the corpus of what I shall call the literature of *délire*.

From the start, questions arise about the unity of this corpus, and the name I have chosen for it. Why literature? and why *délire*? For only two of the texts would normally be called 'literature'. Roussel was a novelist and playwright, Artaud a poet. But Brisset claimed to be a man of science, and Wolfson wrote the story of his life, which he believed would only interest professional linguists. And yet the most imaginative of the four texts are perhaps not those which are presented as fiction. Beneath the veneer of Brisset's grammar and 'science of God' there soon emerges the violent story of how the frog became man, an epic of cruelty and pain, of war and cannibalism, a tale told by a prophet, full of croaks and fury, signifying much. And Wolfson's true life story reads like a *Bildungsroman*. On the other hand, Roussel's fiction is written like a technical description of machinery, an encyclopaedia of things, and how they work. And Artaud's is the classic poetic stance of the *vates*, whose concern is urgent truth, not the superficialities of civilized art. Poetic science, scientific or inspired poetry, truth and fiction are inextricably mixed. Literature is the name for this unholy brew. If confirmation were needed, we might find it in the fact that three of the writers were discovered or rediscovered by the Surrealists: Wolfson is an exception only because he came too late to be hailed as one of the tribe.

So 'literature' is an apt characterization of this paradoxical situation. But why *délire*? Because all four texts engage in shady dealings with language, all four manifest a love for language and interest in its workings both extreme and dubious. As we know, Michel Pierssens has coined a word for this: logophilia, or the love for language that knows no bounds, certainly not those of common sense. The word sounds like the name of a perversion. And a perversion it is: instead of using language as a transparent and docile instrument, and looking through it at the world outside, the four authors focus their attention on its workings, on its dark, frightening origin in the human body. They refuse to conform to the common-sense rule which forbids the users of language to reflect on the material existence of words as produced by certain organs of the body. Stated like this, the position may sound extreme, for after all the linguist does, among other things, just that (he calls it phonetics). But this is precisely what the logophiliac text teaches us: that there is a link between grammar and madness; *délire* indeed can be defined as the point where they come together. The linguist, extracting *langue* as a system of differential values out of the concrete situations where language is used, represses its material origin. The denied origin returns in the *délire* that threatens any linguist in his love for language. Brisset the mad grammarian, Wolfson, who calls himself 'the demented student of languages', are exemplary cases. But so, as we have seen, is Saussure.

So I shall adopt a provisional definition of *délire*: *délire* is a perversion which consists in interfering, or rather taking risks, with language.

For there are indeed risks. The personal risks of mockery and confinement (all four authors were treated, at some point in their lives, for mental illness, and three of them spent periods in a mental asylum) are perhaps less serious than the risks to personal integrity. Meddling with language, risking *délire* and madness, means accepting disintegration and struggling to restore the unity of the self. It means abandoning control of and mastery over language. The logophilist no longer speaks through language, he is spoken by it. This is the core of the experience of language in *délire*: an experience of madness in language, of possession.

But the reward may be greater than the risk. Each of the four authors has experienced that feeling of glory, that conviction that a revelation has been granted to him: a sun burning in Roussel's breast; the seventh angel of the apocalypse speaking through Brisset; even the more modest

16

Wolfson is overjoyed at the astonishing fecundity of his ideas. And the glory comes where the pain was: in language, for the content of the revelation is the key to language, the total and definitive explanation of its origin, of its workings. The great mystery has been explained at last, and each of the four books constitutes a true myth, that is, a myth revealed, where mind and body, words and things, madness and reason, language and desire act their colourful parts, as in one of the *tableaux vivants* that one finds on every page of Roussel's novels.

At this point, it is no longer so easy to dismiss the corpus as one of madness, an instance of delirium in the medical sense, even if, for instance, Roussel's feeling of glory was described by Janet in his *De l'Angoisse à l'Extase* (*From Anxiety to Ecstasy*). Logophilia, because it turns the writer, or the mental patient, into a linguist, concerns each of us: in its glorious myths, there is at least this element of truth, that madness inhabits language, that whether one practises literature, philosophy or linguistics, one has to *experience* language. The corpus, the strangeness of which I will now attempt to describe, has its unity in the fact that each of the four texts is an experience of language, pursued, without cheating or hesitation, to its ultimate end.

Corpus

Roussel

Raymond Roussel was born in Paris in 1877. He led the life of a wealthy eccentric, publishing novels (*Impressions d'Afrique*, 1910; *Locus Solus*, 1914) and verse (*Nouvelles Impressions d'Afrique*, 1932) which were received with indifference or ridicule. In an attempt to capture the interest of the public, he turned his novels into plays: they were utter failures, except among the Surrealists. After the completion of his first novel he had an experience of ecstasy followed by acute depression, for which he had to be treated, intermittently, all his life. He committed suicide in Palermo in 1933. Just before his death he wrote a short essay, *Comment j'ai écrit certains de mes livres*, intended to be published posthumously, in which he gives the 'key' to his writings. This enables the reader of *Impressions d'Afrique* to understand the logic behind the arbitrary events of the novel. But the explanation, itself rather gratuitous, is already the second given by Roussel, for the novel itself provides one. Indeed the structure of *Impressions d'Afrique* is bizarre: in a foreword the author advises the reader to skip the first nine chapters and start at chapter 10, that is, to read the first part of the text after the second. This, of course, is mere provocation: the reader knows the difference between a novel and a textbook; he must, in a novel, 'begin at the beginning' as the King of Hearts ordered the White Rabbit. And, as promised, he is soon lost. On the main square of a purely imaginary African capital, a series of acts, in the theatrical sense, are performed, each more unbelievable than the rest: a marksman manages, by shooting at it, to separate the white from the yolk of a soft-boiled egg; six brothers, because of their extreme thinness and the hollowness of their chests, reflect, by placing themselves at regular intervals, the voice of their father exactly like the echo in the nave of a cathedral; a singer has a mouth and tongue so shaped that he is able to sing, *at the same time*, four tunes, or the four parts of a canon. Many of these impossible acts involve equally impossible machines. The statue of a Lacedemonian slave (a helot) is made of corset stays. It is set on a base supported by wheels, themselves placed on rails made of a pinkish substance, which turns out to be the lights that cats are fed on. A magpie has been taught to operate with its beak a complex mechanism which tilts the statue, back and forth, on its base.

In the first nine chapters dozens of such wonders are presented, one after the other, without the least explanation, to an astonished reader. The next fifteen chapters provide an explanation, by placing them in a narrative framework: the dynastic quarrels in two African kingdoms, a steamer on its way to America stranded on the African coast, an ordeal imposed on some of the white captives by a rather capricious black sovereign, the desire of the rest of the white people to impress him by showing their best tricks. A host of stories provide a 'logical' explanation for each act. Thus, the emperor has, on pain of death, ordered one of the characters to make a statue light enough to be supported on rails made of lights, a substance he had much appreciated when the ship's cook had prepared it for his dinner. Judging that the task was not difficult enough, he added that the machine should be set in motion by a tame magpie. First we have a *tableau vivant*, then a fiction which 'explains' it, if explanation is the right word, so contorted, gratuitous and absurd is the fiction.

In the posthumous essay, 'How I wrote some of my books', Roussel informs us that *Impressions d'Afrique, Locus Solus* and a few other texts were written according to what he calls 'the device' (*le procédé*). This device is in fact threefold, or has three stages. The *first device* consists in taking a sentence, whose words each have two different meanings, and in modifying only one letter in it, so as to obtain another sentence. The writer then proceeds to compose a text which starts with the first sentence and ends with the second. Roussel claims that he used this device for *Impressions d'Afrique*. The sentence he chose is 'les lettres du blanc sur les bandes du vieux pillard' (the letters of the white man concerning the hordes of the old bandit). By changing the 'p' in 'pillard' to a 'b', he obtained the following sentence: 'les lettres du blanc sur les bandes du vieux billard', which, he claims, we must interpret as 'the characters traced in white chalk on the edges of the old billiard table'. And one of his early stories does start with the first sentence and end with the last: the narrator was playing charades with the guests at a party; one of the guests having mimed the title of a novel about Africa and about the letters of a white explorer captured by a local bandit, the narrator decides to give his answer by way of a cryptogram which he writes in chalk on the edge of the billiard table. But although Roussel claims that he used the same device, and the same pair of sentences, for *Impressions d'Afrique*, we need not believe him. We do find white people captured by an emperor who might be called, perhaps unjustly, an old bandit. But the letters have disappeared, and so has the whole of the second sentence. What Roussel has used is in fact another device, derived from the first.

The *second, or extended, device* is based on the systematic use of the pun. Although Roussel dropped the second sentence, he decided to use words associated with the word 'billiards', which had two different meanings, as in a pun. Thus the chalk used for billiard cues is stuck with glue to a piece of paper: but 'colle' (glue) also means, in school slang, detention: so, in the novel the emperor imposes a detention on one of the white men because he failed to recite the words of the national anthem. Roussel gives about fifty instances of such puns, which account for most of the episodes in *Impression d'Afrique*. In each case two semantically linked words are chosen; their meaning is transformed by punning, and two new words, or meanings, are produced, which have no semantic link. The *tableau vivant*, or the machine, and the fiction in the second part, are there to provide such a link. From a 'natural' (semantic) link one proceeds to an artificial (fictional) link. We now understand why the marksman chose for his target a soft-boiled egg: the calf of the leg is called in French 'le gras du mollet'; 'un oeuf mollet' is a soft-boiled egg; and 'Gras' was the name of a gun used in the French army. Hence, in the first part, the champion marksman shooting at a soft-boiled egg with a Gras gun.

In the second part, the narrative explains how he came into possession of a Gras gun, a model which was apparently obsolete. To take another instance: with a little luck one can sometimes see whales ('baleines') sporting themselves round an islet ('îlot'). But 'baleines' also means the stays of a corset (which used to be made of whalebone), and by adding an 'e' to 'îlot' one obtains 'ilote', helot: hence the statue of a slave, made of stays. Also, in the classroom, a sluggard ('un mou') is often mocked ('raillé') by the other boys. But 'mou de veau' means 'lights', and 'raille' is pronounced like 'rail': so we find this incredible rail made of a pink sponge-like substance. And the narrative explains how such an object came to be built. We now understand the complexity and the apparently arbitrary character of the stories: they must establish a link between two words which are homophonic but have little or nothing in common in the world of reference.

Although Roussel gives many instances of the use of the second device, it appears that it did not permit him to diversify his fiction sufficiently: for the stories become more and more complicated, they seem to acquire a life of their own. Also, perhaps, simple punning is too static, fit for the individual scene rather than the whole narrative. So Roussel started using a *third, or modified, device*. It is also based on systematic punning. He takes a sentence, any sentence, for instance the first line of a French folk-song, 'j'ai du bon tabac' and divides the phonetic sequence into segments, so that other patterns, other words appear: in this case, the sequence of words 'jade, tube, onde, aubade ('onde' means 'wave' or 'water'). He is not the inventor of this device, often used in party games like picture puzzles and charades, and also in the type of verse called holorhyme verse (an extension to the whole line of the punning rhyme for which Thomas Hood is famous). The punning, instead of being confined to the word, concerns the whole sentence: it gives a series of words, again without referential links, and the fiction develops in order to provide those links. One can understand the admiration the Surrealists felt for Roussel: what we have just described is a typical Surrealist game, where the text is produced, almost mechanically, from a totally different subtext. Indeed, to produce stories with this device, Roussel used lines by Victor Hugo, some of his own lines, and the address of his bootmaker. Here the hermeticism of the text reaches its acme: the first device was obvious, and revealed at the first reading; the second device, although extremely difficult to puzzle out, was still public, since it was based on ambiguities existing in language; the third is completely private unless

20

explicit clues are given (the pictures in a puzzle, the acting and setting in a charade), or unless the subtext is so well known as to be recognized by all. This is the case when the device is used to go from one language to another, in cases of 'translation' according to sound, the best-known instance of which is L. D. Van Rooten's *Mots d'Heures, Gousses, Rames*. The lines are now famous; they correspond exactly to Roussel's third device:

> *Un petit d'un petit*
> *S'étonne aux Halles.*
> *Un petit d'un petit*
> *Ah! degrés te fallent . . . .*

It is now time to assess Roussel's attitude to language, to justify his inclusion in a corpus of *délire*: I shall try to show that in his work madness is linked with fiction in so far as both are experiences of language.

That Roussel's fiction is preoccupied with language and its workings is obvious. His fascination in fact goes further. Language is no longer the medium, the transparent instrument of fiction, it is the source and the master of fiction. Fiction no longer uses language, it is merely a pretext for the unfolding of language. Take for instance the structure of *Impressions d'Afrique*: static scenes, their narrative explanation, and many years afterwards, in the essay, the key to their linguistic structure. The order is the same as in a textbook on language: first, a vocabulary, lists of words to be learnt; then, examples of grammar, sentences which give meaning to the words by presenting them in their context; and last the philological commentary, the grammarian's metalinguistic explanations of the syntactic and semantic properties of the words and perhaps their etymology. For Roussel, the novel has the form of a grammar.

Or again take the charades in his novels: Roussel is obsessed with the theatre and many of his 'scenes' are actually acted on a stage, in the manner of *tableaux vivants*. But the use of charades is a well-known part of the classic realistic novel (for instance *Jane Eyre* or *Vanity Fair*). Their function is to provide an *abyme*[1] of the text, an ironic commentary on the plot. In Roussel, the relation is reversed. Since the only role of fiction is to fill the gap between two homophonic words, the plot is used by the charade as its commentary, rather than the reverse: fiction is an instrument for the exploration of language. The absurdity of the objects described, of the adventures narrated, springs from this inversion: an extremely logical form of *délire* in which reason is made to stand on its head.

Roussel's fiction is primarily an experience of language: experiencing language means playing with it, but not in the sense of party games, where the player remains firmly in control. The experience is that of a passion for language in which language, not the author, soon gains the upper hand, and imposes its own rules. Roussel's madness lies in the fact that he does not stop, he does not stay within the bounds of common sense (which provide the social limits for the game of picture puzzle or charades, and the linguistic rules for the production of normal fiction). The party turns sour, the guests take fright and disappear, and the author remains alone with his *délire*.

But he too is frightened at his own audacity; he has both a fascination with disorder and a commonplace desire for order. So he tries to balance his *délire* by the ponderous seriousness of his writing. The most striking paradox in Roussel's work is that the flights of extreme and inventive imagination are rendered in a prose made deliberately flat and banal by the constant use of cliché. The French language has a particularly apt phrase for this: because the experience of language is one of madness, clichés constitute a protection, a *garde-fou*[2] against dissolution and incoherence. A paragraph from *Locus Solus* will give an idea of Roussel's style: 'Tendres époux, Florine et Lucius connurent l'absolu bonheur lorsqu'après dix années de cruelle attente la naissance de leur fille Gillette combla leurs voeux les plus ardents.' ('A tender couple, Florine and Lucius found absolute happiness when, after ten years of cruel waiting, the birth of a daughter fulfilled their most ardent wishes'.) None but the most predictable adjectives are used: after all, the experience of disorder is also, paradoxically, one of extreme order.

And indeed a strong preoccupation with order pervades Roussel's fiction: the dangerous words soon become embodied in things, especially in machines; for Roussel, who acknowledges Jules Verne as his sole master, lives in the positive world of the Great Exhibition. The workings of the machines are described in the minutest details, and the style increases the reader's impression that he is reading a Technical Encyclopaedia gone mad (in the manner of Borges) or the famous *Catalogue de la Manufacture d'Armes de St Etienne*, which Carelman parodied so successfully in his *Objets Introuvables*. The constant use of repetition (actions repeated, acts rehearsed, imitated, parodied) and the fascination for the process of reproduction (from animal mimicry to all sorts of photographic machines) also tend to produce an overall effect of strict order.

There lies Roussel's own brand of *délire*, a rather mild variety: on the frontier between the attraction of disorder and the love of order, in the contradictory disruption of language at one level (the semantic, or the referential level), and the strict respect for the merest of its rules on another, syntactic or morphological, level. The narrative sentence is 'impossible', the scenes that constitute its words defy belief, but the language which conveys these wonders is conservative and stilted. Between psychosis and grammar, says Pierssens, something emerges: Roussel's *délire*. His portrait, *en abyme*, can be found in *Locus Solus*, in the character of Lucius Egroizard: a sculptor, gone mad after the horrible death of his daughter, who thinks he is Leonardo, and between his fits spends his time making animated sculptures of his enemies and trying to reproduce, with the help of a ruler made of bacon (*la règle de l'art/la règle de lard*) the voice of his daugher on a machine strangely reminiscent of a phonograph.

Brisset

We know little about the life of Jean Pierre Brisset (1837–1923): he was an officer in the French army, a private tutor in languages, and ended up working for the railway station at Angers. He published – at his own expense – a number of books on language and religion. He would have remained one of those obscure paranoid circle-squarers of whom Raymond Queneau was so fond, had he not been discovered by the Paris intelligentsia: in 1913 he was the victim of an elaborate practical joke devised by Jules Romains, who invited him to Paris and solemnly appointed him 'thinker laureate' ('prince des penseurs'); a few years later, the Surrealists were the first to take him seriously (he is mentioned in André Breton's *Anthology of Black Humour*); in 1970 his two main works, *La Grammaire Logique* (1878) and *La Science de Dieu* (1900) were republished, with an introduction by Michel Foucault.

To most people, Brisset is known as the author of two curious theses: Latin does not exist, and Man descends from the frog. The first thesis is asserted in *La Grammaire Logique*. Latin is not a real language, but an artificial slang, the language of ancient Roman banditti, who used it as a secret code to confuse the common people. There is little historical evidence to support the thesis, but the context in which it appears is interesting. *La Grammaire Logique* begins like a perfectly straightforward textbook of grammar, with a definition of the parts of speech. In the first chapters, the only odd element is a certain tendency, which Brisset shares with Lewis Carroll, to correct language where it does not behave according to logic. Then comes the first revelation which, although false, is in no way absurd: the conjugation of French verbs (the suffixes for the various tenses) is formed with the Latin verb *ire* and not, as is usually believed, with *habere*. But it is already a *revelation*: the key to the workings of language, capable of dispelling all obscurities about words and their origin. From then on, the innocuous textbook seems to plunge into some sort of *délire*: as Brisset himself puts it, 'it is all a little incoherent, but the fever of the spirit is on us, and will not let us rest' (Brisset, p. 114). The revelations are multiplied: they all deal with the logic of language and the ultimate origin and meaning of words. First, Latin: the proofs of its artificiality are all derived from the illogical character of the language. No people in their right minds would have chosen to speak a language in which words occur in reverse order. Instead of 'I wanted to kill my enemy' Livy stupidly says 'hostem occidere volui'. So Latin grammar is a nasty and artificial puzzle: 'how can one teach logic with the help of a language based on illogicality?' (Brisset, p. 91) – which suggests that the purpose of language is to teach logic to the human mind. The other revelations concern the origin of language. Brisset holds a Cratylic view of the origin of language: words do not receive their meaning by convention, but through imitation of natural sounds – language was founded on the process of onomatopoeia. The revelation is that the origin of language lies in the original – should we say 'primal'? – scream, an animal noise through which our ancestors first expressed their emotions.

We now come to the second thesis. *La Science de Dieu* (if the title sounds immodest, we must remember that it is, after all, nothing but a transposition into French of the word 'theology') contains a fully fledged theory of origins: of language and of man. The object of the revelation is what Brisset calls 'the Great law, or the key to Language'. It is strictly philological: 'all the ideas expressed with similar sounds have the same origin and all refer, initially, to the same object'. The word 'idea' is deliberately vague: we notice that Brisset does not say 'all words phonetically similar', for in fact the unit of meaning is not the word, but the syllable. The meaning of a word or phrase is obtained by the combination of the meanings of their constituent syllables. Hence, two

24

sentences composed of entirely different words, but similar sounds, must have the same origin. Origin, not meaning: for meaning is a matter of surface; what is postulated is a link between all the surface meanings, deriving from their common origin. We are very close to Roussel's modified device, except that the link between the various surface sentences is provided through science (revealed philology), not fiction. The similarity between the devices will appear from an example. Brisset takes the word 'logé' (lodged) and analyses it into syllables, causing the surface meanings to proliferate:

1 'l'eau j'ai' (I have water)
2 'l'haut j'ai' (I am high – Brisset's interpretation)
3 'l'os j'ai' (I have a bone)
4 'le au jet' (where I throw that object – Brisset)
5 'loge ai' (I have a lodge)
6 'lot j'ai' (I bear my lot)
7 'l'auge ai' (I have my trough)

The Great Law postulates a 'semantic' link between all seven sentences, and as in Roussel a narrative develops to establish it, this time not mere fiction, but true fiction, that is myth, a myth of origins. In these seven sentences one can read the story of Man's ancestor, the frog, who lived in the water (1), in lake villages built on posts (2) and was carnivorous (3). Sentences 4 to 7 are not interpreted directly, but become the source of new interpretations: 'loge ai' (I am lodged), 'à l'eau berge' (on the bank of the water – 'à l'auberge', at an inn), 'dans les eaux t'es le' (you are standing in the water – 'dans les hôtels', at the hotel).

The example we have quoted is the first philological analysis in *La Science de Dieu*. The rest of the book consists in a multitude of other analyses through which the myth takes form. It is a story of violence, of battle and captivity, of the painful emergence of organs, not least the frog's sex: 'sais que c'est?', do you know what it is? 'ce excès', that excess, 'c'est le sexe'; 'je ne sais ce que c'est', I don't know what it is, 'jeune sexe est', the young sex is; 'je sais que c'est bien', I know it's good, 'je ou jeu sexe est bien', my sex or the sex game is a good thing. We see here that Brisset takes more risks with language than Roussel. The sentence is not only analysed once, as in a picture puzzle or in Roussel's third device, but many times, in a process of disruption and reconstruction which will never be completed. And the myth of the frog

25

is a real, though diseased, creation myth. It tells of the birth of desire and violence, of society, of the family and all the institutions which produce violence ('raîne', frog/'reine', queen/'reine-mère', queen-mother). A myth of the origin of the family, a diseased family romance: Brisset himself notes the phonetic link between 'grand-mère', grandmother and 'grammaire', grammar.

The word is not only the content of the myth ('It is not I, but the Word that speaks', Brisset, p. 123), but its key (the revelation is linguistic) and its guarantee. In the beginning was the word, and it never altered, for it is more durable than diamond (p. 179). The sediments of history, the post-Babelian multiplication of idioms, the hypocrisy or blindness of priests and scientists alike have hidden it; the Seventh Angel recovers it, through an effort of memory that defines true man, where it has always been, in language. For the word is the true son of God, the spiritual son whose animal counterpart is Man, and Brisset gives a linguistic equivalent of the Christian Trinity: He who speaks, He who is spoken to, and He who is the object of speech. The system of personal pronouns is the linguistic embodiment of the Trinity.

We may now try to assess Brisset's achievement. The mirth that some of his discoveries provoke in us (his exhilaration is often contagious) is not free from embarrassment. He reminds us that it is a short step from prophetic truth to delirium. Behind Brisset's obvious paranoia, there emerge a creation myth and an experience of language where again madness and grammar are mixed. The missing term here is fiction: this is the main difference between him and Roussel. Whereas Roussel's devices were explicitly presented as fictions, that is as (albeit serious) games, Brisset's version of the device is presented as science and truth. Whereas Roussel was cautious, aiming to reduce disorder, Brisset's experience is, from the beginning, one of anarchy and disruption. Language in Roussel was a source of anxiety, a danger to the sanity of the writer: in Brisset, it is the only source of truth and the scribe must lose himself in it, let it regain its mastery, without which no remembrance of origins is possible. On the one hand a poet, for ever fighting for a mastery over language which constantly threatens to evade him: on the other hand a prophet, joyfully and gratefully possessed by language. On the one hand fiction, but controlled and blocked by the common-sense style of clichés; on the other hand science, in which fiction is denied, but where it makes its presence felt even more. For the myth of the frog is unbridled fiction, more extraordinary, if that is possible, than Roussel's.

26

Because fiction in Brisset is ultimately given free rein in the guise of prophetic science, he was able to broach a subject which was repressed and displaced by Roussel: the relation between language and desire, language and the body. 'Sexual suffering, he says, impelled the first men to speak' (Brisset, p. 137): the history of man is the history of his sex, and the secret that the word ultimately reveals is a primitive scene. Michel Pierssens finds evidence of paranoia and homosexuality in Brisset's books; we shall discover a new and stronger form of *délire*, in which linguistic disruption has triumphed over the forces of order, in which grammar and the love of language, are linked with desire, the body, and the sexual history of the individual within the family. A new version of the contradiction that produces *délire*: grammar versus sex.

Wolfson

Louis Wolfson's *Le Schizo et les Langues* was published in 1970 in Paris. Wolfson, 'the demented student of languages', is an American of Jewish origin whose parents emigrated in their youth from Eastern Europe to the United States. He wrote this book, which tells the story of his mental illness and of his attempts at curing himself through the study of languages, directly in French: he rejected his mother tongue, English, and refused to speak or write it and could not listen to it, because each English word was a source of pain to him.

The last sentence had to be written in the past tense, for Wolfson appears to have cured himself, to a certain extent, of his 'linguistic' illness in two ways: he has become addicted to horse races – which implies that he must have recourse to his mother tongue to read the names of the horses and place his bets – and, after the death of his mother, he has emigrated to French Canada. These events are narrated in his second book, a celebration of his mother in her last illness, *Ma mère est morte de maladie maligne en mai mardi à minuit au mouroir Memorial à Manhattan*. The alliterative title and the fact that the second book is also written in French show that Wolfson's linguistic interests have not been completely superseded by the horses. Nevertheless, I shall concentrate on the first book, where his passion for language is most evident.

In *Le Schizo et les Langues*, then, we learn a lot about Wolfson's life, sometimes indirectly: his parents' divorce, his mother's remarriage to a rather weak character, his difficulties at school because of his slowness, and numerous episodes of psychiatric treatment, sometimes ending in his discharge from hospital, and at least once in his escape. He lives with his mother and stepfather, and spends most of his time at home, studying foreign languages, except for trips to the library or visits to his father. Relations with other people are difficult, because of his rejection of English: most of all with his mother, who apparently insists on addressing him in a loud piercing voice, when he least expects it.

As one may imagine, life is complicated, for Wolfson makes few compromises. He refuses to read English, and therefore cannot read the labels on tins of food. He is forever at risk: at every moment he is threatened with inadvertently hearing words pronounced in the hated tongue, or with deliberate verbal aggression by his family.

Yet one cannot help admiring his courage, his determination to overcome obstacles and to live in spite of difficulties. At first, he tells us, he developed purely defensive techniques, sitting with a foreign book open on his knees, a radio set tuned on a foreign programme near his right ear (the earphone is a great help), and a finger of his left hand ready to stop his other ear on the slightest provocation. But one cannot live like this, not all the time. So he had to find an instrument of liberation: since language caused the pain, only language could provide the help. Not unsurprisingly, he found his *first device* in the course of a conversation with his father, who suggested, as it happens incorrectly, that the word 'tree' was translated in Russian by a very similar word, 'tri'. The device is discovered: instant translation into another tongue. The word, although it has not changed, has ceased to be an English word. The word 'milk' no longer causes pain, because it instantly becomes 'milch' (in German), 'maelk' (in Danish), 'mleko' (in Polish) or 'moloko' (in Russian) (Wolfson, p. 41). And Wolfson's linguistic studies are useful, for the number of words which can be transposed without transformation from English into another language is necessarily limited: but there are cases of regular, recurrent transpositions, from English to German for instance, and these can be admitted, become 'legal'. A strange game has started, where the student of languages plays against his mother (tongue). The rules are strict, and any illegal move is punished: the translation is blocked, and, ugly and painful, the word remains English.

An example will give us an idea of the complexity of the game. Wolfson is often compelled to read on labels the words 'vegetable shortening'. The first word offers no problem for it has ready French ('végétal') and German ('vegetabilisches') equivalents. But the word 'shortening' is more difficult, it has no such easy transposition. The only way is to cut it into its constituent syllables and phonemes, as Roussel and Brisset did. The first consonant, /sh/ becomes the Hebrew word 'chemenn' (meaning 'grease') and the German 'schmelz' (which has the same meaning). The sound 'or' becomes the Russian 'jir'. The suffix 'ing' quite regularly becomes the German 'ung'. The task is more or less completed: the word has been decomposed, it has lost its power, it no longer causes pain. But we notice that Wolfson has extended the range of possible moves, that his rules are no longer so strict, for the English word no longer has one equivalent in another tongue, but several partial equivalents in three different languages. We have insensibly passed to *the second, or extended, device*, a stroke of genius according to Wolfson, where words associate more freely, where a single word, or a single sentence can be translated into several languages at the same time. Thus the sentence 'I'm mad' (which often 'irresistibly' comes to his mind) becomes '-âm' (a Persian suffix meaning 'I') 'malade' (French for 'ill'). 'Don't trip over the wire' becomes 'tu nicht trébucher über eth he zwirn', where 'tu nicht', 'über' and 'zwirn' are German, 'trébucher' is French for 'trip', and 'eth he' is a Hebrew group where 'eth' is a marker for the accusative case and 'he' the definite article. Sometimes the device becomes so extended that a vague semantic similarity and one or two common phonemes are enough. Thus 'early' becomes the French words '*sur le champ; de bonne heure; matinalement; dévorer l'espace*'. The last instance shows that, as with Roussel and Brisset, the extended device ends in *délire*.

Another recurrent feature of Wolfson's book must be mentioned: the link he establishes between language and feeding, two oral activities which, for him, are exclusive. Wolfson tells us that he is extremely thin. He refuses to eat normally – exactly as he refuses to speak English. He has two reasons for this: he is afraid of swallowing the eggs of various larvae and parasitic worms, and food prevents him from studying languages (his mind becomes heavy and sluggish, he is unable to act, a prey to feelings of anxiety and guilt). But he is only gaining time by practising this form of retention. An overriding desire for food eventually compels him to rush to the refrigerator and eat indiscriminately, opening the tins without looking at the labels and swallowing the food, sweet or sour, without even cooking it. Wolfson calls this an orgy; after it the feeling of guilt is even greater and he can no longer work, for food has destroyed the protection provided by foreign words. The dilemma is either fasting and studying or eating and anxiety. Knowledge is incompatible with food.

From this description one could form the impression that life for Wolfson is so difficult that it is not worth living, that the course which has been imposed on him can only end in suicide. Yet that is not so: in the very moving last chapter, a sort of reflective afterword to his tale, he considers the question of suffering, suicide, and the justification for life, and ends on a note of hope, of confidence in the eventual restoration of his lost freedom. The reader is left with the conviction that in his case the 'talking cure' has really begun to work, even if we know from the second book that his compulsive study of languages has been replaced by compulsive betting (if this is madness, at least it is more common than a passion for linguistics) and that, apart from the horses, his main preoccupation is the nuclear holocaust: not because he is afraid of it, but because he looks forward to it. Collective suicide, blowing up the planet (the second, definitive, version of his first book, which was never published, was entitled *Point final à une planète infernale*) is the only solution to a condition which is not individual but cosmic. In spite of these grim views (Wolfson has always supported Ronald Reagan as the politician most likely to bring about the desired state of affairs), the author's struggle, his human qualities, his sense of humour and his courage command one's respect and forestall the instinctively patronizing attitude of a reader who, having to go through the confessions of a schizophrenic, finds himself placed in the position of a doctor. This is the diary of a struggle, with language, with the family.

The situation is now familiar: a *délire* which has nothing to do with delirium; risks, which in Wolfson's case are imposed by his illness rather than taken; a threatening disorder and a struggle to restore order. But the configuration is inverted. Disorder is not where we are used to expect it, in incoherence, in the dissolution of social ties. It is within, in the heart of the family, in the author's head. His mother is the embodiment of this disorder, the mother tongue its carrier. Order, as a consequence, lies without, in the escape from mother and the family, in the destruction of the mother tongue (Wolfson, p. 262, uses the word 'massacre'). The ordering process starts with apparent disorder and refusal. It is a process of slow, painful reconstruction, a form of *bricolage*,[3] 'formally illegitimate' to use Deleuze's phrase (but legitimacy, the relation to one's parents which society sanctions, is precisely at the root of the problem). A complicated process, reflected in Wolfson's style: long sentences, a taste for extreme detail, a deliberately pedantic diction, not without ironic distance, in a French which is both remarkable and flawed – remarkable in its sheer readability, in its knowledge of the idiom, in the quality of the philological reflection; but full of obvious grammatical mistakes, which all have the same characteristic: an English turn of phrase, with no strict equivalent in French, is transposed literally into French, thus betraying the nationality of the writer. One cannot escape one's mother tongue; in Wolfson, it always reappears in the end, sometimes even invades the text.

But Wolfson's *délire* is not in the impossible dream of being able to escape his own language. It is, as it was in Roussel and Brisset, a struggle for mastery, an attempt at settling the question of who talks. Mother, or me? Language, or the author? As we now know, there is no simple answer to this, and *délire* expresses this contradiction. On the one hand, the speaker claims mastery over language, on the other he feels it elude his grasp, impose its own mastery on him, its own deep disorder. Wolfson's attitude is at first defensive: silence, then escape, the passage from a language which he will not call his own into a proliferation of other languages. But defence is not sufficient. Wolfson resumes the offensive by writing his book even if, to achieve his aim, he has to make a compromise: he writes in French, in the conditional mood instead of the narrative past, in the impersonal third person instead of the authorial 'I', all of which makes his mastery doubtful. This, then, is the contradiction of *délire*: to master language, or be mastered by it. Like Roussel, like Brisset, Wolfson fights, often a losing battle, against disorder, the disorder, violence and cruelty of language which are again perceived as emanating from the instincts of the body, and from the social organisation of bodies, the family.

Artaud

I shall deal here with two works by Artaud: his translation of a chapter from Lewis Carroll's *Through the Looking-Glass*, and a letter to Henri Parisot in which he comments on his translation. Both were written in 1945, when he was interned in the psychiatric hospital at Rodez.

His choice of a chapter for translation is not arbitrary: it is chapter 6, in which Humpty-Dumpty comments, for Alice's benefit, on the poem 'Jabberwocky', in which also he asserts his mastery over language (words mean, he says, exactly what I want them to mean; if I want them to assume more meaning, I pay them extra). This choice places Artaud's text right at the centre of the problem of *délire*, as we have tried to delimit it: adapting a text where Carroll expresses highly original – and seminal – views about language, he too gets to grips with the question of the power of language.

In Carroll's text, it will be remembered, Humpty-Dumpty adopts a complex position, with a mixture of conventionalism on the level of discourse (conversation is a rule-governed game, and each player moves in turn) and Cratylism at the level of words (a word imitates its reference: Humpty-Dumpty himself, who looks his name, is a case in point). The main aspect of his position, however, is the assumption of mastery over language, an assumption subject to strong dramatic irony since, as every one knows, pride comes before a fall, and especially since Humpty-Dumpty, self-styled master of words, is himself only a creature of language, mastered by the words of the Nursery Rhyme which determines both his shape and his fate.

But Carroll's irony sets limits to the reflection on language, it transforms the whole affair into a game where the question of mastery is posed only to be evaded, for this is after all nothing but a dream. Artaud was extremely resentful of this lack of seriousness in Carroll, of the timidity, the superficiality he discerned in Carroll's disruption of language. So his text is not a real translation, but rather a betrayal, a deliberate misprision, as the subtitle shows: 'an antigrammatical attempt against Lewis Carroll'. In those few words the refusal, the revolt are expressed twice. Artaud does to Carroll what Carroll did not quite dare to do to language: he 'massacres' his text. His rage is everywhere apparent in the letter to Parisot (himself the author of the standard French translation of the Alice books): 'the work of a castrated, half-caste hybrid who ground consciousness like coffee beans to get a text out of it'; 'when one digs into the shit of being and language, one's poem must smell bad, and 'Jabberwocky' is a poem which its author has carefully kept away from the uterine essence of suffering'; '*Jabberwocky* is the work of a coward, who did not want to suffer for his work'; '*Jabberwocky* is a bowdlerized plagiarism of a work which I wrote but which was suppressed so that I hardly know myself what was in it.' (Artaud, pp. 185, 188).

'Suffering' is the important word here: Artaud reproaches Carroll for wasting his opportunity, for hesitating before the risks of *délire*, for denying the link between language and pain, language and the body which – in its violence and cruelty – *délire* alone can express. Carroll fails to do what all four authors of the corpus do: he does not take language seriously. His preoccupation with it is obvious, but it is timid and reticent. Treating language as a game is a way of deprecating its obscure and dangerous power. Shut up in the asylum at Rodez, Artaud cannot afford to play games, he can only give vent to his rage and anguish: hence his disruption of Carroll's text.

The translation begins in a fairly straightforward manner, except that in the first paragraph 'clearly' is translated as 'intropoltabrement', a made-up word, though no more strange than Carroll's own portmanteau words: like them, it conforms to the phonotactic rules of language.[4] But soon the translation goes off course, new fragments of text appear, as if the text generated itself according to its own laws, forgetting the strict relation of translation. For instance, here is a short paragraph of Carroll's text: '"I said you *looked* like an egg, Sir"', Alice gently explained, '"And some eggs are very pretty, you know"', she added, hoping to turn her remark into a sort of compliment.' And here is the translation: 'J'ai dit que vous me faisiez penser à un oeuf, monsieur, s'excusa griliment Alice. Mais il y a des oeufs qui sont plus que jolis, ourla-t-elle comme pour amadouer la tapette, au reste de ce su-Turlet si bien rilé et riptionné.' (Artaud, p. 157). As we can see, the first sentence is a real translation except for 'griliment', a coined word, which represents 'gently'. The betrayal starts in the second sentence: Carroll would never have called Humpty-Dumpty a queer ('une tapette'), and the verb 'ourler', which translates 'added', is not used properly (it means 'to hem'). But it is phonetically similar to 'hurler', to scream, which does *not* translate 'added', but is perhaps a good indication of Artaud's (Alice's?) emotions towards Humpty-Dumpty. The last clause sinks into incoherence, although 'su-Turlet' suggests 'suturer' (to stitch), which is semantically linked to 'ourler', and 'rilé' and 'riptionné', two coined words, are instances of the proliferation of the sound 'r' (which occurs in 'griliment' but *not* in 'gently'), a sound which pervades Artaud's additional text. We have reached here the first type of disruption which Artaud imposes on Carroll's text: the attack takes the form of semantic addition (new words, new clauses, new themes) and phonetic dissemination. Carroll no longer speaks in his text: nor in fact does Artaud. The text speaks for itself, develops according to its own laws of semantic association and alliteration.

The chapter goes on, a mixture of straight translation and disruption, until Alice asks Humpty-Dumpty to explain 'Jabberwocky'. This is how the title of the poem is 'translated' in Artaud's text:

NEANT OMO NOTAR NEMO
Jurigastri – Solargultri
Gabar Uli – Barangoumti
Oltar Ufi – Sarangmumpti

Sofar Ami – Zantar Upti
Momar Uni – Septfar Esti
Gonpar Arak – Alak Eli (Artaud, p. 165)

Instead of one, we have a multitude of coined words: left to its own devices, language proliferates. The use of language for purposes of communication implies a certain restraint, a capacity to discern and differentiate, that is, *not* to say things, an ability to stop when one's meaning has been expressed. But language on its own does not express, conveys no meaning, certainly not somebody's meaning. It develops according to its own rules, in this case the poetic rules of rhyme (including internal rhyme), syllable count (eight syllables per 'line'), and caesura. And if the last line is an apparent exception to the rule of internal rhyme, it is only because another type of rhyming (Arak/Alak) has been introduced. Nor are the words produced entirely at random: it is true they are not possible words in French in the way that 'Jabberwocky' is a possible word in English, but they nevertheless form a definite system of phonetic dissemination. We notice the use of the 'ar' sounds as word rhymes ('Gabar/Oltar/Sofar/Momar'), and the strategic dissemination of the sound 'g' in the first two lines. So language proliferates according to self-imposed rules (the 'author' has an experience of possession: the words are forced on him). And proliferate it does: what was supposed to be a title becomes a poem in its own right, with its own title.

The passage from possible coined words to impossible ones is important. It is even more apparent if we look at Artaud's 'massacring' of the first stanza of 'Jabberwocky':

'Twas brillig, and the slithy toves
Did gyre and gimble in the wabe:
All mimsy were the borogoves,
And the mome raths outgrabe.

This is Artaud's French version:

Il était Roparant, et les vliqueux tarands
Allaient en gibroyant et en brimbulkdriquant
Jusque là où la rourghe est à rouarghe à rangmbde et rangmbde à rouarghambde
Tous les falomitards étaient les chats-huants
Et les Ghoré Uk'hatis dans le GRABUGEUMENT. (Artaud, p. 165)

In spite of appearances a text like 'Jabberwocky' poses few problems of translation, provided the translator manages to coin convincing portmanteau words in his own language: there are excellent translations of the poem in French and German (these are the first lines of Parisot's version: 'Il était grilheure, les slictueux toves/Gyraient sur l'alloinde et vriblaient . . .'). Some of Artaud's words, like 'vliqueux' belong to this type, and his Dodu-Mafflu explains 'falomitard' as a combination of 'falot' (weak) and 'miteux' (moth-eaten, seedy). But, as early as the second line, something changes: again, language develops of its own accord, according to phonetic laws, as appears in the third line, and articulated speech gives way to incantation and animal noise, the scream (*le cri*). For the portmanteau word is yet another attempt to control language in its phonetic development by establishing the validity of phonotactic rules, to reduce its capacity for ambiguity by concentrating two meanings (but not more) into one word. Ambiguity, then, is only the ultimate and perfect state of the portmanteau word, where the two component words are the same: which is a way of stating – and dictionaries are built on this basis – that each word has one and only one basic meaning. Artaud's incantations disrupt this fine order. They show that the phonetic laws of language go beyond the rules of phonotactics, that the sequences of sounds that emerge from the body and are a cause of pleasure or pain go beyond the conventions that specify possible words. They also show that the attribution of one meaning to a word does not correspond to the instinctive working of language (by 'instinctive' I mean deriving from the instinctual drives and desires of the body): left to itself language screams, in meaningless utterances, or is riddled with ambiguity, which gives it an appearance of meaninglessness. Thus the coined word 'Goré Uk'hatis' is explained by Artaud as the portmanteau combination of the words 'ukhase, hâte, abruti, cahot nocturne sous Hécate' ('ukase, haste, stupefied, nocturnal jolt under Hecate' Artaud, p. 169). As in Roussel, language becomes enigmatic, it becomes impossible to retrieve the multiple meanings packed beneath the incoherent surface of the words. At this point language is no longer an instrument of communication (of translation), the privileged vehicle of social practice, it has become the bearer of the violent passions of the human body: no longer the word, but the scream.

What Artaud has discovered is that there are two languages: the language of surface, of social communication, where order (phonotactic – syntactic) reigns; and a language of the depths of the body, where the articulate word becomes a scream, where only affects and the passions of the body can be expressed. Correspondingly, there are two masters: the speaker dominates the surface language which he uses; but language itself, as an oral activity, as a production of the body, possesses the individual who utters its screams, and whom society expels by calling him mad. Games played with language recognize this duality, only to deny it in most cases: they can be arranged on a scale according to the degree of denial. In Carroll, it is maximal: the game is meant to preserve order, at all costs; in Roussel a serious risk is taken, the risk of *délire*, but the self-conscious style and aesthetic ambitions limit it; in Brisset *délire* overcomes the attempts at control: the truth of the revelation can no longer be doubted; in Wolfson disorder has already triumphed, from the very beginning: there is no longer any question of controlling language, but only a long struggle to escape from the mastery of the mother tongue, to recover the power that from the start was denied to the speaker; in Artaud, there is no struggle: language is installed in the position of absolute mastery: the contradiction between order and disorder that gave their form to the three other texts has been resolved: disorder reigns, or rather another order, a new language, a tongue that nobody understands, not even he who utters the words, the language of suffering, the screaming of the flesh. This must have been the contents of the lost book which 'Jabberwocky' plagiarizes: a lost meaning, a text of which only fragments remain, 'attempts at language', in which the rhythm above all is important:

> *ratara ratara ratara*
> *atara tatara rana*
> *otara otara katara*
> *otara ratara kana.* . . . (Artaud, p. 188)

Analysis

The unity I have imposed on the corpus so far consists in a largely implicit attitude towards language. But the corpus also has a historical and cultural unity, beginning with the recurrent analysis of the texts by the same philosophers or critics. Apart from Artaud's works, the texts were first discovered in the 1960s by people who were also reading the critical analyses of Foucault, Kristeva and Deleuze. Thus, from the beginning, the criticism is almost part of the text, as in the prefaces which Foucault wrote for Brisset, and Deleuze for Wolfson. And there is an element of involvement in it: Kristeva on Roussel and Deleuze on Wolfson both refer to Foucault's volume on Roussel. My own reading of the texts has already been influenced by this criticism: it is now time to render unto the philosophers the things which are theirs. The unity of this critical corpus will be found in a fascination with language in its marginal aspect of *délire*: disaffection with the all powerful structural linguistics, and the concomitent demise of the author as the sole source of textual meaning have moved the productions of *poètes maudits* and madmen to the centre of interest.

The device and the experience of language

In his book on Roussel and his preface to Brisset, Foucault gives a detailed analysis of the similar devices used by Roussel, Brisset and Wolfson. Behind the purely mechanical aspect of the device, there is an experience of language, the real object of his analysis. This experience is essential to Man: language is the process in which sheer existence is given form, the abstraction through which the subject apprehends the concrete world, which gives form to the concrete world. But the relation of the subject to this abstraction is not one of instrumentality: language has something to do with time, because of its capacity for repetition, always tending towards death as the end of the process of repetition, always tempting the subject to try to discover the secret of his origin which always evades him. There is no beginning, only language, by which the subject is carried along. But the subject is always fighting for mastery, always trying to use as an instrument that which carries him like a stream, always trying to appropriate the world through the word, to name things, to give them order through syntax and narration. This attempt is bound to fail and to be forever repeated, because of the contradiction inherent in the relation between language and reality, words and things. At the heart of language there is a deficiency, an 'exiguity': there are fewer words than there are things waiting to be named. This is not economy (on another level, that of its double articulation, language is based on economy), but sheer lack: it does not help communication or expression, it rather hinders or complicates them, for with synonymy come ambiguity, equivocation and all the dangers pertaining to tropes. For the other side of this lack of words (reality is always in excess of language) is a proliferation of meanings, the best illustration of which is the unlimited possibility of creating new meanings through tropes (the whole discussion is based on a reading by Foucault of the eighteenth-century French tradition of grammarians and rhetoricians). If the same word or sentence can have two utterly unrelated meanings (as appears in Roussel's devices) there is no reason why the multiplication of meanings should stop at that: Brisset's analysis of 'logé' is a good example of this process of multiplication. So the speaker's mastery is twice defeated: signs are too few for the adequate naming of reality, meanings are too numerous for the precise and unequivocal expression of the speaker's 'own' ideas. The result of this contradiction is the 'anxiety of the sign'. The various forms of the device are means of illustrating the situation and coming to terms with the anxiety. The obsessional punning in Roussel and Brisset proclaims the possibility of multiple meanings; it also illustrates the loss of mastery by the subject who is compelled to give in to this proliferation. Madness and *délire* are the deepest experience of language, they express the truth about it.

This is the intuition which Foucault recognizes in Roussel's work. The device, then, appears to be a symptom of the struggle, within language, between order and disorder. But why a symptom? Because the struggle is symptomatic of the fact that language is also produced by the speaker's body, the passions of which it reflects. The science of linguistics, and the instrumentalist conception of language treat the latter as an abstraction, a system belonging to a community of speakers, of a different order of being from the physical existence of the individual speaker. What the device, or Artaud's disruption, forces us to acknowledge is that language has a material existence in the speaker's body and its passions: hence the link, in Wolfson, between speaking and eating, in Artaud between words and excrements.

In his preface to Brisset, Foucault distinguishes three types of device, corresponding to a deliberate mishandling of three types of linguistic relations: from words to things (designation), from sentence to sentence (signification), from language to language (translation) (Brisset, p. xvi). The first device operates on the things within the words, not in order to purify language and enable it to designate, but to purify the things themselves, to reject the diseased nefarious things, which threaten to invade the hearer's body like the larvae of parasitic worms. The second device operates on signification, the relation of paraphrase between sentences: instead of comparing and insisting on equivalence of meaning, it separates them, establishes a discursive gap between them, filled with a multitude of scenes, adventures, speeches, or machines. The distance which the relation of signification was meant to deny becomes maximal. The third device creates a disruption between different languages or different states of the same language in place of the regular relation of translation. The origin emerges within the present state of the language and destroys it, as the translation ruins the translated text; what emerges from the ruins is the cruelty of passion, cannibalistic scenes in Brisset, scatological violence in Artaud.

Although each form of the device is present in all three authors, it is obvious that the first dominates in Wolfson, the second in Roussel, the third in Brisset (whose philological device is a diseased translation from the modern text into its original subtext). Foucault points out a relation between each form of the device and a physical organ: the mouth in Wolfson, the eye in Roussel, the ear in Brisset (the primitive scenes are described in terms of noises). In all three cases language has become an affection of the body.

Language and the body

In his preface to Wolfson, Deleuze gives another version of this conception of language. Wolfson's insight, as he sees it, is that language carries 'a story of love and sex', the story of the passions of the individual body. There are three ways of coming to terms with this central characteristic of language. One can – this is the 'normal' reaction – deny it, maintain that the relation between language and sex is one of designation. The speaker makes obscene jokes and feels the embarrassment implied in an act of denial. Or one can displace it: the relation, then, is one of signification; the speaker is no longer conscious of the relation, which, however, becomes more vigorous; we are in the realm of humour, of the slip of the tongue, where we are no longer masters of the sexuality carried by our language, where on the contrary it masters us. But in the psychotic's discourse the relation is not one of designation, or of signification, but of experience: the story of love and sex is no longer carried by language, it has got 'caught' in it, like cement. There is no longer any displacement: the passions of the body, its breathing and its screams, are directly turned into words, and the 'device' enables them to come to the surface.

So the device is, in each case, a personal solution to the enigma of the body as the source of language: the experience which Roussel and Wolfson undergo is that of the body, and their device is truly a talking cure. But there are two moments in the experience, at least in the case of Wolfson: a moment of destruction, and a moment of restitution and totality. For, as we have seen, the first stage of the experience is one of suffering, of intense pain. Life means pain and injustice; it is associated with the words of the mother tongue and the dangerous foodstuffs the patient must absorb if he wants to live. But both English words and foodstuffs are 'part-objects' (a psychoanalytic concept, originally found in the work of Melanie Klein: the object of the drive is not always a whole person, but can be a part of the body – the breast, faeces, the penis – or its symbolic equivalent), they are 'threatening, noisy, toxic' (Wolfson, p. 14), fragments which resist totalization and symbolization, any attribution of identity or meaning. As such, they endanger the integrity of the subject. But Wolfson's story is one of struggle: the second moment of his experience is that of recaptured totality, of the restoration of his identity. He finds it in knowledge, the knowledge of foreign languages, the chemical knowledge of the periodic law (the scientific equivalent of the linguistic device: it provides a means of analysing the noxious foodstuffs). And as the part-objects originated in the mother, the guarantee of science is sought in the father figure. In foreign tongues, words become whole again, and the atomic structures guarantee the completeness of the objects. The experience is summarized by Deleuze in an 'equation' (Wolfson, p. 14)

$$\frac{\text{Words of mother tongue}}{\text{foreign languages}} = \frac{\text{foodstuffs}}{\text{atomic structures}} = \left(\frac{\text{life}}{\text{knowledge}}\right)$$

The top line (the numerator) designates the intricate relation between words and things, between the fragmented word and the part object. The bottom line (the denominator) shows how knowledge is 'breathed' into the words (the whole word, 'le mot souffle', which can no longer be analysed or fragmented) and the objects (the complete object). The experience, which of course goes from the breaking up of the subject to the restoration of identity, is that of Wolfson's cure. *Délire*, then, is the experience of the body within language, of the destruction and painful reconstruction of the speaking subject, not through the illusory mastery of language and consciousness, but through possession by language. The subject understands that he does not speak language, he is spoken by it. 'The psychotic's cure does not consist in becoming conscious, but in living *through words* the story of love' (Wolfson, p. 23).

The term 'subject' here is misleading: it implies a centre of consciousness, a mastery over mental processes, including language. But all the texts in our corpus, especially those of Artaud, deny that this is a valid way of describing what happens when words are produced.

For there are two organizations, two languages, and perhaps two *délires*. Carroll's language belongs to the surface, it abides by all the rules and conventions, it is highly grammatical and engages in games (e.g. the portmanteau words) which do not threaten, but on the contrary reinforce it. His form of *délire* is Nonsense with a capital N, a literary genre, a social activity, whose apparent madness and freedom from meaning is only meant to ward off the dangers of meaninglessness and so to promote communication. His is the world of little girls, of politeness, of idealized language. But there is another dimension, that of depth, the depths of the body, where another language emerges, raucous, violent, full of consonants and unpronounceable sounds, of screams and hoarse whispers. This is always threatening to emerge from the orifices of the body, to overcome and destroy the fragile language of the surface, to plunge the subject who is made to utter the sounds into the deepest madness: it is the scream – or breath-language of schizophrenia. Its similarities with the surface game of Nonsense are only apparent. It alone deserves the name of *délire*, for its effect is to disrupt language as the vehicle of meaning. It carries with it the much deeper nonsense of the body: language is no longer *effect* (a system of differential values promoting the exchange of meaning) but *affect*, where the overpowering passions of the body find a direct outlet. It is no longer articulate language: the words cannot be segmented into relevant units of a lower level (as words can be divided into morphemes, morphemes into phonemes). Artaud's portmanteau words preclude analysis: they are no longer means of designation but of action. Artaud is an extreme point in the corpus: if Carroll's language is on the 'normal' side of *délire*, Artaud's poetry is beyond *délire*, at a point where the contradiction has been resolved, by the destruction of the surface organization of language. What Deleuze calls 'the primary order' of the body pervades the text, its violent sounds having replaced normal language.

Semiotic versus symbolic
In Deleuze's analysis, Artaud's *délire* was contrasted with Nonsense, as the primary order of the body and its passions are to be contrasted with the secondary order of normal language. Deleuze does not use the word 'subject' because, for him, any centre of control is forever threatened in its organization by the overriding madness of the depths, because the very notion of a centre of consciousness, of social 'normality', is only the superficial product of a repression of the instincts or drives of the

body, marking the paranoid rather than the schizoid position (cf. Chapters 3 and 5). But even if the difference is not between normal and pathological, the distribution of roles is synchronic: Carroll or Artaud, the choice is made by (or imposed on) each individual.

On the other hand, Julia Kristeva's discussions of Artaud and Roussel ('Le Sujet en Procès', in *Polylogue*; 'La Productivité dite texte', in *Sèmeiôtikè*) deal with the problem of the speaking subject, of who controls linguistic production. Her approach is diachronic. The psychotic makes a breach in the organization of language, and in so doing enables us to look back to the period before the individual acquires language, to the pre-verbal era of the semiotic organization of instincts.

The main opposition here is between what Kristeva calls 'semiotic' and 'symbolic', i.e. between the pre-verbal organization of instinctual drives and language. The centre of control which masters language has been theorized by the philosophical tradition in the concept of the unitary subject. One of its tasks is the repression, the denial of its origins in the semiotic *chora*, or pre-verbal organization of drives. Hence the title of her article on Artaud, 'Le Sujet en Procès' ('The subject on trial – in process').

The term '*chora*' is borrowed from Plato (*Timaeus*) via Derrida (*Positions*): it originally means a receptacle, a matrix, where elements are mixed in chaos before God orders them into a cosmos. In Kristeva's use it means the receptacle where the instincts acquire an unstable and contradictory organization and out of which the subject is formed. The instinctual drives are charged with both psychic and somatic energy (the 'semiotic' is the frontier between the two: one may recall that for Freud drives are on the frontier between soma and psyche), and their energy creates and forms the *chora*. Out of this *chora*, which is fundamentally dynamic, or unstable, emerges the static position of the subject, when the semiotic gives place to the symbolic, or articulate language. The instinctual drives are caught in syntax, in the rules of language: this is when the subject establishes itself above the semiotic *chora* and starts repressing its physical origin.

The subject is generated in the transition from semiotic to symbolic. The movement arises from a primary *rejection* (e.g. Hegel's negation or Freud's death instinct) of the unstable semiotic organization of instincts or drives, which produces the symbolic, where the subject appears and rejection is subdued as *linguistic* negation: the subject is now master over itself, i.e. over language, but only because its material origin is

42

successfully repressed. Since the repressed always returns, its position too is relatively unstable, contradictory. *Délire* embodies the contradiction between the mastery of the subject and the re-emergence of chaos, of the original disruptive rejection. It always hesitates between returning to the pre-verbal *chora*, or protecting language by insisting on its syntactic organization.

If Artaud is the symbol of the first attitude, Roussel represents the second. The concept which Kristeva uses to describe his strategy is that of verisimilitude. We have already noted Roussel's fascination with technical descriptions, with details, and particularly with clichés: all these elements form a style whose main characteristic is its obsession with verisimilitude. Kristeva's theory of verisimilitude is based on the Husserlian theory of meaning. If the authentic will-to-say is the will-to-say-the-truth, the discourse of truth imitates reality, and the discourse of verisimilitude, literary discourse, has a second-order relationship to reality: it imitates the discourse which imitates reality. The reader will have recognized in this conception a transposition of the famous Platonic theory of images and simulacra (the 'real' bed is the Idea in the mind of God, which is imitated by the carpenter who makes the bed; this imitation is in turn imitated by the artist who paints a bed). The literary discourse of verisimilitude, then, lies beyond the opposition between truth and falsehood: it has the appearance of truth, is more 'natural' than truth. Because it is an imitation of a discourse, its only existence is linguistic, syntax and rhetoric are its only principles of organization, internal coherence its only criterion. Kristeva analyses semantic and narrative-syntactic verisimilitude in Roussel: clichés which compensate the extraordinary nature of the events, the well-formedness of the sentence and the narrative which maintains the text within the conventional limits of readability.

In Roussel verisimilitude is always the dominant aspect of the contradiction between verisimilitude and the text as productive/disruptive. The contradiction was there but the rhetoric of the text always filled the breach. Roussel's *délire* is an anti-*délire*; his admiration for the 'natural' discourse of Jules Verne is such that his text can be read as a pastiche; his verisimilitude, then, is second degree: his text imitates a text, which imitates a discourse, which imitates reality. There is excess in this chain of imitations, the excess of *délire*: a vastly different *délire* from that of Artaud, the *délire* of hyper-normality.

Conclusion: the dictionary and the scream

This chapter has moved from a literary to a philosophical corpus. This movement reflects a cultural event: the four texts were assembled into a corpus in the mid 1960s by a group of philosopher–critics. Nor were they the only texts subjected to this treatment: one could add Bataille or Joyce. What the cultural event marked was the discovery of a frontier between philosophy and literature, and its exploration. Bataille, whose work is both fictional and philosophical, is a case in point. *Délire* is the name for this frontier, the point where two theoretical interests meet: literature→language / *délire*←philosophy. What was new was that both sides went the whole hog; they crossed the frontier. But this cultural event was also a theoretical thesis.

As we have seen, language, and its duality, are the objects of this thesis: the opposition between what we might call the 'dictionary', i.e. language as abstract, systematic, an instrument of communication, and the 'scream', i.e. language as material, individual, an expression of the passions and instinctual drives of the human body.

'You may call it ''nonsense'' if you like, . . . but *I've* heard nonsense, compared with which that would be as sensible as a dictionary': thus the Red Queen (*Through the Looking-Glass*, ch. 2) expresses her ultimate confidence in the rules of language.

'This is now the only use which language can have: an instrument of madness, of uprooting of thought, of revolt, a labyrinth of unreason, not a dictionary into which the pedants who dwell on the banks of the Seine direct their mental contractions.' This is what Artaud, writing in 1925, thought of the civilized organization of the dictionary (*Révolution Surréaliste*, n. 3, (1925)): the beginning of his text might be a definition of *délire* as we have described it.

Délire, then, is at the frontier between two languages, the embodiment of the contradiction between them. Abstract language is systematic; it transcends the individual speaker, separated from any physical or material origin, it is an instrument of control, mastered by a regulating subject. Material language, on the other hand, is unsystematic, a series of noises, private to individual speakers, not meant to promote communication, and therefore self-contradictory, 'impossible' like all 'private languages'. It is an integral part of the speaker's body, an outward expression of its drives. It imposes itself on the individual, controlling the 'subject': it is not the transparent medium which the instrumentalist describes, nor the means of consensus which the conventionalist conceives, it is, to misquote a philosophical phrase, a (material) process without a subject. Language which has reverted to its origin in the human body, where the primary order reigns.

This is a real contradiction. Neither of the two languages exists on its own, as an independent entity: material language is repressed and returns to the surface as a disruptive force, and the 'dictionary' is an abstraction which denies the material expression of instincts. *Délire* is the name for this contradiction: the various forms it takes, on a scale which goes from mild to wild, reflect the various modes of dominance in the contradiction. Between the dictionary and the scream, or in both at the same time, *délire* pervades the text, dissolves the subject, threatens to engulf the reader in its disaster, yet saves him – and the text – at the last moment, by preserving an appearance of order, a semblance of linguistic organization. Even screams can become dictionary items; and every word, even an entry in a dictionary, can be a scream.

Notes

1   *Abyme*: an abyss. The term was first used in a technical sense by André Gide, to designate a reflexive process in a work of art – the painter within the picture, the play within the play, as in *Hamlet*, the tale within the tale. More generally, the term is used to refer to the various ways in which a text can reflect itself.
2   The idiom means 'railing' or 'parapet'. Although the metonymy is no longer quite alive, its origin comes readily to mind: a parapet is that which 'protects lunatics', probably by preventing them from throwing themselves into the river.
3   The word means 'tinkering'. It is an important concept in Lévi-Strauss's *The Savage Mind*, where the 'tinkering' of primitive forms of thought is contrasted with the systematic and rational thought of more advanced cultures. For a similar concept, see Karl Popper's *The Poverty of Historicism* (1957), which advocates a form of social and political tinkering, as opposed to 'holistic' (revolutionary) theories of social change – he calls this the 'piecemeal approach'.
4   English words and syllables do not use all the possible combinations of phonemes, but there are rules which govern the combination of phonemes, and distinguish, for instance, a possible coined word from an arbitrary sequence of phonemes: 'splatch' is possible English, 'hjrrckh' is not. These rules, which we often obey without being aware of them, are called phonotactic rules.

Further reading

Raymond Roussel's two main novels are *Impressions d'Afrique* (first published 1910, English

45

translation, *Impressions of Africa* New York: John Calder/Riverrun Press 1985) and *Locus Solus* (first published, 1913; English translation *Locus Solus*, New York: John Calder/Riverrun Press 1985). His complete works have been re-issued by Jean Jacques Pauvert (Paris 1963 onwards): this edition includes a volume entitled *Comment j'ai écrit certains de mes livres* (Paris 1963; English translation, *How I Wrote Certain of my Books*, New York: Sun 1985). Carelman's *Catalogue d'Objets Introuvables* was published by André Balland (Paris 1969). *Mots d'Heures, Gousses, Rames*, by Louis d'Antin Van Rooten, was published in the UK by Angus and Robertson (London 1967).

Page numbers in the section on Brisset refer to Jean Pierre Brisset, *La Grammaire Logique, suivi de La Science de Dieu* (Paris: Tchou 1970). Two other texts have been reissued since then: *Les Origines Humaines* (Paris: Baudouin 1980), and *Le Mystère de Dieu est accompli, Analytica*, vol. 31 (Paris: Navarin 1983) (with an introduction, giving information on Brisset's life, by Philippe Culard).

Page numbers in the section on Wolfson refer to his first book, *Le Schizo et les Langues* (Paris: Gallimard 1970). His second (*Ma mère est morte . . .*) was published by Navarin (Paris 1984). Number 28 of the review *Ornicar* (Paris: Navarin 1984) contains extracts from the second book. A few extracts from the second version of the first book can be found in *Change*, 32–3, 'La Folie Encerclée' (Paris: Seghers-Laffont 1977).

The texts by Artaud mentioned in this chapter can be found in vol. 9 of his *Oeuvres Complètes* (Paris: Gallimard 1971).

Foucault's book on Roussel, *Raymond Roussel*, was published by Gallimard (Paris 1963). His essay on Brisset, 'Sept Propos sur le Septième Ange' is the introduction to Brisset (1970). Deleuze's essay on Wolfson is the introduction to Wolfson (1970). Two essays by Kristeva have been used in this chapter: 'Le Sujet en Procès', in *Polylogue* (Paris: Seuil 1977) (on Artaud), and 'La Productivité dite Texte', in *Sèmeiotikè* (Paris: Seuil 1969) (on Roussel). A selection of articles by Kristeva has appeared in English: *Desire in Language* (Blackwell 1981).

2
The linguistics of délire

Introduction: a philosophical tradition

'What a dreadful mess it's in' Alice remarked, after gazing at it for a few moments in silence. 'What is it, and why is it here?'
'It hasn't any meaning,' said the Cat, 'it simply *is*.'
'Can it talk?' asked Alice eagerly.
'It has never done anything else,' chuckled the Cat.

This passage is taken from the first page of *The Westminster Alice*, Saki's political parody of *Alice in Wonderland*. The creature described is an Ineptitude ('"Have you ever seen an Ineptitude?" asked the Cheshire Cat suddenly.'). A footnote explains that the object of the satire is A. J. Balfour, who was First Lord of the Treasury when Saki was writing. But I choose to interpret the passage as an *abyme* of the text itself. Ineptitudes are what Nonsense and *délire* deal in; for behind the thin disguise of the satire, another character soon appears, the true subject of the description: language as we saw it at work in the last chapter. With his usual acumen, the Cheshire Cat draws Alice's attention to the workings of language, a rather messy object: it grows and proliferates (it never stops talking) in a useless attempt to conceal the ineptitude, the lack of meaning at its centre; but it also has that inescapable solidity which confronts man whenever he comes into contact with reality. As the Cat so aptly says, 'it simply *is*': behind this apparent tautology, there lies a theory of language. It remained largely implicit in the last chapter: it is now time to make it explicit.

In the last chapter I drew heavily on two notions – language and the body – whose exact content is still somewhat vague. In exactly what sense is the term 'language' being used? Is it not merely a metaphor, a rather portentous way of giving an instant solution to whichever problem appears in the course of the discussion? And exactly what is meant by 'the body'? Is it a concept, with a specific place within a definite philosophical discourse, or an empty gesture, an image signalling the presence of a question, and the impossibility of finding a solution for it? The aim of this and the following chapters is to attempt to answer those questions. My contention will be that the concept of language which was implicit in the analysis of the corpus of *délire* is by no means vague or incoherent, that it has become the central tenet of a philosophical tradition, within which it makes sense to talk about *délire* in a non-medical or non-literary fashion. This chapter attempts an exposition of the tradition.

One of the main aspects of the conception of language I am dealing with is that it tries to analyse the relation between language and its physical origins. Of course, this goes beyond the study of the physical organs of speech, or of linguistic acoustics and phonetics. It approaches the production of sounds by the speech organs as a displaced expression of instinctual drives, and also, conversely, the appearance of bodily (psychosomatic) symptoms as depending on unconscious operations of a fundamentally linguistic nature (the metaphor of the *inscription* of a symptom on the surface of the body is often used in this context). In other words, this conception of language remembers that one of the major advances in the understanding of the link between psyche and body was achieved through what an early patient, with considerable insight, called 'the talking cure'. (She used an English phrase because her condition in some ways resembled Wolfson's, and one of her symptoms was that she expressed herself better in English than in her native German.)

But we are not dealing with a simple question of interaction between language and the body: one could formulate a facile mechanistic theory of the influence of the body on linguistic utterance, a linguistic version of a theory of humours. But the tradition we are concerned with has taken a different direction: its main thesis is the central importance of language as the process through which the subject is formed, a process which turns the small animal (*infans*) into a human child. The subject is thus seen as constituted by language and it appropriates the world through language. If we replace 'constitute' by 'dominate', we have the experience of possession which is the main characteristic of *délire*.

The thesis will appear extremely debatable, particularly as it cuts across many respectable traditions of reflection on language, and seems to reject outright the validity of their questions, and to pose other questions which, in the older framework, would appear irrelevant. Thus the classic questions about the relations between language and logic, about sense and reference are shelved; the question of meaning and its construction, will remain, but in an entirely different context. In other words, this tradition deliberately deals with what some Anglo-Saxon linguistic philosophers would call 'nonsense'. And this is one of the reasons why such a tradition finds the utterances of *délire* a relevant object of study.

This position entails at least a partial rejection of the traditions which treat language as an instrument (of expression or of communication) and often try therefore to perfect it, by constructing *logical* languages or grammars. This rejection is perhaps to be interpreted in Freudian terms: as the attempted subversion of a tradition which is, at another level, recognized as valid. We are dealing with a form of transgression, which sets out to explore the dark zones of nonsense deliberately neglected by the older tradition.

I would not like to give the impression that this tradition is based on the (conscious or compulsive) rejection of modern analytic philosophy of language: the relationship is better described as one of blissful ignorance.[1] Nor am I suggesting that this is a totally new tradition, created *ex nihilo* by a few bold spirits. It is enriched by a long succession of philosophical or scientific discussions about language. One can take, for instance, the relationship between this tradition and the science of linguistics. Surely they have something in common, in so far as both insist on the centrality of language. And the relationship is indeed one of filiation (Lacan's debt to Jakobson is well known, and the tradition is full of discussions of the ambiguous figure of Saussure). But it is also one of partial rejection: for linguistic theory often implicitly rests upon a philosophy in which language is conceived as an instrument for communication, mastered by a subject fully conscious of what he is doing when he speaks. In this context, the interest of the tradition is that it has opened up new fields of study for linguists, all centred round the (real or virtual) lack of mastery of the speaking subject: slips of the tongue, jokes and more generally the implicit import of what is being said, fiction as the capacity to say that which is not, and of course *délire*. Rather than focusing on the 'normal' workings of language and communication, the tradition has shifted to what Austin called 'infelicities'. All this, of course, shows how a tradition is established, and that its claims to a creative breakthrough must be considered with calm: for it is built by assimilation of already existing theories (and emphatic rejection of others), in this case not only Freud, but also the Anglo-Saxon tradition of speech–act theory. Thus, fiction, for instance, has long been an object of philosophical thought, from the classic chimera or unicorn to the non-existent beings of Meinong.

One can see why *délire* is an important theme for such a tradition. First, it illustrates its central thesis, of the domination of language over the speaking subject. Second, it also provides a good approach to another essential concept, 'the frontier'. For to assert the central importance of language is not specific enough: it draws our attention to the relationship between language and the subject, but it does not tell us what language is. So the first thesis is coupled with another, more positive one: the crucial point in the study of language is the question of frontiers. 'Positive' is not the right word, for the thesis is much better described as negative. Linguistics has a positive attitude to language when it gives a description of its workings in the rules of grammar. But language has one important characteristic which goes beyond this positive approach: it is imposed on the grammarian, as a part of the material world, as something *given*, the inescapable reality of which forever defeats the theoretical constructions erected by the linguist. So that the real work of the grammarian can be considered as negative. If he is true to his vocation he draws up a list of prohibitions ('one cannot say this', 'this isn't English') and turns into a positive object that part of the territory which is protected by these barriers: from this point of view, a grammar is the set of rules which accounts for the set of sentences *not* under a prohibition. In other words the object of a grammar is to draw the frontier between the grammatical and the a-grammatical. And the work is negative because, fundamentally, the frontiers are imposed on the grammarian by his object: every linguist knows the intense frustration of ultimately not being able to find a convincing explanation of why things are said in exactly the way they are. It is even possible to turn this frustration into a comprehensive view of language: one recalls, in the history of linguistics, the debate between analogists, who maintained that language was a structured object, and anomalists, who drew everyone's attention to its sheer incoherence.

So the problem of frontiers is placed at the centre of the study of language: language is not defined as an instrument for saying all that can be said, but as a structure imposed on the subject and based on the fact that not everything can be said. We can perceive here a link with the 'talking cure', which is also based on the idea that not everything can be expressed (or made conscious), and with *délire* where, from a superficial point of view, nothing is expressed. The paradox of this account of language is that if language is defined negatively, if the problem of the establishment of frontiers becomes crucial, it also means that language will always try to utter what cannot be said, the subject will always be tempted to go beyond the frontier: in order to define a boundary one must at least attempt to cross it. This is exactly what happens in *délire*.

The centrality of language

The thesis of the centrality of language is the point where psychoanalysis meets linguistics. Its two aspects are related to important psychoanalytic conceptions of the subject and the unconscious. The constitutive (or dominating) role of language in the formation of the subject refers to the 'topology' of the subject in psychoanalytic theory, especially to Lacan's conceptions of a de-centred subject.[2] And the idea that unconscious or instinctual phenomena work according to a logic which is fundamentally the same as that of language (the so-called 'logic of the signifier') also stems from Lacan's conception, notably from his definition of what he calls the 'symbolic'. The obvious reference here is his famous maxim about the unconscious as 'structured like a language' and his analysis of the dream-work (notably condensation and displacement) in terms of rhetoric (metaphor and metonymy). It is not my purpose here, however, to give yet another account of Lacan, but rather to illustrate the consequences of some of his theories in the field of language. I shall first try to cast some light on the two main aspects of the thesis I am discussing by briefly considering two articles by Freud (which have become an integral part of the Lacan canon), 'Die Verneinung' ('On Negation')[3] and 'Ein Kind wird geschlagen' ('A child is being beaten').

Both articles offer an account of psychic processes based on a sort of linguistic analysis, in a way which strongly suggests a relation of isomorphism[4] between linguistic and psychic phenomena. In fact the article on negation is based on the hypothesis that logico-linguistic negation and psychological negation have the same origin. By 'psychological negation' Freud means an event which we all experience in our daily life: the absolute necessity of interpreting, often against the conscious volition of its author, a negative sentence as positive in meaning. This is the example Freud himself gives: a patient once said to him, 'you may think that what I am going to say is offensive, but

51

it is not my intention to be so'. Freud interpreted this as an expression of aggression, the (barely) displaced fulfilment of a desire to offend. Or again, according to Freud, if a patient, trying to interpret his own dream, says: 'I don't know who that person was, but it certainly wasn't my mother', the analyst must understand 'it *was* my mother', i.e. he must abstract the linguistic negation from the sentence and consider only the content of the association. In this first superficial analysis negation is seen as reversed affirmation, the price the repressed thought-content has to pay in order to get past censorship. The price is not very high, for the linguistic expression of negation clearly distinguishes the affirmative proposition from the negative particle which governs it, thus at the same time putting forward the affirmative content and negating it: and everyone knows what happened when the man came to bury Caesar, not to praise him. More interestingly perhaps, Freud also contends that this is the way through which unconscious affections of the body manage to reach consciousness: 'I'm lucky, I haven't had a headache for a long time', exclaims the man who, without being yet conscious of it (or refusing to be) feels the first stirrings of pain.

But Freud goes further in his explanation. He relates the linguistic contrast to an early (pre-verbal) instinctual contrast in what he calls the 'pleasure-self', and to a perceptual contrast in what he calls the 'reality-self'. For the position of the primitive pleasure-self is one of oral appropriation of the outside world, through the activities of absorption and rejection. Linguistic negation is the greatly displaced expression of this primitive rejection. But the expression is extremely indirect, for the 'pleasure-self' has given way to a 'reality-self', a subject who has come to terms with the outside world and its constraints. It achieves this through the precise means of a similar movement of rejection, this time perceptual: it learns to distinguish between mere subjective representation, inside the subject, and those representations which can be confirmed, repeated or recovered by perceptions, because they are objective, related to a reality outside the subject. The objective external reality is constituted by a movement of negation/rejection which at the same time constitutes the subject as that which negates reality, that which is inside. This process of negation is typical of what Freud calls 'judgement', (verurteilung: judgement of condemnation) an intellectual act, the capacity to assert and deny, which finds its origin in the interplay of two instinctual drives (Freud relates them to Eros and Thanatos) and its linguistic expression in the operation of negation.

Clearly this line of reasoning is linked with both aspects of our thesis. For the existence of psychological negation shows that the subject cannot master his own discourse: it turns each instance of one of the main linguistic operations into a potential slip of the tongue or symptom. But it also shows an isomorphism between utterances and instinctual drives. Negation, as a linguistic transformation in Chomsky's sense, corresponds to a psychic reality, but not in the classic psycholinguistic sense, where you measure the lengths of response to various utterances: the amount of time, hopefully, increases with the complexity of the sentence. There, the linguistic operation has only a relationship of coincidence with the psychic phenomenon, the reality of which it attests. Our tradition makes the much stronger assertion that the psychic phenomena themselves, in this case the instinctual drives or the unconscious processes, conform to the same basic semiotic patterns as language. Language is only the end-product of a chain of semiotic processes some of which have a physical reality in the body.[5]

The best illustration of these patterns is perhaps given by the famous *fort/da* scene analysed by Freud. In it, a child re-enacts the disappearance and return of its mother through the use of a binary opposition between two sounds (/ɔ:/ and /a:/ – a minimal pair), which therefore take on a distinctive, phonemic, value. This accession to the level of symbolic structure is a crucial stage in the development of the child into a subject. But it is only a *stage*, for there is a continuity between the workings of the instinctual drives (absorption/rejection), the psychic processes of subject formation and the linguistic operations of assertion and negation. Absorption versus rejection; presence versus absence; self versus the other; inside versus outside; assertion versus negation: the semiotic structure of distinctive opposition (the minimal pair) pervades all the processes that contribute to the formation of the subject.

This pervasiveness is also manifest in the second article, 'A child is being beaten', in which Freud analyses a recurrent sadistic fantasy, where the patient imagines a child being beaten (at first by an unspecified agent, then by its father, lastly by a schoolmaster). The interesting point for us is that the fantasy, which is presented as a *scene* (which the patient witnesses) can only be understood and analysed if it is given a linguistic form. Starting from the surface sentence 1 'a child is beaten', Freud obtains two other sentences, one consciously produced by the patient, 2 'my father beats the child (I hate)', and the other a masochistic fantasy, only approached indirectly because it remains unconscious, 3 'my father beats me'. What is fascinating about this (linguistic) analysis is that first, the fantasy does *not* function like a natural language (there is no possible linguistic transformation between the three sentences) and yet second, it uses exactly the same operations as a natural language. Sentence 1, for instance, because it can be 'transformed' into 2, raises the problem of the difference between the subject of the utterance and the speaking subject, which is noticeably absent from the sentence, and only present if we add to it an implicit quasi-performative: 'I say that I see this scene: a child is beaten.' It also raises the question of subject of utterance and topic: the agent in 1 has characteristically been erased, and the analysis that obtains 2 and 3 performs the linguistic work of recovering the subject. Sentence 2 raises the problem of presupposition: analysis gives us another sentence, which conditions 2: 4 'my father loves me alone'. And all the sentences use fantasmatic negation, which functions like linguistic negation, but with different elements: for the unconscious ignores *linguistic* negation, and yet operates something which closely resembles it: 'I love him' becomes by negation of affect 'I hate him', by inversion of personal pronouns (of subject and object) 'he loves me', or by implicit negation of focus 'it is another (i.e. not me) who loves him'.

And yet the fantasy is not linguistic, not a succession of sentences, but rather visual: it takes the form of a succession of scenes in the patient's day-dreaming. But its structure conforms to rules which are isomorphic with those of a grammar, so that it makes sense to talk about 'fantasmatic negation' or a 'grammar of fantasy'. In other words, the semiotic processes, of which language provides the best example, also operate at other, non-verbal or pre-verbal, levels: we have already recalled the similarity, noted by linguists and psychoanalysts alike, between types of dream work and certain rhetorical devices.

The picture these two articles give of the workings of the human psyche confirms the analysis that was inspired by the corpus of *délire* in the last chapter: language masters the subject, the unconscious processes and instinctual drives conform to the same semiotic rules as language. Yet, the corpus we analysed has also convinced us that there is a difference between surface language and the deeper utterances of the body, and that *délire* dwells on this frontier. Any conception of language along these Freudian lines will ultimately be founded on an exploration of this frontier; and the 'language of madmen', far from being the specialized concern of a handful of psychiatrists, becomes a central preoccupation for the theory of language.

The language of madness

The peculiarities of the utterances of mental patients have long attracted notice, and there are numerous studies of, for instance, the language of schizophrenia. But these enlightening studies were in most cases the work of psychiatrists with little or no training in linguistics. What changed in France in the 1960s was that new interest was taken in the subject from two directions: a few linguists decided that it was relevant for the study of language to explore its margins, the dubious no man's land where it begins to dissolve, and certain psychoanalysts found in the internal development of their theory new reasons to do research on psychosis and to pay renewed and more informed attention to the workings of language. The texts we are now going to examine have the advantage of belonging to both trends, for their author, Luce Irigaray, is both a psychoanalyst and a linguist: she belonged to the Ecole Freudienne de Paris and wrote her thesis on *Le Language des Déments* (in which *déments* is to be taken in the narrow technical sense of people suffering from senile dementia). It must, however, be stressed here that we will only consider her early work: she later broke with the Ecole Freudienne and became a distinguished exponent of philosophical feminism.

The new research may not have provided a fundamental breakthrough in the study of the language of schizophrenia, but it significantly changed the emphasis: even the most delirious utterances of patients were now seen not as mere gibberish, but as texts which could be accounted for according to the rules of linguistic structure, even if they broke them repeatedly. We are going from mere delirium to *délire*, i.e. an utterance which, at the very moment when it plays havoc with language acknowledges the domination of the rules it transgresses. The schizophrenic's love of language, his vocation to become a linguist is at last recognized. Characteristically, the first of the two articles I shall comment on, 'The Schizophrenic and the Question of the Sign', tries to assess the relevance, for the language of schizophrenia, of the distinctions on which linguistics, as an independent science, is based: *langue* and *parole*, competence and performance, the signifier and the signified.

The first of these distinctions is ignored by the schizophrenic, who masters neither the collective system of differential values (*langue*) nor its creative use by the individual speaker (*parole*): he is not the bearer of the treasury of words, of the dictionary that all other speakers of the language carry in their minds; his glossary is neither 'his own' nor 'common to all', for it is defined by specific relations to 'the language of the mother' (Irigaray, p. 32). His is a private language, an idiolect, unfit for communicating with. His code is not the pattern of relations of a *langue*, but rather a web, an intricate and fragile structure, the centre of which has been torn away. Because *langue* is absorbed into the private code of his mother's language[6] (a contradiction, but one with which the schizophrenic has to live), no *parole* is possible, no creative use of a shared system: the meaning is not created by the specific arrangements of words in the message. It is given in the mother's corpus of utterances, in her private code, which dominates and limits the patient's own utterances. The meaning can be misread, distorted, destroyed, but not avoided or shared or creatively altered. His 'grammar' provides him with pre-programmed sentences, which he must reproduce, repeat, even out of context, in what appears to be delirium. We understand better now Wolfson's attitude to his mother tongue, and his difficulty in trying to destroy it, his inability to escape it altogether.

The second distinction sounds more promising. As we know, the words 'competence' and 'performance' in Chomsky correspond roughly to *langue* and *parole* in Saussure, with one important difference: competence is not, like *langue*, a dictionary of elements, of words, but a list of rules, a grammar; indeed, the rules of syntax form the core of competence, whereas they were allocated to *parole* by Saussure. As a result, creativity is not the exclusive feature of performance and *parole*: there is also creativity at the level of competence (as shown for instance by the existence of recursive rules). The schizophrenic's competence, however, is not creative, it is determined by his mother's. In *her* language, the creativity of competence can produce a virtual infinity of sentences; in *his* language, the actual sentences produced by her competence become so many programmes beyond which he cannot go. His is a limited competence, devoid of creativity. But he has a form of competence, though a displaced one. He is not only 'spoken' by his mother's utterances, but also attempts to speak in his own right: his competence becomes metalinguistic, he turns into a linguist, trying to find rules beyond the sentences which are imposed on him, playing on language in an attempt to discover the secret of its working, deconstructing the syntax, the rules of which are not his, only his mother's. Here, not unexpectedly, Irigaray refers to Wolfson, whose practice corresponds closely to her description. The schizophrenic, therefore, does not speak, he un-speaks the language of his mother; in generative terms, his linguistic activity does not go from deep to surface structure, but the other way round:[7] the surface structure of his own utterances is an enigma, a cryptogram, behind which we must find the deep structure and the rules that generate it – which is exactly the task of the linguist.

One can understand the meaninglessness, or madness, of his speech, if one turns to the third distinction, between the signifier and the signified, whose union forms the meaningful unit which is the sign. The schizophrenic stands in a peculiar relation to the sign: for him, the only source of 'meaning' is in the meaningless signifiers of his mother's discourse. The signifier for him does not *represent* a signified assigned to it by the speaking subject as a member of a community of native speakers: it *repeats*, imperfectly, after the event, a signification which escapes the schizophrenic himself. We have here the by now familiar structure of a central absence (the lack of meaning) compensated for by an excess, the excess of signifiers which, through repetition, transformation or derivation, forever try to reconstruct the absent meaning. This language, in its eccentricity, is ex-centric in the etymological sense. An excess of signifiers, a lack of signifieds: this indicates both the failure of the sign and the power of the signifier. And with this comes a disquieting conviction: this type of language may not be exclusive to the schizophrenic; it may be the dark side of all language, ignored and denied by the speaker but nevertheless virtually present in every utterance. One cannot escape one's mother tongue.

Let us return to Irigaray's article to note a paradox. For I have already stated that the new departure in the study of the language of schizophrenia was the emphasis on similarities with normal language and the avoidance of such terms as 'word-salad', sometimes used by psychiatrists in this context. But what Irigaray actually does is to show the inadequacy of the classic concepts. And the paradox is undoubtedly present in the text: for her study is confined to these concepts, even if it is intended to show their inadequacy. I have no solution to this paradox, but I think that it is meaningful, and can help to clarify the concept of language. The theory of language which is being expounded is based on the unstable and paradoxical coexistence under the term 'language' of several meanings (to which specific concepts will be assigned later). By 'language' is meant first what the linguist describes: a *natural* object, and, once the grammarian has finished with it, a *structured* object (I leave aside for the time being the difference between the faculty of language – *langage* in

French – and the concrete object which is called *a* language – *une langue*). But both the natural object and the structured description abstracted from it imply a frontier, which is inevitably crossed: language is also what lies on the other side of the frontier, in delirium and nonsense, in jokes and symptoms; it is also that part of the natural object which escapes the structuring process, which in the course of the process is left aside, because it resists it and transgresses its rules: having read Wolfson and Irigaray, we could call this *maternal* language. One could give a simple epistemological picture of the process: a flow of phenomena on which the observer imposes a structure, thus leaving a residue of irrelevant phenomena. But the study of Freud's articles has enabled us to go further: linguistic structure is not an abstraction imposed on the flow of discourse from outside; it is rather the fragile and complex surface form of a more general semiotic process. Saussure already maintained that linguistics was only one part – albeit the essential part – of the wider field of semiology. 'Language' is in fact sometimes used in a third, more general sense, where it stands for the whole *semiotic* process: non-verbal or pre-verbal phenomena are also part of this process, which is the process of the emergence of the subject in its subordination to the semiotic law. The thesis of the centrality of language can be summed up thus: the subject is nothing outside the order of language by which it has been formed, where 'language' is the unstable combination of natural and structural elements, of maternal and semiotic processes.

The second article by Irigaray, 'Communication Linguistique et Spéculaire', deals with this problem: exactly what part is played by language, or more generally by the semiotic process, in the constitution of the subject? Its goal is to enable us to draw a map of the languages of madness, and it ends in a rather brief sketch of such a typology, where an attempt is made to distinguish between the languages of schizophrenia, of obsessional neurosis, of hysteria and of clinical delirium. This part is very sketchy, but the real interest of the text lies in the theoretical construction which precedes it, in which Irigaray tries to elaborate significant ways of understanding the language of madness, the various forms of *délire*, as distortions of a semiotic process which every speaking subject undergoes: the process of construction of the subject by 'the reciprocal integration of language and the body'. It is the impact of the discourse of others on *this* body which turns it into *my* body: the purely imaginary relationship I have with it is mediated by the symbolic law, the law of language, and in the process appears the 'I', the self that this body is after all; it is both dominated by the law of language and capable of using it for purposes of communication, of entering the world of intercommunication, where a place has been assigned to me.

The whole article is based on a parallelism between the structuring of the subject when it goes through what Lacan calls the 'mirror-stage', and the linguistic constitution of the subject when it masters the proper use of personal pronouns. Lacan borrowed the idea of a mirror-stage from the French psychologist, Henri Wallon, but reinterpreted it in psychoanalytic terms. (We must remember that the idea that every child goes through a mirror-stage has been denied by some psychologists.) The mirror-experience, the crucial moment of the mirror-stage, is supposed to occur at the age of about six months, when the child has not fully mastered its own body, and in fact does not yet realize that this body is different and separate from that of its mother. In the mirror-experience it confronts its own image in a mirror, and realizes that this other body it sees is in fact *itself*, a recognition that is a source of intense glee. The experience, however, can only occur if an adult is present, whose look both confirms and guarantees that the experience was genuine. This is the core of what Irigaray calls 'specular communication'. It can be symbolized thus: before the experience, the child's body is not unified, nor is it clearly perceived as separate from other bodies, an indistinct whole composed of fragments, not a single, organized body; the experience begins with a feeling of alienation, as the child is confronted in the mirror with an image it perceives as alien; this feeling is reversed by the realization that the body is a self; it is confirmed by the adult observer.

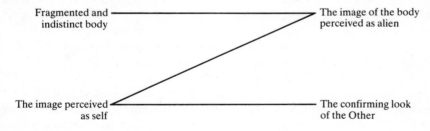

So far, Irigaray is more or less repeating Lacan. But she goes on to suggest a parallel between this 'specular communication' and linguistic communication: the process through which the subject acquires the mastery of speech and, by learning to use the personal pronouns, becomes a speaking subject (a pleonastic phrase, on this theory) is parallel to the sequence of events in the mirror-stage. As Lacan drew on Wallon, Irigaray draws on Benveniste's famous articles on personal pronouns, which she re-interprets in psychoanalytical terms. Benveniste's analysis of the system of personal pronouns in French distinguishes genuine personal pronouns, the 'shifters' of the first and second person, from the non-personal pronouns of the third, which are not shifters: the third-person pronoun designates the absent third party in the dialogue, or the party who is present but does not or cannot talk. The reference of third-person pronouns, in a given context, is constant, and does not shift whenever the speaking subject changes, whereas 'I' and 'you' change reference whenever the person who speaks changes. So 'he' or 'she' are not shifters; they are the same sort of pronouns as impersonal '*on*' (a French pronoun which is used when the action of the verb is not assigned to a specific agent: it is usually translated into English by 'one', 'you' or 'they', or by putting the sentence in a passive form).

Irigaray, too, arranges the pronouns into a system, but with a different meaning: the system is the synchronic image of the diachronic process through which the *infans* becomes a subject, by going from impersonal '*on*' to the correct use of 'I' and 'you' in a situation of communication (and linguists like Jakobson have noticed the peculiar difficulties attached to learning the correct use of shifters). In the beginning, there is only the impersonal '*on*' of indistinction (before the mirror-stage the child does not conceive its body as separated from its mother's). But the family situation, to the child's dismay, turns out to be triangular, and mother and father do exchange the 'I' and 'you' of communication, in discourses where the child has no part – even if it is the topic. This situation of exclusion, which is an experience of absence, of emptiness, of death, in which the child is a non-person, is at the same time a point of entry into the linguistic system: through its very exclusion from dialogue the child is included in it as the object of discourse, the non-person which conditions the linguistic exchange (according to the classic structuralist account, it is the circulation of the empty element, of the blank, which produces meaning within a system). The English language, which allows the use of the pronoun 'it' for a child, suits Irigaray's argument here better than French (she has to compensate for this by using the symbol 'il_o' for this stage). The next stage occurs when the child, no longer a mere blank, is named; it becomes a person, a he or a she (in Irigaray notation, 'il_1') by receiving a name, the means of insertion into a

cultural system of differential values, the best instance of which is the
linguistic system: he or she now occupies the place in the social system
assigned by the linguistic law, becoming, by being named, the son or
daughter of so and so. In acquiring a name, he or she becomes a separate
element in the linguistic exchange: the only thing that he or she lacks is the
ability to use shifters; when he or she learns this, he or she becomes a person, a subject, in both senses of the word ('subjective' and 'subjected').

To show the parallel with the mirror-stage, we can draw another
diagram:

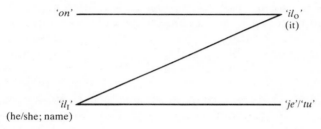

The word 'diachronic' which we used at the beginning of the last
paragraph raises a problem: it is not Irigaray's contention that a child
actually says '*on*' or '*il*' before '*je*' and '*tu*'. We are to understand that
the linguistic system bears the traces of the diachronic process of the
emergence of the subject, and that this process is inscribed within the
system of personal pronouns. This is not surprising since the process
is one of entry into the structure of language. Benveniste had already
noticed that the only definition one could give of 'I' was a circular one:
by 'I' is meant the person who, in a given context of communication,
says 'I'. We have here a similar circularity: by a subject, an 'I', is meant
the result of the process by which a human individual learns to say 'I'
and to accept the linguistic law. And the parallel between the two
diagrams (above) shows how language and the body are connected: for
both experiences (the gleeful experience of the mirror-stage, and the
acquisition of language) involve the emergence of the subject. They are
experiences not only of unification (of the self), but also of separation
(of the child from its mother, and of the subject from the ineffable truth
of its pre-verbal being) and of alienation into a semiotic system (the
Oedipal triangle of the family or the linguistic system). What we have
reached here is the third, and better known, diagram, Lacan's '*schéma L*':

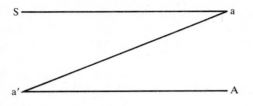

The subject, in this topological figure, is de-centred, attracted to the four corners at once. 'S' represents, in Lacan's terms, its 'ineffable and stupid existence', 'a' its objects (the objects of desire), 'a'' what is reflected by its objects, i.e. the self (not to be understood as another term for the unitary subject), and 'A' the place of the Other, of the Law, of the Name of the Father (the old triangle, within the subject, can be found in a–a'–A). And this too is the synchronic representation of a diachronic story: it reminds us that the subject is not the origin of his discourse, that on the contrary he is formed by language, a social order anterior and exterior to him; what Lacan, following Lévi-Strauss, calls the symbolic. The story is one of victory and defeat, of gain and loss: as the *infans* becomes a subject he loses the truth about his own being, from which he is irretrievably separated by his subordination to the social order. But he gains access to the mastery of language and the relative freedom of the individual *person.*

If we go back to Irigaray's article, we can see how this can be useful for an analysis of the languages of madness: each of the varieties of *délire* she distinguishes can be described as the result of a mishap in the subjective process and of attempts to compensate for it; the schizophrenic's linguistic strategy, for instance, can be understood as a failure of full subjective status owing to the impossible separation from his mother and consequent excess in the domination of a symbolic law which he cannot master or understand, but which he is ceaselessly trying to decipher.

The frontiers of language

In the last section, I concentrated on one aspect of the thesis of the centrality of language: the role of language, or language-like processes, in the constitution of the subject. Our discussion has enabled us to clarify a little what we mean by language: an unstable combination of structural and maternal elements, and the surface form of wider semiotic processes governed by the symbolic law. This heterogeneity and instability can be traced to the relationship between language and the human body, a reciprocal relationship of utterance (where language in its materiality is produced by the body) and inscription (where the symbolic-linguistic system gives unity and form to the self and its body, and is inscribed on the body in the form of symptoms). The interest of *délire* in this context is that its texts provide a source for studying this relationship: in the infelicities that distinguish *délire* from the language of communication, the utterance of screams and the inscription of symptoms are, albeit distortedly, transcribed. In other words, in the texts of *délire*, the frontiers of language are crossed. We will now attempt to explain this, the second aspect of the thesis of the centrality of language.

But the previous section was also excessively abstract, concentrating as it did on a linguistic system (of personal pronouns) rather than on an individual text. It was, necessarily, more concerned with the global construction of linguistic subjects than with the concrete utterances in which meaning is conveyed. The time has now come to consider more closely how the subject masters (or fails to master) the text he or she produces, how meaning is exchanged (or not): this is what the study of frontiers is about. And we shall start empirically, by asking ourselves how meaning is produced in the first sentences of two novels.

Here is, then, the first sentence of Mary Webb's *Precious Bane*: 'It was at a love-spinning that I saw Kester first.' And here, rather predictably, I confess, is the first sentence of *Finnegan's Wake*: 'riverrun, past Eve and Adam's, from swerve of shore to bend of bay, brings us by a commodius vicus of recirculation back to Howth Castle and Environs'. Obviously, the two sentences may be contrasted because the second breaks a certain number of 'rules' which the first one respects: 'meaning' cannot be obtained in the same way from the two sentences. *Precious Bane*, a mimetic text,[8] maintains distinctions between well defined linguistic levels. For instance, there is a *lexical* level in which every word receives a meaning, and at which the meaning of the sentence is – at least partially – obtained by combining the meanings of individual words.[9] Rules of compatibility (projection rules in the vocabulary of standard generative grammar) ensure that the sentence fares better than the celebrated 'colourless green ideas sleep furiously'. And there is even a space for creativity, for one word in the sentence, 'love-spinning' may be meaningless at first for the reader (the second sentence of the novel says roughly: if you do not know what a love-spinning is, you will soon learn), but it is itself composed of perfectly respectable elements, and is a well-formed compound word, whose meaning, if not clear straight away, may be guessed at or retrieved from the context. Besides, it occupies a regular syntactic slot (the position of a noun, following a preposition and an article). So there is a second, *syntactic*, level which contributes to the construction of meaning. It does this not only in the obvious etymological way (the meaning varies according to the various ways the words are 'put together', i.e. the purely semantic rules of projection are dependent on the syntactic arrangement of words: here, for instance, the meaning is affected by the grammatical operation of focus, which stresses the importance of 'love-spinning') but also in a more devious way. The very well-formedness of the sentence contributes to its meaning, through what Roland Barthes called '*phrasé*': a syntactically correct sentence forms a whole, and this tends to reinforce, and even to harden or freeze its meaning, by turning it, too, into a fixed unit. This is the source of his famous maxim accusing language of being fascist.

Syntactic correction freezes meanings. But there is also a third, *implicit*, level: the sentence uses presupposition (for 'I saw Kester first' implies subsequent meetings), and what we might call narrative presupposition. This is indeed the first sentence of a fairly conventional novel, a genre which often uses circularity (the end of the novel is already hinted at in the first pages). We know that Kester is a man's name, and something (which we derive both from the way the sentence is phrased, and from our cultural expectations about the way such novels are written) tells us that the 'I' refers to a woman: indeed, if we extract the three relevant words, all present in the text (but in the wrong order), we have the argument of the novel: 'I . . . love . . . Kester'. The heroine duly marries her Kester on the last page.

So the construction of meaning in the sentence rests on specific rules, which apply at various levels of the linguistic structure. We ought in fact to have added a fourth level to the three we mentioned: the phonic/graphic level, taken for granted in the mimetic text, except when it (painfully) tries to reproduce the dialect of Cockneys, foreigners and country bumpkins. Thus the very first sign of the text, a capital letter, conforms to a graphic rule which hardly reaches our full consciousness until we read the first page of *Finnegan's Wake*. And if we glance at that first page, we come across this fine rendering of 'the fall', which is not even an onomatopoeia, since it contains the words for 'thunder' in various

languages (French and Greek for instance): babadalgharaghtakammina-
vronnkonnbronntonnerronntuonnthunntrovarrrhounawnskawntoohoo-
hoordenentthurnuk!' A 'word' like this plays on sounds, and makes it
clear that the overall construction of meaning is also obtained by the
careful marshalling of sounds, as even the most incompetent poet knows.
But what it also suggests (and this goes beyond conventional poetics)
is that playing with sounds can also be the symptomatic expression of
instinctual drives, as we saw in Artaud's demolition of Carroll: here,
'meaning' may well escape the subject's grasp.

The exact number of levels varies according to the theory (it is
questionable, for instance, to isolate what I have called the implicit level),
but what is imposed on the linguist by his object is the existence of levels,
the best image for which is still the pyramid: it is language, not the
linguist, which insists on double articulation. Language is an inescapable
part of reality and this is how it works: a pyramid of levels, a system
of systems.

But this is only half of the picture. For at every level there is a frontier,
which must not be crossed, and therefore often is. This is what the concept
of frontier is about, the central paradox of language. On the one hand,
language is founded on the impossibility of saying everything (the
grammatical implies the existence of the non-grammatical, and the
linguistic structure is based on exclusion: 'one cannot say this'); on the
other hand, there is nothing that cannot be said (or nothing need be
left unsaid), provided one is prepared (and even, sometimes, compelled)
to break the rules. This paradox, a genuine one, for we must maintain
both propositions, and they are incompatible, has correspondences on
other levels, in the contradiction between the normative and the
descriptive approach (there must be rules; there isn't a rule that isn't
transgressed, through error, exceptions, creativeness, or even rhetorical
devices like conversion: 'grace me no grace, nor uncle me no uncle!',
exclaims the righteous uncle before his imploring nephew), or in the
controversy between the analogists and the anomalists, to which I have
already alluded.

So, beyond these various frontiers appears the other side of language,
and a different process of meaning-formation: the contrast between the
two sentences and the two novels is that *Finnegan's Wake* relies heavily
on this dark side of language. What we have to draw now is a map of
infelicities, we might say a grammar of *délire*. Let us try, on one level
after the other, to cross the frontier.

If we cross the frontier at the phonic level, we find something resembling Joyce's pseudo-onomatopoeia: the unpronounceable word or the inarticulate scream. Our discussion of Artaud and Brisset in the last chapter showed us how language is disturbed by the mad poetics of the scream. If we cross the lexical frontier, we have the portmanteau word ('riverrun', or 'recirculation'). On the other side of this frontier, we can roam far and wide: some coined words are tame, like 'recirculation', and can be assimilated without damage by the system, as happened to the Carrollian 'chortle'; some are wilder creatures, as the second paragraph of *Finnegan's Wake* will show: 'Sir Tristram, violer d'amores, fr'over the short sea, had passencore rearrived from North Armorica on this side the scraggy isthmus of Europe Minor to wielderfight his penisolate war.' The wildness of these fakes (we might call them forgeries, seeing that words, like coins, have exchange value) is due to two characteristics: first, meaning proliferates, and is no longer obtained by the combination of fixed units; as with Brisset, words are analysed more than once: 'passencore'→'pas encore' (not yet), 'passe encore' (well and good), etc. second, meaning is weighted with the tabooed affections of the body; Freud had already suggested that portmanteau words were fragments of sexual words put together. This is only another way of stating the paradox of language: not everything can be said, because of repression and censorship, but nothing need be left unsaid, because censorship can always be lifted or circumvented through the rhetorical devices of the joke or dream work. Crossing the frontier, then, is sometimes an unconscious and always a significant act, in which meaning is not composed or constructed by the subject, but woven into the text in a rather desultory and unsystematic manner. In the sentence we have just quoted, the tabooed words appear clearly enough beneath the portmanteau or the foreign words (and the river Oconee is duly mentioned in the next sentence). Here is a less obvious Carrollian example: the last line of *The Hunting of the Snark* occurred to Lewis Carroll one day, out of the blue. He never knew where it came from, yet it formed the foundation of the whole poem. The line reads: 'For the Snark was a Boojum, you know.' Research shows that the line is an echo from a poem written by one of his cousins. But this source is, unfortunately, of no interest, for it does not contain the two coined words 'Snark' and 'Boojum', which are Carroll's specific contribution (the poem by Mrs Hart, Carroll's cousin, mentions, using the same words and the same rhythm, a dog and a mouse). The first of these two words has often been analysed, and there is no reason to diverge from the classic explanation: it is clearly a portmanteau word, which conforms to phonotactic rules, and could, for instance, be obtained by condensation from 'snail' and 'shark'. And if this seems too tame to the reader, any dictionary of historical slang will provide convenient sexual words to replace these two. But the second word, 'Boojum' has not been explained: I suggest – this is my own modest contribution to *délire* in this book – that it is a childhood word, the Carrollian equivalent of the Freudian *fort-da* experience. It does sound like a child's word, it *is* founded on the opposition between a long vowel (/u:/) and a short one (/ʌ/), and the name is after all about a disappearance (because the Snark is a Boojum the Baker vanishes at the end of the poem). If Freud describes the child acting out the scene of his separation from his mother, a game which enables him to cope with the situation and embrace his separate existence and individuality, perhaps we have here the trace of Carroll's own experience of a similar separation from his mother, a separation rendered all the more traumatic as it occurred early, for the young Lewis Carroll, like most Victorian children, was soon displaced by a younger baby.

I have commented at some length on coined words to show how, beyond the frontier, a different process of meaning develops. The rules are no longer explicit and clear cut; meaning is no longer obtained by definition and composition through projection rules: the winding paths of allusion, echo, private play on words and figures of speech must be tentatively explored; they never yield more than fragments of meaning, which it is almost impossible to assemble into a coherent whole, a totality.[10]

Let us now cross the next frontier on the semantic level: we shall find sentences like the one quoted above ('colourless green ideas . . .'), which contradict the rules of semantic construction; we shall also find rather more common forms, for figures of speech are, in some accounts, nothing but semantic anomalies: if 'I meet Kester' is semantically well-formed because the verb 'meet' requires that both subject and object be human, what about 'roads meet'? It is a metaphor (frozen into cliché),[11] the conscious misuse of language for creative purposes. But this type of account, which derives metaphors and figures of speech from 'normal' language clearly underestimates their quantitative and qualitative importance: perhaps the capacity to produce them is a vital characteristic of language, at least as important as the straightforward conveying of information. This is certainly what a conception of language based on the existence of frontiers – and therefore bent on the exploration of the other side of language – suggests; and it is confirmed by the fact that metaphor and metonymy, as we have seen, are the linguistic forms of a more general semiotic process, and can be equated to the main operations of the dream-work as described by Freud.[12]

So far we have breached the phonic, lexical and semantic frontiers. The new country is both strange and familiar, full of old schooldays friends, but also of traps and pitfalls. If we now cross the syntactic frontier we shall soon meet two of these old friends, anacoluthon and solecism. For not all sentences are examples of grammar, nor are all writers worthy of Dr Johnson: either deliberately or unwittingly they cross the frontier into dubious or incorrect syntax. e. e. cummings's famous line, 'he sang his didn't he danced his did', or most of *Finnegan's Wake* belong to the first category: a deliberate misuse of syntax, sometimes called anacoluthon. The second, solecism, is less easy to illustrate, for an aura of opprobrium still surrounds the term: yet the psychopathology of everyday life predicts that even the most conscious stylist will occasionally make a slip. Often those slips reveal a depth of meaning of which the author was probably not aware (this, of course, can hardly ever be proved).

Since it is too iconoclastic to accuse Conrad or Dickens of having committed solecisms, I have taken the easy option of quoting from the autobiography of John Merrick, better known as the Elephant Man: 'Being unable to get employment my father got me a pedlar's licence to hawk the town, but being deformed, people would not come to the door to buy my wares.' In this sentence present participles with erased subjects are used with verbs whose subjects are different from the erased element. This, according to the best English grammars, constitutes a solecism (known as 'the unattached participle'). Two things have to be said to qualify this: this construction only became a solecism in the nineteenth century, and was still established practice, often found in the best authors, in the eighteenth century; one may therefore suppose that it remained established in popular dialects long after this (it probably still is), and John Merrick, an almost illiterate man, must have used it as a matter of course. Yet the very frequency, in the short text of his autobiography, of the turn of phrase, suggests another explanation, added to the historical–philological one: for the erased subject of the unattached participle is 'I', and as a result of this the sentence becomes impersonal, or rather the function of the erased subject is transferred to the other subject. What fails to emerge here is the 'I', the subject of mastered communication, the linguistic representation of the unitary subject, of the individual person, whose mirror image assures (and reassures) him that he is indeed a person, *this* person: the implications of this failure in the case of the Elephant Man are clear.

But both anacoluthon and solecism have a reassuring appearance: they both refer to a subject, either master of his language (the poet) or mastered by his unconscious – the frontier is crossed by someone. What if language itself crossed its own frontiers? The structure of language, as a *system*, is based on the existence of units at each level, and on their grouping into relevant units of the next level (phonemes into morphemes, etc.): what if language denied or destroyed its own structure by allowing multiple or irrelevant groupings to emerge, by inciting the users to cut up the utterances into incorrect fragments? I am alluding here to various phenomena well known to linguists: folk-etymology (where the etymological helico/pter has become heli/copter, hence the abbreviation 'copter'), syntactic ambiguity ('the workmen tore up the street'), or what is sometimes called 'sentences within sentences', which can be illustrated by the old joke:

> *Oh, John, do not kiss me!*
> *Oh, John, do not kiss!*
> *Oh, John, do not*
> *Oh, John, do*
> *Oh, John,*
> *Oh!*

Apart from its unrepentant male-chauvinist attitude, the joke shows, in a rather exaggerated fashion, that there may appear in a sentence other, parasitic, sentences only obtained by hesitant segmentation or by the outrageous (but not impossible) removal of essential elements of meaning: in the joke, the meaning changes when the negation is removed; we have already seen that Freudian analysis assigns general relevance to the possibility of such removal (this is confirmed by the need for the feminist reminder that 'when a woman says no, it means no').

I want to insist on the ludicrousness of the whole proceedings: the sentence within a sentence, except in cases of genuine ambiguity, only appears when the rules of segmentation are not broken but forced, producing impossible phrases, and creatures like Carroll's

'Mock-Turtle' (from 'mock turtle soup'). Thus the sentence 'Jeeves waits on Bertie' is not really ambiguous: only if we divide it, wrongly, into 'Jeeves waits/on Bertie' (notice that 'Jeeves waits' is a sentence within a sentence) does a second, ludicrous meaning appear.[13] But this is the whole point: there is provocation, the structure induces us to explore its possibilities, and in so doing to cross the frontier – illegitimate ambiguity is produced by the system. This soon becomes clear if English is not your own language and you happen to make a mistake in understanding the above sentence (errors in translation often make pleasant reading).

Perhaps the last of our transgressions will be the crossing of the borderline of the whole text: for the text as a whole, and not only the sentence, is a relevant linguistic unit, with specific rules of formation. If we cross this frontier we enter into nonsense, as in the non-sequiturs, in which Richard Corbet, a minor seventeenth-century poet, specialized, or in this old Nursery favourite, 'The Great Panjandrum':

> She went into the garden
> To cut a cabbage-leaf
> To make an apple-pie.
> Just then a great she-bear,
> Coming down the street
> Poked its nose into the shop-window.
> 'What! no soap?'
> So he died
> And she very imprudently married the barber . . . .

But beyond this frontier we may also enter into *délire*, the *délire* of Roussel and Wolfson, of Artaud and Joyce.

Let us take a look at the whole map. A natural language can be described as a system of subsystems: at every level, a relevant unit is defined by its place in the system. But at each level there is a borderline between the system and what it excludes. The paradox of language is that first, the term is used to designate both the system and what lies outside it and, second, that this is not a terminological mistake, to be remedied by the invention of a new name for what lies outside the system, but a necessary situation, for the two sides of language (the systematic and the subversive) are inseparable. One could here use the famous metaphor of the two sides of a sheet of paper, used by Saussure to demonstrate the solidity and closeness of the relation between signifier and signified in the sign. The reverse side of language is the subversive opposite of the 'normal' side, and as such hardly distinguishable from it. On the bright side, meaning is constructed by differentiation and composition, and the totality, and the closed character of the system, guarantee its correct construction. On the dark side, meaning proliferates, in short threads that can hardly manage to weave a coherent text: there is no totality, no guarantee, and the field is never closed. Language has both a bright and a dark side to it. The best picture of this can be admired when the borderline is crossed at the ultimate level, that of the national language: when, as in Wolfson and Joyce, several languages at once interfere with each other in the same text. When this occurs, no satisfactory global meaning can be obtained, only fragments which can never be synthesized. The system gives way to mere chance, or, in other words, to the semiotic processes of the unconscious.

The concept of frontier which we have used so far is simple: there are two sides to language, one normal, one subversive, and each rule of grammar draws a borderline between what can and what cannot be said. Crossing the frontier, then, is just breaking the rule, an activity which, however, acquires a new value as we realize that everyone does it, and that we cannot help doing it anyway. But this paradoxical definition of language, based on negation, can be improved if the concept of the frontier is made more precise. We will attempt to do so by examining the work of the linguist Judith Milner.

Her starting point is the taxonomy of jokes given in Freud's *Jokes and their Relation to the Unconscious*. She tries to isolate a set of jokes which deal specifically with language, or rather with *langue* (not the faculty of language, but the concrete system of a natural language). Here is an example of such a joke, deliberately chosen from among the *French* examples discussed by Freud: 'j'ai voyagé avec lui tête à bête' (I travelled *tête à tête* with him; he is a blockhead – *une bête*). This joke has two noticeable characteristics: first, it cannot be translated, but only explained, because it is based on a given situation in the French language (the arbitrary phonetic closeness between 'tête' and 'bête'); and second, its production and its decipherment involve a metalinguistic activity, which establishes, and jokingly denies, a distinction between two relevant linguistic units – a minimal pair. The following are the two aspects of Milner's explanation: in order to understand such jokes one must both consider language as *langue* and pay attention to the descriptive characteristics of linguistic units. The first point is further explained by a definition of *langue* as based on dividing possible from impossible, grammatical from non-grammatical. This activity is ultimately intuitive: there is no logical reason why a language should use one turn of phrase and prohibit another; one side of the division is turned into a positive totality, a system, and yet the division can be crossed, that is denied (in *délire*) or forgotten (in jokes or nonsense).

This explanation of linguistic frontiers is confirmed by an analysis of the use of the identity principle by Guarani Indians, which Milner takes from the work of the French anthropologist Pierre Clastres. For the Guarani, according to Clastres, the positive identification provided by the identity principle, 'A is A', is to be interpreted as a double negation, 'A is not not-A'. Thus 'a man is a man' means that he is not a god or a jaguar: it is an indication of limitation, of incompleteness. This sense of incompleteness is reflected in Guarani myths in the form of (Freudian) negation: the powerful and terrifying beings (like the jaguar) which man is not, are presented in the myths as weak and stupid, objects of derision or ridicule. The myths have a cathartic function: to free the Guarani from their fear of the powerful creatures, by denying the frontier that separates gods from men, by doing in the imaginary world of myth what is forbidden in the world of reality. But they also have an educational function: crossing the borderline is a way of reminding themselves of its existence, of handing down to generations to come the essential elements of their culture.

The analysis of jokes about *langue* has convinced Milner that the most apt definition of it is also negative: a set of elements defined by its separation from another, complementary, set of elements. Hence it is inadequate to define *langue* as a system, for this neglects the fact that there is always a moment when the speaker has to decide whether a given form falls *within langue* or outside it. The frontier is therefore essential to the definition of *langue* as a negative object. Can we say this? If the answer is 'no', the utterance lies outside the system: but the system itself is what remains when the negative judgements have been made; not a logical construction or structure, but a fragment of reality, a complex and contorted object, the outlines of which the linguist proceeds to map out. And because the concept of frontier is essential to the definition of *langue*, because it separates the system from what lies outside it (one natural language from another), it is also imported into the system, which is structured along a series of internal borderlines: between discrete units (phonemes for instance) or between different linguistic levels.

A good illustration of these frontiers which should not, but can, be crossed is found in Carroll, in the famous definitions of the Red Queen ('*I* could show you hills in comparison with which you'd call that a valley'). A hill cannot be a dale; there are, in language, such things as discrete elements. One must say either 'pig' or 'fig', but not both at the same time, or something ambiguously situated in between. Yet hesitation is possible, language always offers superficial ambiguities one can play upon, thus crossing the borderline: 'did you say "pig" or "fig"?' asks the Cheshire Cat, and indeed one is never sure whether it is a baby or a pig (the baby turns into a pig in Alice's arms), Alice or Mabel (Alice convinces herself, in the wood where she forgets her name, that she must be Mabel), a serpent or a little girl (the pigeon uses a syllogism to prove to Alice that she is a serpent), a waist or a neck (and consequently Alice takes Humpty-Dumpty's tie for a belt, a mistake at which he is greatly offended). The reference to Carroll enables Milner to take a bold step, from language to the body. 'In the speaker's life, language is not the only experience he has of a reality articulated on the disjunction between two sets of elements, each of which is *not* the other (each set is defined only negatively, and their addition does not form a totality)' (Milner 1977, p. 135). The first of these other disjunctions, he experiences in his own body, in the disjunction of sex; to experience one's body as a woman's is to recognize a limitation – the impossibility of experiencing it as a man's (a transvestite does what no woman can do: he *makes* a woman of himself). Because of this primary disjunction, the human body is experienced not only as a unity but as a set of discrete parts (this is my head, distinct from the rest of my body). Humpty-Dumpty is the character who blurs all distinctions, and therefore causes uneasiness (is he an egg or a man? Is this his waist or his neck?): it is not a mere coincidence that he is also the character who claims mastery over language. The analogy is reinforced if we realize that the distinction is more than biological. Milner distinguishes between (biological) gender and what she calls 'sexuation', the distribution of sexual roles as prescribed by social norms. The jokes about language which she analyses are very close to jokes about homosexuals, in so far as both types explore a norm which they transgress but implicitly recognize. The relation here goes further than mere Freudian displacement (jokes about language being seen as repressed and displaced versions of sexual jokes): the semiotic processes of disjunction are common to the experiences of language and of the body.

There is another aspect to the analogy, implicit in the comparison between 'specular' and linguistic communication in Irigaray. In the cases of language and the body, an experience of learning is crucial: learning, or internalizing, the frontiers, learning to distinguish between bodies (mine and others), between sounds ('pig' and 'fig'), between what the norm allows and what it does not. There is the general education in the symbolic function (of language as opposed to *langue*), of the distinction between presence and absence, in the *fort/da* experience. And there is the specific learning of *langue* and of the body as a sexual entity, in the playful exploration of borderlines. Laughter at jokes about language is educational and also complex: '(i) the subject, by laughing, remembers that language imposes strict limits, even "distortions" on what "one would like to say" – at least what is trying to emerge in the utterance cannot be expressed beyond the frontiers of language; these frontiers are external to the subject in so far as he cannot master or escape them; (ii) at the same time, he is reminded of other, inescapable, frontiers, which are disclosed by language: the speaker has a sex, experiences a body which he did not choose to be, which imposes limitations on him, etc.' (J. Milner, 1977, p. 150).

This learning process enables us to distinguish two attitudes towards the frontiers: denying them and forgetting them. If we deny them, the whole system of language crumbles away: the more exotic forms of *délire* are examples of this. If we simply forget them, temporarily, we recognize them and with them the norm, we come to terms with reality – our relation to language is tame and educational, a matter of playing and control, not of disruption. Our attitude towards the frontiers is that of the smuggler, whose very profession is based on the recognition of frontiers, and of the necessity of their protection by customs officials. This attitude of fundamental respect for the norm can be found in literary nonsense: we come upon the contrast between Artaud and Carroll again.

Nonsense and *délire*

We have presented a conception of language based on a central paradox. *Langue* is a system based on disjunction, which is defined negatively, with an in-built possibility of breaching the system's boundaries,

deliberately or unwittingly. The paradox arises not only at the level of
the system itself, but also affects the subject, who is both responsible
for his utterances and ex-centrically dominated by language. Nonsense
and *délire* are two different responses to the paradox: presented in literary
texts or deciphered from symptoms, they are only mythical solutions,
but after all one of the less trivial definitions of myth, found in Lévi-
Strauss's *Anthropologie Structurale* is that it is the imaginary solution of
a real contradiction. We shall now spell out the myth, and distinguish
nonsense from *délire*, by commenting on a well-known poem by Lewis
Carroll. It is presented as evidence at the Knave of Heart's trial; the
White Rabbit reads it, and the King of Hearts gives a rather biased
interpretation of it, which so deeply shocks Alice's British sense of fair
play that she interrupts the proceedings and eventually escapes from
her dream.

> *They told me you had been to her,*
> *And mentioned me to him:*
> *She gave me a good character,*
> *But said I could not swim.*
>
> *He sent them word I had not gone*
> *(We know it to be true):*
> *If she should push the matter on,*
> *What would become of you?*
>
> *I gave her one, they gave him two,*
> *You gave us three or more;*
> *They all returned from him to you,*
> *Though they were mine before.*
>
> *If I or she should chance to be*
> *Involved in this affair,*
> *He trusts to you to set them free,*
> *Exactly as we were.*
>
> *My notion was that you had been*
> *(Before she had this fit)*
> *An obstacle that came between*
> *Him, and ourselves, and it.*
>
> *Don't let him know she liked them best,*
> *For this must ever be*
> *A secret, kept from all the rest,*
> *Between yourselves and me.*

Three things must be noted at once. First, the poem is interesting to professional linguists because of its play on shifters: the reason why its meaning remains so obscure is that the reference of personal pronouns is never made clear. And the fact that the poem indulges in the old game of declension (several personal pronouns being used in each stanza) is hardly sufficient compensation for this lack. Second, the context makes it clear that the principal difficulty of the text is that its author remains unknown: it is read by the White Rabbit, the prosecution maintains that it was written by the Knave of Hearts, who denies this and advances as proof the fact that the poem is not in his handwriting and that he did not sign it (which is the cause of one of the King of Hearts' brighter sallies: 'if it is not in your handwriting, you must have imitated somebody else's hand; and if you didn't sign it, that only makes the matter worse; you *must* have meant some mischief, or else you'd have signed your name like an honest man'). The third element is that the last stanza makes the whole poem appear as a joke, and the joke is on the readers: if the whole thing must be kept a secret 'between yourselves and me', two pronouns behind which we cannot help seeing ourselves – the readers – and him – the author – we will remain all the more silent as we have understood nothing, because he has not told us anything at all.

The passage from the first stanza, where the play on the empty pronouns begins, to the last, where the author declares his hand, and we acknowledge our defeat, can be seen as a progression. The myth I want to describe (the myth in which we shall find the solution that Nonsense offers for the central paradox of language) follows the various stages of this progression. There are six stages; the first and last constitute the two terms of the paradox, and the other four enable us to go from one to the other, thus giving a solution to the paradox (again, the progression is genealogical, rather than strictly diachronic). This structure is particularly apt, since it is based on the Carrollian game of doublets, in which the player must get from one word to another (e.g. 'evil' to 'love') in as few moves as possible.

The *first stage* is expressed in the words 'language speaks'. No subject has uttered the text, for language speaks directly, in its own right. In the beginning was the text, and it dispensed with an authorial subject. A coherent *délire*, the *délire* of the structure, the independent logic of the signifier precedes the emergence of the subject. The absence of referents for the shifters and the declension constitute the surface manifestations of this stage. This kind of *délire* says language is an inseparable part of reality, or in Milner's words, which refute Humpty-Dumpty's theories: 'of language, there is no master: it simply *is*' (Milner, 1977, p. 136). The only subject of the text is *langue* itself: this is why the text refuses to inscribe within its words the presence of an author (and the Knave of Hearts denies the authorship with considerable vehemence).

In the *second stage*, 'language speaks through me': this is an experience of possession, in which language finds a subject; the text imposes itself on a subject, it is foisted on a reluctant Knave, and is read by the White Rabbit; but they are not his words. What has begun here is the process through which language creates the speaking subject. Alice repeatedly finds herself in the same situation in the course of the tale, when she recites poems, the words of which 'come out very queer indeed', i.e. are imposed on her.

The creation is achieved in the *third stage*, 'language speaks to me'. In the previous stage, the structure had produced potential (but still empty) subjects, the personal pronouns. Now it 'interpellates' a subject, or rather it interpellates an individual into a subject, a process described by Althusser in his famous essay on ideology. In the case of our poem, it interpellates the Knave of Hearts into a defendant, perhaps also ourselves into readers of the text. Biographic details cling to the empty subjects ('but said I could not swim', 'before she had this fit'), on which the King of Hearts will pounce to build his interpretation (he asks the Knave whether he can swim, at which the Knave reminds him contemptuously that they are both made out of cardboard, not a very promising start for potential swimmers). Fragments of dialogue appear, in which subjects attempt to communicate ('He trusts to you to set them free/Exactly as we were') and the question of truth is mentioned ('We know it to be true'), which shows that the text is ready to enter the realm of verisimilitude, the existence of which presupposes a subject mastering his utterances (so that they can 'imitate' reality). Nonsense as a genre always strives towards the linguistic security of the mimetic; hence the strictures of Artaud, whose poetic stance is that of modernism: a position of negation and rejection. The modernist text asserts itself by rejecting mimesis – often pejoratively labelled 'realism': this is no longer a source of surprise to us, since modernist texts by definition attempt to cross frontiers.

At the end of this stage, then, a subject appears and takes responsibility for the text. The mastery, however, remains partial and doubtful: the subject is not in full control, and *délire* still rules the text. But it now has an author, and a garrulous one at that. In the *fourth stage*, 'mine is an empty speech'. Although the speech is mine, it has no object except to fulfil the author's buttonholing sense of urgency. My utterances never end, because I am not sufficiently master of my own language to bring them to a conclusion: I am still possessed, and my *délire* takes the form of raving. In *Alice*, the characters repeatedly recite not the best but the longest of the poems they know.

The only way to end this raving is to become a linguist, to make language the object of my speech. In the *fifth stage*, therefore, 'I speak about language', or 'mine is a metalinguistic speech'. When the emptiness of *délire*, or logorrhea, becomes too obvious, only language can fill it: the subject avoids being possessed by language by reflecting on it, finding its laws, commenting on the words. This is what the King of Hearts does to our poem. He explains the words, and thus imposes meaning on the text, forces it to imitate reality; he also reflects on its rules (in another passage, he answers Alice's 'I beg your pardon' with 'it isn't a very nice thing to beg'). Humpty-Dumpty is the embodiment of this stage: he is obsessed by rules (of language, of conversation), and his interest in words comes close to preciosity.

But Humpty-Dumpty, the master of words, is also the embodiment of the *sixth and last stage*, 'I speak through language', where the subject has at last assumed full mastery. The addition of 'through language' to 'I speak', which appears to be mere pleonasm, is meant to indicate this mastery: at this stage language is used like a tool. And in the last stanza of the poem the author appears. So there was an author after all. He *did* mean something, since he was laughing at us; he *was* constructing meaning, even as he denied us access to it. The last stage is the reverse side of the first, and contradicts it. The paradox, which we have described in these pages, is that language, in its daily use, in its daily production of texts, occupies both positions: it both is and is not mastered by the speaking subject; it is and is not self-generated, imposed on a helpless and something unwilling subject.

The progress of the myth also enables us to distinguish *délire* from nonsense. As we have stated it, the myth describes the progress of nonsense, in which the frontiers are temporarily forgotten. The last stage is always reached, and is both the starting point and the ultimate goal, and nonsense is only a playful detour, which the author makes for educational reasons. Carroll's timidity is deliberate, and the risks he takes are strictly controlled. Working its way back from 'normality' (the sixth stage) through nonsense (the first five stages), the nonsense poet is like Alice: his forgetting of frontiers is especially comfortable because he knows he will wake from his dream, and that the ghosts he conjures up will vanish into thin air, as in a trick. So it is all a pedagogic trick. In order to teach children their way into communicative language, one must pretend to put it at risk.

But the risks can become real: not everyone is so fully in command that he can take them with impunity (it takes a professional logician to do it). Wolfson, the schizophrenic, also passes through the stages of our myth: but in his case the genealogical becomes chronological, and he never reaches the last stage, but can only repeat his progress through the first five, as he continuously rewrites his book. For him, in the beginning, 'language speaks', for it has an opaque material existence, which escapes his control; it may be uttered by a subject, but the subject is not himself, but his mother, or rather a linguistic entity, the mother-tongue. And it does 'speak through him', repeatedly, painfully: he is penetrated by it, the word 'through' taking its most concrete meaning. The language that speaks *through* him also 'speaks *to* him', assigns him a place in society, 'interpellates' him as his mother's son, an English speaker (and a mental patient); this interpellation is both physical (when his mother hails him) and psychiatric (when he is arrested and confined to a hospital). The two stages are inseparable. The interpellation is a form of possession: language, the English tongue, is in his head, and in spite of all his efforts he can never completely escape it. But he tries to, and so he writes, in an unceasing flow of words, which puts him in a paradoxical situation: he is a man who feels physically attacked by language, and yet he has become a writer (and as the characters in *Alice* recited the longest poem, he writes sentences as long as he can make them – this is a striking characteristic of his style). We can understand the paradox: his goal is the fifth stage, where the speaker becomes a linguist, in order to benefit from the talking cure. There he stops: the mythical sixth stage of recovery never comes. The difference can be summarized thus:

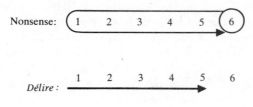

79

Conclusion: *langue* and *lalangue*

The purpose of this chapter has been to show that the literature of *délire* is part of a broader tradition: a philosophical tradition which attempts to articulate linguistics with psychoanalysis. For this tradition, the central characteristics of language are not those which are purified and built on in logic (language as unequivocal) but the infelicities of linguistic usage which are inseparable from concrete utterances or texts. The main characteristic of language is therefore *excess*: more meaning creeps into the sentence than the author intended, echoes and involuntary repetitions disturb the careful ordering of linguistic units. Phrases are analysed, and re-analysed, symptoms and word plays proliferate. But to this excess there corresponds a *lack*: the absence of the central all-mastering subject, who means what he says and says what he means. Things fall apart, the centre will not hold. The utterance is full of involuntary admissions, echoes of other voices, traces imposed by the structure itself, distortion and displacement which irretrievably conceal the truth. An absent subject, an unattainable truth: the lack of the signified and signifying subject is compensated for by the excess of signifiers. Such is the 'logic of the signifier', the main operation of which is *suture*,[14] to use Jacques Alain Miller's concept: the compensating semiotic operation by which the place of the absent signified is made to generate the chain of signifiers, the utterance.

There is a philosophical tradition (Leibniz and Frege, for instance, belong to it) which insists on the imperfection of language, on the need to purify natural languages, or improve it by creating artificial languages (logical languages for instance) where nonsense becomes impossible. But any attempt to improve language will leave impurities, and our tradition takes these residues as the centre of its interest. 'Saying more than one means, not being fully aware of the import of what one says, saying something different from what one means, speaking without purpose, all these acts are not, in Freudian analysis, defects of language, which justify the construction of formal languages, but unavoidable, positive characteristics of speech acts. Psychoanalysis and logic: the former uses as its material what the latter eliminates. The dustbins of logic provide psychoanalysis with its objects. Or, if you like, psychoanalysis unleashes what logic masters.' (Miller, *Ornicar?*, pp. 23–4.)

This is of course an acknowledgement of the validity of the 'logical' tradition. *Délire* is based on a prior concept of *langue*. But the first step in the construction of *langue* is negative: linguistics has to do with reality because it is not possible to say everything ('the impossible' is the Lacanian definition of 'the real').[15] In the simplest terms, linguistics, when it deals with the grammar of a particular language, aims to specify all the possible sentences of the language, and to exclude all impossible ones. Linguistics, however, is not an art, but a science. I am now following the line of reasoning of another French linguist, Jean-Claude Milner. His epistemological views are based on two ideas: the construction of a mathematical system of notation, and the promotion of every effective technique. The constitution of linguistics into a science therefore involves four stages:

1   The object of linguistics is *langue*, which becomes an object of science through the rejection of all causes external to itself. This postulate is generally known as the arbitrary character of the sign.
2   *Langue* can be represented by a calculus, which governs a system of discrete units with differential values.
3   Linguistics is concerned with the speaking subject only as the origin of utterances specified by the calculus: he must be considered as a sort of angel, without past or future, without a body, without an unconscious, etc.
4   Linguistics is concerned with the society of speaking subjects only as two ideal points, an encoder and a decoder, creating a perfect symmetrical communication system of extreme simplicity.

This construction is purely ideal: for nothing guarantees that it gives the whole picture. On the contrary, our daily experience of language shows us the limitations of this scientific reduction; many aspects of language are left out. For we constantly come up against the asymmetry of speaking subjects (language carries with it an assignment of hierarchical places – therefore relations of power), the non-arbitrary character of the sign (onomatopoeia for instance) and the equivocal character of utterances, which gives the lie to the differential principle: echo, ambiguity, etc. are cases in point. Two general remarks are called for here: first, these infelicities are all due to the impossibility of keeping language within the limit of the third stage – the speaking subject has more depth and complexity than is required for calculus; he does have a body, and an unconscious, which inescapably affect his language. And second, the purpose of the four stages is to build the object into a totality, a structure covering the whole field. This turns out to be a contradictory aim: there can be no single totality built out of language, and the remainder cannot be built into another, complementary totality (the obverse face of language) for it escapes totalization, and cannot be formalized for calculus.

This 'residue' has been given a name in Lacanian theory: *lalangue* in one word, as opposed to *la langue* in two. The theory of *lalangue* will be found in Jean-Claude Milner's book: it is the concept that covers what we have been describing. If *langue* is the name for the object of the first, 'logical' conception of language, then *lalangue* is the object of our tradition. It is defined negatively: that which *langue* excludes; that which condemns all language to equivocation; the fact that language will always be in excess of any theory that attempts to describe it. The best image of *lalangue* is in the phrase 'the mother tongue', and illustrations of its workings can be found in the *délire* of mad linguists: Brisset, Roussel, Artaud, Wolfson. *Lalangue* is the absence, in any given text, of coherent structure, or rather the proliferation of structures: those which the linguist analyses, but also those which he rejects (anagrams, homophonic relationships, tropes). It is the pattern of points where the system fails (this is why the term 'infelicity' is so apt): and at these points the subject – not the angelic subject of calculus, but the desiring subject – appears in the text. A new territory is waiting to be explored, more terrifying than Wonderland, but every inch as fascinating.

Notes

1 I mean active ignorance on the part of the tradition as a whole, for certain members of it are well acquainted with analytical philosophy. The history of the importation of Anglo-Saxon philosophy into France has yet to be written.

2 cf. Lacan's '*schéma L*', explained in the section on the language of madness in this chapter.

3 *Verneinung* is sometimes translated as 'denial'. I retain the term 'negation' in order to emphasize the link between the psychic process of denial and the linguistic operation of negation, a link which the French translation ('*dénégation*') makes clear.

4 Isomorphism characterizes two objects or states which have the same form. The term is used in chemistry (when two substances with similar chemical structures produce similar crystals) and also in Gestalt psychology.

5 This formation is, perhaps unavoidably, ambiguous. It can be understood as a biological conception of instinctual drives and therefore, by implication, of language. Freud's texts on drives confront the reader with a paradox: two accounts of drives are given, one in biological terms (in terms of tension, discharge and relief: a biological urge), and one in psycho-semiotic

terms, where the reality of psychic life, of the unconscious order, is composed of *representations* of drives. The drives, therefore, are conceived as a frontier between psyche and soma (in Kristeva's conception, we recall, the *semiotic* is that boundary). The relation between language and the body can therefore be read in two directions. Deleuze interprets it through the metaphor of depth and surface: language is the outward surface of the fantasized body, and the relation goes from the body to language. For Lacanian psychoanalysts the relation is reversed, the body as a set of erogenous zones is informed and formed by a semiotic process of inscription (see my discussion of Leclaire in Chapter 4), and the relation goes from language to the body. In both cases 'the body' is not a biological entity, but a fantasized one, the body as experienced by the subject, at the frontier between psyche and soma.

6 The phrase takes a dead metonymy (the mother tongue) literally. What the child learns, the mother tongue, is a symbolic system. If language were Lacanian, it ought by rights to be called the father tongue. But language is never wrong: the metonymy indicates the difficulty of acceding to the symbolic order, the danger of being trapped by imaginary (specular) relationships. This is what happens to the schizophrenic: he reduces the collective symbolic code to an idiolect, his mother tongue to his mother's tongue.

7 This *psychological* interpretation of 'deep' and 'surface' structures is obviously debatable, and goes against Chomsky's very explicit remarks that his theory is not concerned with the psychological mechanism of either the production or the reception of utterances. But the present concern is with the use of linguistic concepts (even at the price of distortion) to describe the schizophrenic experience of language.

8 The term 'mimetic' implies *a* a relation of imitation to the world of reference and *b* the respect of certain linguistic rules. Contrary to appearances *b* is more important than *a*, for the relationship between the world of reference of a text and 'reality' may be rather strained.

9 As a *general* theory of sentence-meaning, this may be erroneous; but it is undeniable that word-meanings contribute to sentence-meaning.

10 We seem to go here from a simplistic definition of word-meaning as denotation and of sentence-meaning as the composition of word-meanings to a more acceptable theory of meaning as *use* (for *The Hunting of the Snark* is nothing but a large context of use, which indicates how the word 'Snark' is used and therefore assigns meaning to it – it even describes an ironic way of verifying this meaning by giving 'five unmistakable marks' (pleasantly incoherent) which are supposed to enable one to recognize a Snark). But this conception goes further than a theory of use: it denies the possibility of constructing *one* meaning, i.e. a totality.

11 This metaphor is as old as the hills, almost as old as the word itself, and therefore lexicalized. But the *OED* states that only persons meet; when the word applies to inanimate objects, the meaning is said by the *OED* to be *transferred*.

12 This conception of the central role of metaphor in language is by no means new. Here again, we find a long philosophical and rhetorical tradition (from Coleridge to I. A. Richards, from Nietzsche to Derrida).

13 The device can be used to produce poetic effects, as in Shakespeare's Sonnet 104:

> *Three winters' cold*
> *Have from the forests shook three summers' pride,*
> *Three beauteous springs to yellow autumn turned*
> *In process of the seasons have I seen.*

The first reading of the third line inclines readers to interpret 'turned' as a verb in the past tense or part of a compound past tense ('have turned'). But the next line compels us to reinterpret the word as a past participle.

14 The image is of sewing up a wound; but the term is also used, figuratively, for a text: when you have made cuts, you have to 'join up' the remaining material.

15 On the distinction between reality and 'the real', see below, Chapter 4, p. 154. Lacan's distinction between 'the symbolic' (language), 'the imaginary' (specular relationships, relationships of similarity) and 'the real' (sheer existence) is expounded in his Seminar XXII, *RSI* (mimeographed).

Further reading

1 For Deleuze's interest in Meinong, see below, Chapter 3, and *Logique du Sens*, passim. On Meinong and Russell's criticism, cf. J. M. Findlay, *Meinong's Theory of Objects and Values* (Oxford University Press 1933); K. Lambert, *Meinong and the Principle of Independence* (Cambridge University Press 1983); and L. Linski, *Referring* (Routledge and Kegan Paul 1967).

2 Freud's article, 'On negation', can be found in the *Standard Edition*, vol. XIX; his article 'A child is being beaten', is in vol. XVII. The two articles can also be found in the Pelican Freud Library, in vols. XI and X respectively. On the linguistic origin and structure of fantasies in Freud, see A. Lecercle-Sweet, 'Grammaire, figures et lettres du fantasme', in *Tropismes*, 3 (Paris 1985).

3 On psychiatric analyses of the language of schizophrenia, see J. S. Kasanin (ed.), *Language and Thought in Schizophrenia* (New York: Norton 1964) (1st edn 1944).

 The two articles by L. Irigaray mentioned in this section are: 'Le schizophrène et la question du signe', in *Recherches*, 16 (Paris 1974) (tr. in *Semiotexte*, 1974), and 'Communication linguistique et communication spéculaire', in *Cahiers pour l'Analyse*, 3 (Paris 1966). Her thesis is *Le Langage des Déments* (The Hague: Mouton 1973). In 1967, she contributed three articles ('La production des phrases chez les déments', 'Négation et transformation négative chez les schizophrènes' and 'Approche d'une grammaire d'énonciation de l'hystérique et de l'obsessionnel') to *Langages*, 5, 'Pathologie du Langage'. Her works as a philosophical feminist include *Speculum* (Paris: Minuit 1974); and *Ce sexe qui n'en est pas un* (Paris: Minuit 1977).

 Lacan's article on the mirror stage is 'Le stade du miroir comme formateur de la fonction du Je', in *Ecrits* (Paris: Seuil 1966). The 'schéma L' appears in the seminar on Poe's 'Purloined Letter', ibid., and is developed in 'Du traitement possible de la psychose', ibid. cf. *Ecrits, a selection*, tr. by Alan Sheridan (Tavistock 1977). On Lacan in general, cf. David Archard's *Consciousness and the Unconscious* (Hutchinson 1984); and Catherine Clement's *Le pouvoir des mots* (Paris: Mame 1973), and *Vies et Légendes de Jacques Lacan* (Paris: Grasset 1981).

 Benveniste's article on personal pronouns is in his *Problems in General Linguistics*, and Jakobson's article on shifters, 'Shifters, verbal categories and the Russian verb' is in *Selected Writings*, vol. II (The Hague: Mouton 1971).

4 Barthes's concept of *phrasé* appears in ch. LV ('Le langage comme nature') of *S/Z* (Paris: Seuil 1970). His maxim on language as fascist comes from *Leçon* (Paris: Seuil 1978). English translation of *S/Z* by Richard Miller (Jonathan Cape 1975).

 The autobiography of the Elephant Man was published as an appendix to M. Howell and P. Ford, *The true history of the Elephant Man* (Allison & Busby 1980). Most anthologies of Nonsense include verses by Bishop Corbet and *The Great Panjandrum*, for instance, R. L. Green (ed.), *A Book of Nonsense* (Everyman's Library 1927). On sentences within sentences, cf. Y. Lecerf, 'Des poèmes cachés dans les poèmes', in *Poétique*, **18** (Paris 1974).

The articles by Judith Milner referred to in this section are 'Langage et langue – ou: de quoi rient les locuteurs?', *Change*, **29** (Paris 1976), and 'De quoi rient les locuteurs (II)', *Change*, **32–3** (Paris 1977). She deals with similar problems in two recent articles: 'La voix publique', in *DRLAV*, **21** (Paris 1979), and 'Les monstres de la langue', in *DRLAV*, **27** (Paris 1982). The text on Guarani Indians which she mentions can be found in P. Clastres, *La société contre l'Etat* (Paris: Minuit 1979).

5   On Nonsense, see my thesis, *Le Nonsense: genre, histoire, mythe* (University of Paris VII 1980) and my book, *Le Dictionnaire et le Cri* (in press). Lévi-Strauss's theory of myth appears in 'La structure des mythes', in *Anthropologie Structurale* (Paris: Plon 1958) (tr. *Structural Anthropology* (Penguin 1972)). On Althusser's conception of interpellation, see 'Ideologie et appareils idéologiques d'Etat', in *Positions* (Paris: Editions Sociales 1976) (the article first appeared in 1970; tr. in *Essays on Ideology* (Verso 1984)).

6   Jacques Alain Miller's article on *suture* is 'La suture – Eléments de la logique du signifiant', *Cahiers pour l'Analyse*, **1** (Paris 1966). On the Lacanian concept of *lalangue*, cf. J. A. Miller, 'Theorie de lalangue (rudiment)', in *Ornicar?*, **1** (Paris 1975), and the two books by Jean-Claude Milner, *L'amour de la langue* (Paris: Seuil 1978), and *Les noms indistincts* (Paris: Seuil 1983).

3
The philosophy of délire

Introduction

Feste   To see this age! A sentence is but a cheveril glove to a good wit; how quickly the wrong side may be turned outward!

Viola   Nay, that's certain. They that dally nicely with words quickly make them wanton.

Feste   I would therefore my sister had no name, sir.

Viola   Why, man?

Feste   Why, sir, her name's a word, and to dally with that word might make my sister wanton. But indeed, words are very rascals, since bonds disgraced them.[1]

There is danger in words. They fail to convey the utterer's meaning, or convey it too well, or enable him to cheat. They threaten the integrity of the body, they make it wanton, they lie: they create bonds between men, yet they are the means of breaking them. They are very rascals.

But man has always distrusted them, and attempted to reassert his power over them because he knows they will always escape again. Humpty-Dumpty has a mythical status because every reader knows that his claim to mastery over words is an instance of Freudian denial, because every reader has made the same attempt, and experienced the same failure. There is a long tradition of reflexion on the danger of words, on their noxious effects on the hearer (if he is deceived by the lie) or on the utterer (if he is taken over by words, and produces *délire*).

To take a single example: students of myth are aware that, among the many theories of the origins of myths, one, put forward in the nineteenth century by Max Müller and much derided, concerns language. For Max Müller, myth is a symptom produced by a disease of language. The myth of Daphne, who was turned into a laurel to escape Apollo, has a linguistic origin: the word comes from a Sanskrit word meaning 'dawn', which itself comes from a root meaning 'burn'. The myth is explained: the disappearance of the dawn when the sun emerges becomes the Daphne myth through a linguistic shift, a displacement (and the word 'Daphne' itself means 'laurel' because laurel wood is supposed to burn quickly).[2] Myth is produced by the unruly movements of language, the displacement of the signified which loses its privileged relationship with the signifier (a one-to-one relationship that has, in fact, never existed except in the fantasies of linguists). Take the word 'nothing'. Müller says it is a mere word, and yet, because language is diseased (mythopoiesis is the name of the disorder), the sole origin of whole mythologies: le Néant, Nirvana, etc. Language has created something *ex nihilo*: a nothing, the Great Nothing.

The line of argument is familiar, and definite descriptions can be used to rid man of metaphysics and myth – diseased growths according to Müller. But the point is that they never go away, and in the last resort, they find a lasting protection in fiction. If in 'the Nothing', an unjustified use of the definite article creates a new and illicit entity, it is only a common trick of fiction, the false anaphora of the opening sentence of a piece of fiction. This is the first sentence of a Mills & Boon novel: 'The slim, fair girl came aboard alone, a mink coat draped around her shoulders with orchids on the lapel.' Which girl? How do I know her? *The* girl, of course, for language (here the definite article) is enough to make a person out of her, to create her, thus starting the necessary process of identification (helped, no doubt, by the slimness, the blonde hair and above all the mink coat and orchids).

But what the thin line of fiction protects is, in fact, the communicative use of language. Behind the line the threatening torrent of words gathers strength, waiting to break into *délire* and carry everything with it. *Délire* has a deep relationship with fiction because of their common ambiguity: each of them embodies the mixture of danger and usefulness that words contain. *Délire* is the incarnation of the dangerous side of language. And yet, perhaps, it is also the origin of all language. Lacan says that the only thing which assures me that another subject is facing me, addressing me, is the possibility of my being taken in by his discourse, the possibility that he is lying. The only proof that language *does* communicate a content is the possibility of the utterer bursting into *délire*. The thin line, the bursting of a flow of delirious words, the mirror in which I perceive my image as alien to me: the tradition which I explore is indeed concerned with frontiers. But which frontiers? And which tradition? The terms remain problematic.

For I have attempted to describe a *tradition* within which this conception of language has developed. But, as usual, the term conceals a retro-spective rereading and reordering of the texts, and raises problems. First, and least important, the theory is too new to form a real tradition: it finds predecessors as far back as Carroll and Brisset (as far back, in fact, as the ingenuity of the retrospective linguist can go), but it makes them fit into the framework of a theory which has come into its own only in the last twenty years. (No doubt this is only the normal process of tradition-making.) More important, it places the corpus within the limits of a *single* tradition: a debatable point, which must be contested now. In fact, this and the next two chapters will deal with the separation of the tradition into two divergent, and ultimately opposed, branches: a philosophical analysis of sense and nonsense, and a psychoanalytic study of *délire*. *Anti-Oedipus*, Deleuze's major mature work proclaims this separation in its very title.

Both branches belong to the same tree: reference is made to the same literary corpus, understood as a corpus of *délire*. The separation begins with their attitude to language, and especially to linguistics. The account given in the last chapter was based on linguistics (even when it criticized it for failing to analyse concrete uses of language), and presented a theory of language, broadly inspired by the work of Lacan, making extensive use of the concept of frontiers. But it is not so certain that this concept provides an adequate means of dealing with the corpus, for it involves the paradox that when one breaches a frontier of language – what appears to be a constitutive rule – one ought, logically speaking, to be outside language, in utter absurdity and meaninglessness: this, in principle, is not the case, for what lies outside language is still within language. If you break the lexical frontier of language by interpreting the phrase 'mock-turtle soup' as denoting soup made with mock-turtle, you are outside the frontiers of conventional language, but still within language. For this soup is either an ersatz of turtle soup or soup made with mock-turtle, but not both: Tenniel's illustration reassures us that in the world of fiction the mock-turtle exists, and that the organization of language has not been destroyed. This type of analysis provides an adequate account of the mild *délire* of Nonsense, of the tame ravings of fiction: Carroll and Roussel, rather than Brisset and Artaud. But what if the mock-turtle is also a mock soup? What if *délire* dissolves the whole structure of language, reducing the utterance to a mere collection of fragments, of words without syntax, of sounds which can no longer be abstracted into words, as seems to happen in Artaud's 'screams'?

The concept of frontier turns out to be self-contradictory. It implies the existence of a territory outside language, on the other side of the frontier, and at the same time denies the possibility: outside language, there is nothing, at least nothing that can be conceived. I shall try to indicate a way out of this contradiction by using an analogy. In the opening pages of his book on Nietzsche, Deleuze raises the problem of genealogy: Nietzsche's method is not history, the establishment of causal chains and the discovery of origins, but genealogy, the circular tension between constitutive rules and that which constitutes the rules. Nietzsche's philosophy is a philosophy of values: each phenomenon is related to the value which it represents or enacts. But if values serve to evaluate phenomena, what will evaluate the values? A differential element (in Nietzsche, the difference between the high and the low, the noble and the lowly) which gives value to the values, regulates the circularity, both maintains and solves the paradox of the chicken and the egg (which comes first, the value which allows evaluation, or the evaluation that creates the value?).

Frontiers play the part of a differential element in the paradox of language: there are linguistic values, which distinguish correct or 'normal' language from *délire*, and yet the rejected elements play a part in the constitution of linguistic values. One never gets away from language. The problem is not to find out what lies *beyond* the frontier or, if one tackles the historical problem, *before* language (a fertile ground for myth, where the bow-wow theory forever contends against the pooh-pooh or the yo-he-ho theory.)[3] The problem is the genealogy of language: how can mere sounds cease to be the manifestation of the actions and passions of the body and become words expressing meaning?

In the last chapter the answer to this problem – a central one for our corpus – was given through the centrality of language (in Leclaire's terms, it is language which constitutes the body as experienced by the subject, by inscribing on it the 'letters' around which erogenous zones develop). We shall now consider a philosophical answer, Deleuze's *Logique du Sens*. Deleuze's theory of sense explores the structural relationships between soma and psyche, sounds and words, words and things; it seeks to account for the *délire* which lies at the heart of every utterance, even the most rational and communicative.

An addition to the corpus

The four authors in my corpus have aroused a certain amount of critical attention (from Foucault and Judith Milner, for example, as we have already seen). But there is one work in which they are considered not among others, but *before* others. *Logique du Sens* contains a systematic consideration of the contrast between Carroll and Artaud (one of the chapters is entitled: 'The schizo and the little girl'). Yet it does not, like Pierssens's book on logophilia, treat the corpus as literary: it begins by going back to the old debate between Plato and the Stoics, and places the four texts in a philosophical tradition – albeit a slightly idiosyncratic one. Deleuze's book combines a critical with a historical approach to philosophy, and mixes theory and literature: a mixture at once odd and fascinating.

Indeed, Deleuze occupies a rather special position on the French philosophical scene. He teaches philosophy at the university of Vincennes, a choice which implies a modernist stance. When he published *Logique du Sens*, in 1969, he had already written a number of books, most of them on the history of philosophy. One of the paradoxes of Deleuze is that he started as a conventional historian of philosophy: he successively produced a volume on Hume (*Empirisme et Subjectivité*, 1953), one on Nietzsche (probably the first in France which took Nietzsche seriously as a philosopher: *Nietzsche et la Philosophie*, 1962), one on Kant, meant as an introductory textbook (*La Philosophie critique de Kant*, 1963), one on Bergson, in which again he deals with a philosopher whose influence has waned (*Le Bergsonisme*, 1966), and last, a year before *Logique du Sens*, a book on Spinoza (*Spinoza et le Problème de l'Expression*, 1968). But the conventional historian of philosophy was also a rather unconventional literary critic: in 1964 he wrote an essay on Proust (*Marcel Proust et les Signes*, revised edition 1980), and in 1967 he wrote a long introduction to an edition of the works of Sacher-Masoch. In 1969 he stopped writing on the history of philosophy, and entered the field of critical philosophy, with *Différence et Répétition* (1969) and *Logique du Sens*. Since then, in collaboration with Felix Guattari, a psychoanalyst, he has published the two volumes of *Capitalisme et Schizophrénie* (vol. 1, *L'Anti-OEdipe*, 1972, vol. 2, *Mille Plateaux*, 1980), with two smaller books in between (*Kafka*, 1975, *Rhizome*, 1976: I shall deal with these in Chapter 6). The progression in his work, then, is from history of philosophy to critical philosophy to literary criticism: and all three stages are present in the later books. *Logique du Sens*, for instance, starting with a rereading of the history of philosophy, deals with many literary texts, and indeed is itself, in a way, a work of literature, an addition to our delirious corpus: the historian and the *littérateur* still haunt the original philosopher.

Deleuze is original not only because he has abandoned the more academic fields of the history of philosophy to come into his own (the originality was already obvious in the early books), but because he is, on the French philosophical scene, an outsider. He has remained aloof from the master-disciple relationships in which so many of his colleagues are involved. Important French philosophers, like Lacan and Althusser, both *have* masters (orthodoxy is a philosophical value: the authentic Freud and the real Marx, those well-known fabulous monsters, are the object of expert, but basically pious, (re)interpretations), and *are* masters: the terms 'Lacanian' or 'Althusserian' are still in use. In spite of Foucault's pronouncement ('Perhaps, one day, this century will be called Deleuzian') there are no Deleuzian philosophers (although one can meet the odd devotee of the Vincennes seminar), and Deleuze has attracted little critical attention. Several factors, in my opinion, combine to place Deleuze in that peculiar position. First, there is no orthodoxy in Deleuze, no limitation imposed on his trajectory by an already thought and expressed truth. This does not mean that he refuses to acknowledge influences: but instead of a selective reading of a great text, he provides a comprehensive rereading of the whole history of Western philosophy.[4] Second, he refuses to focus his attention on the problems which appear urgent or important to masses of students or philosophers. Until *Capitalisme et Schizophrénie*, his attitude to philosophy was technical, both in topic and in treatment. (This is the one characteristic he appears to have in common with English-speaking philosophers. It certainly singles him out in France.) In a short essay on Deleuze, Clément Rosset quotes a reader's reaction to *Logique du Sens*: excellent, but dry, very dry. The dryness of the biscuit, or the sheer difficulty of the text, discourages prospective followers. Last, his own attitude to his work produces a similar effect: the disconcerting agility with which he jumps from subject to subject, from abstruse philosophy to the modern novel, the off-handedness with which he sometimes treats both the reader and the text he is commenting on provoke fascination, but also resistance. Is he being serious? Does he really mean what he seems to be saying? He never seems to be where the reader expects him to be, like the egg in the sheep's shop in *Through the Looking-Glass*, an episode of which he makes much use.

The title of *Logique du Sens* is slightly odd. It seems to suggest that meaning possesses a logic of its own, different from logic as we know it, i.e. a system of axioms and rules enabling us to analyse the truth and falsity of propositions. Or rather, what the title suggests is a displacement: the sphere of meaning is autonomous; in it the values of truth and falsity (and their system of mutual exclusion) are replaced by the values of sense and nonsense (their relationship is based on coexistence). There is, of course, an element of provocation in this: we are in fact leaving the realm of logic to enter metaphysics. Yet the term 'logic' is not to be understood metaphorically as meaning something like 'a systematic construction of the concept of meaning' but as pointing to a process of substitution: what we call logic, 'the logic of truth' concerns, if not the relationships between propositions and things (what Deleuze calls 'designation'), at least the relationships which hold between propositions (what Deleuze calls 'signification'). His concern is not with these two dimensions, but with another, outside the realm of 'the logic of truth': sense.

The second noun in the title is equally problematic. In the last paragraph, I have used the word 'meaning', the usual translation for the French word '*sens*'. (For reasons which will be explained later, I prefer the word 'sense'.) At first sight, the field is familiar: even if 'meaning' or 'sense' have no logic of their own, various theories of meaning have been developed on the frontier between philosophy and linguistics, especially in analytical philosophy: Russell, Frege, Wittgenstein, Strawson, etc. But that familiar ground is completely ignored by Deleuze: he sometimes raises his cap, *en passant*, to the theory of types, but Russell and Frege are only mentioned as the authors of paradoxes (in which Deleuze revels), and a reader who limited his reading to this work would conclude that Meinong is by far the more important philosopher. What Deleuze is doing is, in fact, by-passing centuries of reflection on meaning, and going back to the very beginning, exploring a long neglected dead-end, the logic and theory of meaning of the Stoics. Behind this bold move, there lies a conception of philosophy.

This conception has three main characteristics. First, philosophy is not a subject in which progress can be achieved. As Russell practises it, philosophy does indeed progress: reading ancient philosophy is important for cultural reasons, but the solutions offered by Plato and the Stoics have little influence on contemporary developments; they have been replaced by more correct explanations. For Deleuze on the other hand philosophical analysis is circular, it must always go back and reread the whole tradition in a new light. Because the problems raised by the classics remain valid, their solutions must be considered again, set in new contexts, and re-activated. It is true that in a sense all philosophy does this: Kripke's theory of meaning, for instance, goes back several decades to re-activate an old-fashioned solution. But on the whole such retrospective attitudes are limited: for instance, against a long established tradition which considered that in logic the Stoics were cretins (the word sounds un-philosophical, but it echoes the treatment of the Stoics by the German historians of logic, Prantl and Zeller), historians now hail them as the precursors of propositional logic, as opposed to the Aristotelian logic of classes. But this turns the Stoics into a mere curiosity, almost as irrelevant to modern logic as Democritus' atoms are to modern physics. Deleuze adopts an entirely different attitude: he takes the Stoics seriously, reads their texts not in the spirit of the historian, but as living texts, raising problems which he sets out to solve. His is a genuine return to classical philosophy: the only progress consists in working one's way along the tradition, reconsidering the questions posed at each stage.

Logique du Sens can still be construed as the work of a historian (of a special kind), who has become involved in his subject matter. Philosophy is still a technical subject, separated from other fields, and perhaps superior to them. But in his critical period – this is the second characteristic of his philosophy – Deleuze abandons this position: the philosophers he reads still provide the questions, but the answers are sought variously in literature, psychiatry or philosophy. Theory is no longer superior to fiction: the teller of tales tells us as much about the abstruse question of meaning as the professed philosopher, and his delirious texts are as useful for the understanding of schizophrenia as the reports of the psychiatrist. Philosophy is not dispersed in an unholy mixture of fiction and theory, but it loses its conventional limits, it is seen appearing on unexpected ground. We knew Carroll was a logician: who would have thought he was a philosopher of meaning and surfaces? In a way, philosophers have always used Carroll, and, as illustrations of philosophical arguments, Humpty-Dumpty and the Cheshire Cat have powers of seduction which authors find difficult to resist. Deleuze, too, uses Carroll, but much more extensively, in a much more vital and urgent manner: Alice provides not only illustrations, but also philosophical questions and answers.[5]

Third, this widening of the field of philosophy does not mean that the subject loses its autonomy. In a way, the autonomy is greater than in many contemporary theories. For, in Deleuze, philosophy is a serious activity, and must never reduce itself to an ancillary to the exact sciences (as it does both in logical empiricism and in Althusserian Marxism).

Instead of limiting its field, philosophy enlarges it, and unwitting philosophers (unlikely ones too, like F. Scott Fitzgerald) are received into the fold.

The title is not the only surprising element in this book: the text is divided into what seems to be fairly conventional, if rather short, chapters – except that they are not called chapters, but 'series' (the first two are called 'series of paradoxes'). The term, which is used on every page, is never explicitly defined (its meaning must be grasped through its use, through the innumerable language games in which it is involved). In one of the later chapters ('On different types of series'), indirect explanations are given of its use in Freud, who talks of 'sexual series' (this is not the origin of Deleuze's use of the term: only a convergent use). Freud describes the emergence of sexual series in the pregenital sexuality of erogenous zones: an erogenous zone is a series of points, organized around a centre – in this case an orifice with its membrane. This is not an explanation, because it presupposes that we understand what a series is: it provides, at best, an illustration of the inscription of a series on the surface of the human body.

In a way the term 'series' does not have to be accounted for, because it is already defined in the dictionary: an ordered set of elements, governed by a principle of distinction (one and one and one) and a principle of totalization, or synthesis. Deleuze mentions several types of synthesis: the *succession* or *connection* of the single series, the *coexistence* or *co-ordination* of the dual series (the two parts of which converge), the *disjunction* of a series, the parts of which branch out to form two distinct, 'resonant', series. Here we have already parted from the dictionary definition: for a series in Deleuze is always part of a couple, each half reflecting the other or being attracted to it. The image that comes immediately to mind is that of a line and its projection on a surface, or of two parallel lines. Indeed, Deleuze's concept of series originates in Spinoza's conception of the parallel between ideas and things, as explained in Deleuze's book on Spinoza (pp. 100–1). But in *Logique du Sens* Deleuze develops and transforms the concept: the image of two parallel lines fails to insist on the contact between the two (halves of the) series. So the best image is that of a mirror, and we can understand why Deleuze is so keen on Lewis Carroll, for the looking-glass is indeed a good example of the frontier, a surface which both links and separates two series, distinct yet similar. On the other side of the mirror, Alice finds the same objects as in her mother's sitting-room, but with a slight

94

difference: on the face of the looking-glass clock there is a broad smile (I have chosen this example to show that what links the two series is not only a physical process – reflection – but also an ideal one: the pun on 'face', or rather Carroll's decision to take a dead metaphor literally).

The reference to Carroll shows that series are involved in language. In Spinoza the two parallel series are those of ideas and things. In Deleuze, the parallel series are those of causes and effects, of corporeal things and incorporeal events. But the concept of series first appears within a theory of expression: effects, or events, are caught in language from the beginning, and cannot be separated from the proposition in which they are expressed. So that the first duality is transformed into another, of things and propositions, of bodies and language. This is why this theory of sense concerns us: if *délire* is concerned with the relationship between language and the human body, sense as Deleuze analyses it dwells on the frontier between them; indeed it *is* the frontier. The best examples of serial processes are linguistic, and Carroll's works abound in them (as they abound in doublets, like Tweedledum and Tweedledee, that embryo of a series). This is one of the lines used as a leitmotiv in *The Hunting of the Snark*: 'they pursued it with forks and hopes'. In rhetorical terms, this trope is a zeugma, the sentence links two incompatible nouns. This is what the series does: it links in a problematic synthesis a subseries of designations (referring to things – forks) and one of manifestations (referring to emotions – hope).

We can now understand why the concept of series has a structural role in the book: Deleuze's writing is reflexive, and there is an element of *abyme* in it. The series of which the book is composed enter into contrapuntal relations: the book is composed like a fugue, a series of resonant series. There are two points here, and a potential contradiction. The first is order, or organization: in *Logique du Sens* Deleuze is still at heart an academic philosopher, preoccupied by the structure of what he writes. So one has the sense, as one goes from series to series, of an ineluctable progression, but also of a pedagogic one, step by step (even if the difficulty of the text defeats the attempt at pedagogy; this looks like a well-known ironic stance: 'to put it more simply . . .' the Duchess says before she produces her unintelligible sentence). But, at the same time, series may well proliferate in length or in number. Here lies the contradiction: proliferation is always a threat to order. Deleuze answers with two opposed metaphors: the tree for order (as a structured network of roots, trunk and branches), and the rhizome – a subterranean root-like stem – for anarchic and proliferating growth. In his later work, Deleuze uses the metaphor of the rhizome to describe his own writing. In *Logique du Sens*, however, the tree is still present, and the contradiction lies at the heart of the text.

So the text proliferates, grows in unexpected directions, refuses to follow the straight line of demonstration, but on the contrary sometimes changes its course, for no apparent reason. This is where the philosophical text becomes literary, where the theory of *délire* becomes practice. And the erratic progression is reflected in the writing, in the fluidity of an essentially oral style (the solution is never complete, there are always further distinctions to be made), in the author's wondrous capacity to jump from subject to subject, far outstripping the breathless reader. In fact the text never ends, except by an arbitrary gesture at the end of the thirty-fourth series (and some of the threads left dangling will be taken up in the later books: most of the central concepts of *Capitalisme et Schizophrénie* are already present, *in ovo*, in *Logique du Sens*). Yet there it must end: again we find the contradiction between the closure of the construction of a theory of sense and the openness of the proliferating series. On the level of style, the reader cannot fail to be struck by the fact that Deleuze makes systematic use of division (points are carefully numbered, the result of an analysis is often a distinction between two, three or four concepts), yet the text grows and multiplies in an extremely disquieting manner.

Following a root

This tension, best represented as the struggle between two metaphors of order and anarchy, rules the text. There is, therefore, a main root, which we shall follow: the theory of sense. It provides the text with a structure, and involves a definition of the concept of structure itself. Rather predictably, too, it will enable us to go further in our analysis of *délire*.

'To overthrow Plato: which philosopher has not tried to achieve just this?' (Foucault on Deleuze). Deleuze duly obliges, and starts with a critique of Plato's theory of images (copies and simulacra). In the world of Plato, things are defined by their resemblance to an Idea. Each element of the world belongs to a class which subsumes its members according to a common characteristic. To take the celebrated example, all beds are alike in being images of the ideal bed. Plato's sensible world, therefore, is a world of copies, of 'good' images. Which implies that there are bad ones: this is where the poet comes in, with his second-order resemblances, his 'bad copies'. The painted bed is only a simulacrum, an unauthorized and inadequate copy.

In all this there is a value judgement (soon to be reversed by neo-Platonists) which relegates the poet to the position of a dubious fabricator of fictions (at worst no better than lies). Deleuze reverses the value judgement. He does not claim direct access to the Idea for the poet, but praises him for the inadequacy of his forgeries. The copy is limited and measurable, fixed and permanent in its approved relation of resemblance: 'limited' is the important word. The simulacrum, because it rejects, or is denied, any direct relationship with the Idea, loses that permanence, that capacity to be encompassed by the limits of reality: it is mobile, animated by the irrepressible movement of fiction, and it escapes the control of its creator, because it avoids the action of the Idea. The world of Deleuze is not a world of classifiable things, but of events and fictions: in the terms of *Sylvie and Bruno*, not 'bits of things', but 'bits of Shakespeare', or rather, as it happens, 'bits of Alice'.

Deleuze finds the weapons he needs for his attack on Plato in Stoic logic and physics. For the Stoics, a being is not defined by resemblance, but by growth. It is not one element among others, but a singularity, a unit in itself and not part of a higher unit. The typical being for a Stoic is alive: it develops, becomes, germinates or is subject to corruption. This explains the shift of emphasis in Stoic logic from objects to events, and this is why Stoic logic now sounds so modern: it is a logic of propositions, not of classes. The proposition does not consist of two nouns, joined by a copula, but of a subject and a verb: not 'the tree is green' but, so to speak, 'the tree greens'. The predicate expresses a certain aspect of the object, in so far as it acts or is acted upon. What is expressed in the predicate is not a quality (of the object) but an attribute, an event attributed to the object, and distinct from it.

We have reached a famous Stoic distinction, between bodies and incorporeal entities. The Stoics hold a version of materialism which is sometimes called pansomatism. For them, indeed, everything is a body (they solved the problem of the relationship between body and soul by deciding that the soul, too, was a body). Bodies act on one another and are acted upon, they are causes among themselves. This action of body on body is conceived in terms of mixtures: bodies penetrate one another, in a sort of cannibalistic orgy. The knife that cuts and the flesh that is cut become inextricably mixed. But from these very material mixtures there rises (to use Deleuze's metaphor) an incorporeal vapour: the event, which is produced by these mixtures, but which must not be confused with them. Indeed, the event 'cutting/being cut' belongs to a different order of being from the knife, the flesh and their conjunction. It is not a physical property but an attribute of things: it does not *exist* in things, it *insists* in them and *subsists* in language.

To have a clearer picture of what an event is (and, as we shall see, Deleuze's theory of sense is also a theory of events), we can take Deleuze's own example: battles. On the field, a battle consists in innumerable actions and reactions between bodies: sabres cut into the warm flesh, bullets penetrate it, cannonballs dismember it, blood and sweat seep into the earth, trees are blown to smithereens. Nature itself is wounded. But the battle does not exist in any of those unholy mixtures: it does not exist at all, as Stendhal, Tolstoy and Stephen Crane realized; it is everywhere, but nowhere in particular; it clings to every object like a film, yet the actors never perceive it (the hero of *The Red Badge of Courage* takes part in it, at one point tries to escape from it, and yet never perceives it as a single entity, as *the* battle). There it stands,[6] bodiless and impassive, indifferent to the actions and passions that constitute it (and the tall soldier in *The Red Badge* . . . does undergo a Christ-like Passion in the strongest sense), neutral between the victors and the vanquished, the brave and the cowardly. This is why Crane never gives names to his heroes: they are the variables, the 'x's and 'y's in a formula, an event, the battle. And this is why only the novelist can give a satisfactory account of it: for fictions, or phantasies are incorporeal, too, like events. Like them they dwell on the surface of things, they do not exist, but insist in things.[7]

And they subsist in language. For there is an intricate relationship between events and language. First, the Stoic distinction between physical depth (things and states of things) and metaphysical surface (events) corresponds to another distinction, within the proposition: the proposition designates things and expresses events.[8] Or, to put it another way, events are attributed to things and expressed in propositions. The phrase 'a logic of sense' first appears in the book on Spinoza. Deleuze places Spinoza in a logical tradition (from the Stoics to Meinong) which distinguishes between designation and expression: 'that which is expressed' becomes a non-existent entity, neither the thing nor the proposition.

But here we reach a second level in the relationship between events and language. For the Stoics, entities other than events are incorporeal: space, time, the void, and what they call '*lekta*'. The word is sometimes translated as 'the significate'. On most accounts, Stoic logic makes a threefold distinction between the sign (which signifies), the referent (which exists) and the significate (which is signified). Both the referent and the sign (the word as sound) are bodies (remember that for the Stoics the extension of the concept of bodies is very wide); but the significate is incorporeal. It is not a thought, however, but rather 'the actual entity indicated or revealed by the sound, which we apprehend as subsisting together with our thought'.[9] The Greek and the barbarian who hear the same word, hear the same sounds and see the same object. Yet the barbarian does not understand, because he has no access to the *lekton*. For the Greek, but not for the barbarian, the object has an attribute: it is expressed in the word. Sometimes, for Stoic terminology is fluid, and the theory of *lekta* is complicated and controversial (Deleuze follows the account given by the French historian of philosophy, Emile Bréhier), the *lekton* is the predicate in a proposition: the incorporeal predicate expresses the equally incorporeal event. It is neither an individual (a noun) nor a concept (a noun or adjective) but an attribute (a verb).

We have now reached grammar. The Stoic analysis is, in the end, based on oppositions between parts of speech. States of things are expressed by nouns, and incorporeal events by verbs in the infinitive; finite tenses correspond to the actions and passions of bodies, whereas the event is impassive, unaffected by them.

We can now perceive the relationship between events and language: *a* events are to states of things what *lekta* are to propositions; *b* events and states of things form the two halves of a Deleuzian series, separated by a frontier, a surface of contact, the proposition; and *c* the relationship between events and *lekta* is one of partial identity, for a proposition is also an event, and like all events is deployed on the surface of things. In a way this is not new, as any theory of performative utterances and speech acts shows. But here the relationship is closer: one dimension of the proposition, its sense, has a privileged relationship to events, which occur outside language (they are realized as modifications of states of things), but are dependent on the language that expresses them. Like Meinong's chimeras, they do not exist, but only subsist in language.

Deleuze finds in the Stoic concepts of 'events', 'states of things', 'incorporeal entities', and 'the surface of things', the materials he needs to construct a theory of sense. He begins with an analysis of the proposition. A proposition fulfils three functions: it indicates the things it refers to (*designation*: the typical linguistic element which corresponds to this function is the deictic, 'this'); it transmits the beliefs and emotions of a subject (*manifestation*: the utterance manifests its utterer; the linguistic embodiment is to be found in shifters like 'I'); it implies general or universal concepts which guarantee that the assertion is valid or felicitous (*signification*: the proposition is meant to establish relationships with other propositions, in a proof for instance; its linguistic embodiment is connectives like 'therefore').

This threefold distinction already implies a theory of meaning. But Deleuze goes on to state that there is a fourth aspect to the proposition, which corresponds to the Stoic *lekton*: sense. The Stoics, he claims, discovered that sense or meaning does not reside either in designation (there is no strict correspondence between words and things), or in manifestation (the meaning of a proposition is distinct from the beliefs and desires of the utterer), or in signification (for signification is concerned with the conditions of truth and falsity of the proposition, whereas a proposition may have meaning even if it is neither true nor false). Sense, then, is the fourth dimension of a proposition. The Stoic analysis of events leads to their conception of sense: 'sense is, in the proposition, *that which is expressed*, a complex incorporeal entity, on the surface of things, a pure event which insists or subsists in the proposition' (Deleuze, p. 30). A rather elusive object, it is best defined negatively, as something which is neither the state of things designated, nor the images and beliefs manifested in the mind of the utterer, nor the universal concepts (or the linguistic rules) on which the proposition depends: a likely candidate for Ockham's razor.

Deleuze proceeds to argue for its existence by creating a tradition for it, as we have seen (it also includes Ockhamite logicians like Gregory of Rimini), and by finding a place for it to subsist, in language: a frontier, the surface of a mirror.

We can now understand why Deleuze's theory of sense is not concerned with logic: the field of logic is signification (truth and falsity; implication and demonstration; in Carrollian terms, syllogisms and sorites). The field of sense is equally wide, but the landscape is different: we are now concerned with linguistic events, like those of fiction, with paradoxes and nonsense. A logic of sense can be constructed, in which *délire* can take its place.

100

THE PHILOSOPHY OF *DÉLIRE*

Describing this landscape is a way of giving a positive account of sense. Deleuze proceeds in two stages: first, he lists a series of paradoxes which are specific to sense; then, he describes the structure within which sense functions, in other words, language as structured by sense.

The first paradox of sense is the paradox of infinite regression. When I say something, I imply, but do not state, its sense. But I can state, through another proposition, the sense of the first. In turn, the sense of the second proposition is implied, but not stated: to be stated, it requires a third proposition, and so forth; there is no end to this proliferation of propositions. This is a simple form of a Carrollian paradox: in *Through the Looking-Glass*, Alice asks the White Knight the name of his song. The answer, as one recalls, is complex and confusing: the song is 'A-sitting on a gate', it is called 'Ways and Means', its name is 'The old, old man', and its name is called 'Haddock's eye'.

The second paradox concerns the neutrality, or sterility, of sense: the sense of a proposition is a mere phantasy, a neutralized image of the proposition, indifferent to the actions and passions of the bodies involved in the event (as in the instance of the battle), and indifferent to assertion and negation. In the fourteenth century, Nicolas of Autrecourt expressed this paradox thus: 'contradictoria ad invicem idem significant'. 'God exists' and 'God does not exist' have the same sense. Propositions contrary from the points of view of quality, quantity, modality and relation have the same sense, for these aspects concern logic, i.e. signification, not sense, which is neutral towards them. The paradox has another consequence, taken up by Meinong: propositions which involve contradictory or impossible objects (round squares, etc.) have sense, they are devoid of signification, i.e. absurd, but full of sense, i.e. nonsensical. Which shows that the two notions of nonsense and the absurd must not be confused.

This account of Deleuzian sense remains indirect. Its positive definition will be found in the series of concepts with which it forms a system: series, signifier and signified, paradoxical element, nonsense, structure. Sense, as we have seen, constitutes an articulation between propositions and things. But here we find the necessary elements for a Deleuzian series: two heterogenous sets, somehow made to converge. In this case, a set of signifiers (the proposition) and a set of signified entities (things or states of things). How are they made to converge? What guarantee is there that the two parts of the series correspond to each other? Deleuze here provides a brief commentary on Lacan's famous seminar on

The Purloined Letter. In Poe's story, two series of events are opposed: 1 the king fails to see the letter his wife received; the queen hides the letter by leaving it where everyone can see it; and the villainous minister sees everything and purloins the letter (this series corresponds to the first half of the plot); 2 the police fail to find the letter in the minister's house; the minister hides the letter exactly as the queen did; and, finally, Dupin recovers it by seeing through the minister's ploy (this is the second half of the plot, which obviously repeats the first). But this repetition implies a displacement (the position of the minister changes),[10] and the link between the two series is provided by an object, the letter, which goes missing, which is never where it should be (it is best hidden when it is most in evidence). This element links the two halves of the series, it circulates between them, and is never where one expects it to be; and, conversely, it is never found where it is: Deleuze calls it the paradoxical element (*l'instance paradoxale*). It is in excess in one of the series (the signifying), and lacking in the other (the signified): we are back with the Lacanian 'logic of the signifier' mentioned in the previous chapter. Jumping to anthropology, and quoting Lévi-Strauss, Deleuze finds a paradoxical element in the concept of *mana*: a term in itself devoid of meaning, a 'floating signifier' that can, therefore, accommodate any meaning, the 'zero symbolic value' whose only function is to maintain the system of values.

We have landed in structuralism, for the paradoxical element is very close to the 'empty square' (*la case vide*) which produces meaning in a structure. Each element of the structure is defined by its differences from all the others: in so far as it has value (in Saussure's sense), it is only an empty receptacle of differences. Imagine a chess board, where each square represents an element of the structure. In order to obtain the values, move a pawn across the board, stopping at every square. At each point the pawn, which replaces the element (the square) whose place it occupies, will produce a system of differences involving all the other squares – a singularity. The 'meaning' of the structure is the sum of all the singularities it contains: it is given by the 'empty square' which itself lacks meaning, which is in itself one too many (the 'empty square' is the n + 1 square on a board with n squares), and one too few, for when it occupies a space, it empties it (the number of relations in the singularity is n – 1). And this is how Deleuze defines the structure: 1 there are two series, one signifying, one signified, 2 each term in each series exists only through its relation with other terms; and 3 systematic difference is produced by a paradoxical element, which functions as the differentiating agent: it glides along the series, organizing the relationship between the terms.

This paradoxical element is closely connected with the production of sense: it gives meaning, though itself meaningless. In order to make the picture more precise we have now to understand the relation between paradox, common sense and sense. Sense, as we have seen, is indifferent to the determinations of signification and logic, to contradiction. It develops, therefore, in two directions, producing paradoxes: 'God exists' and 'God does not exist' have the same sense. To use a spatial metaphor, the paradoxical element, moving along the frontier between the two series travels in two directions. This is what distinguishes sense from 'common sense', which belongs to the world of signification. The French word 'sens', like its English counterpart, can mean either 'meaning' or a sensory modality, like the sense of hearing; but it can also mean 'direction', and Deleuze relies on this ambiguity to develop his spatial metaphor: the frontier between the two series is conceived as a line along which the paradoxical (the nonsensical) element glides in both directions, giving sense, but indifferent to the direction taken. Signification, on the other hand, is not neutral: it is oriented. 'Good sense', then (*le bon sens*: the standard translation of Plato's *doxa*) is also the right direction, separating truth and and falsity, and 'God exists' and 'God does not exist' are no longer equivalent. An alternative translation of *doxa* is 'common sense' (*le sens commun*), where sense means not a direction but a sense organ,[11] the 'organ' which orders the impressions of the various senses into a unity, a single organizing ego, guaranteeing both the identity of the subject and the permanence of the object (it is the *same* object that I see, hear or remember). 'Remember': for the metaphor is a second-order one, it metaphoricises the well-established metaphor which describes time in terms of space. The contrast between the indirection of the paradox and the oriented vector of common sense was already known to the Classics as the opposition between the regular and irreversible flow of time (Chronos) which has only an ever-renewed present, and the reversible time of memory and anticipation (Aion), which does not exist, but insists in my mind or in the propositions of fiction. (This can be compared with the famous analysis of time in book eleven of Augustine's *Confessions*.)[12] One can understand better, now, the deep complicity between sense and fiction, the opposition between sense and truth or falsity.

I have not yet made clear the role of nonsense in the structure: it lies in the paradoxical element and is produced by the contradictory duality (excess and lack; empty square and supernumerary object: both one too many and one too few). This is why it is often expressed by doublets (verbal dualities), like the Stoic nonsense word 'blituri', always used with its doublet, 'skindapsos'. Or like the Snark (which was a Boojum, you know) – for 'the Snark is sense'.[13] But it is best embodied in the Carrollian nonsense words, the famous portmanteaux of *Jabberwocky*. Deleuze interprets portmanteau words as compressed paradoxes. And he distinguishes two kinds. First, the *esoteric* word, or the name which designates its own sense. It involves either a contraction or a connection, as in the word 'Snark', which circulates both along the series of things (foodstuffs: 'and its taste was meagre and crisp') and along the series of words ('and it looked distressed at a joke'). The Snark is always missing where it is sought, but present in dreams and premonitions, and its name glides along the text, marking the frontier and organizing the two series: it is sought with thimbles and care, with forks and hope. It designates what it expresses, and expresses what it designates. The second type is the *portmanteau* word proper, composed of two recognizable words (as interpreted, for instance, by Humpty-Dumpty) like 'fuming' and 'furious' in 'frumious', or 'lithe' and 'slimy' in 'slithy'. Each part, says Deleuze, designates the sense of the other, or expresses the other part, and in turn is expressed by it. This kind of word operates not through contraction but disjunction.

These nonsense words structure the text: they have no meaning, but they prevent the text from lacking sense. The function of nonsense is to create sense, to *make* sense. The best instance of this process is again the Snark, whose absence (the Snark as character) and lack of sense (the 'Snark' as name) structure the text, cause 'the hunting'. It is the Snark's absent presence, from fit to fit, that makes sense in the text. Once again, we must not confuse nonsense and absurdity. At the end of this analysis we can offer a positive definition of sense: sense is produced, as a linguistic effect, by the circulation of the nonsensical element on the frontier between the two series. Where language is, *on the surface*, there sense emerges.

This theory of sense involves a theory of language: of its origins, of its relationship to the human body, and of its fragility and dissolution into *délire*. Once again, we turn to Deleuze's interpretation of a philosophical tradition, but this time a tradition not of philosophers, but of the image of philosophers. The popular image of the philosopher, Deleuze argues, goes back to Plato: he emerges from the cave and ascends to the heights, towards the sun and the Ideas. Philosophy, in this conception, operates by conversion and ascent. In opposition to this philosophy of heights, Nietzsche finds in the pre-Socratic philosophers a philosophy of depth: the pre-Socratic thinker refuses to leave the cave, he considers he has not gone deep enough into it; his model is Empedocles jumping into Etna. In the Megarics and the Stoics Deleuze finds a third image of philosophy: a philosophy of events, without height (the height of ideas) or depth (the depth of the body) where everything happens on the surface. By a typical Deleuzian leap, this tripartition involves a corresponding tripartition which accounts for the workings of language.

The Stoics provide a theory of events, and therefore of sense (in which events are expressed). But it is this dimension, which they analyse, of incorporeal effects, on the surface, that makes language possible. There sounds cease to be the actions and passions of the body, and become signifying sounds, distinguished from mere noise, abstracted from their oral determinations. This is expressed in Chrysippus's ironic paradox: if you speak of a chariot, a chariot goes through your mouth. Of course, Chrysippus knew the difference between the word and the object it denotes. His 'paradox' insists on the material origin of the word and on the process of abstraction by which the uttered sounds become language, and the spoken chariot ceases to be a chariot. On the surface, then, language develops its organization: we have described this 'structure', where sense emerges out of nonsense. Deleuze calls this *secondary organization*. It is secondary only because the surface coexists with height and depth, the two other philosophical dimensions. The first move is towards the heights. The surface organization accounts for the emergence of language, in its pristine paradoxical state, where sense is indifferent to the needs of signification. This may be where the poet dwells, but not the logician. If Carroll remains on the surface, Dodgson strives to ascend, to the *tertiary ordering* ('*ordonnance tertiaire*') where designation, manifestation and signification provide the rules for our day-to-day use of language as an instrument of communication, expression and proof. But what if the emergence fails to occur? Then the madman and his delirium appear: the organization of language disintegrates, words become sounds and noises, parts of the body, and are engulfed in the actions and passions of bodies, the *primary order*[14]

105

on which the whole edifice rests, but which must be denied if language is to be used to communicate. We have fallen into the depths.

Hence the difference between the pseudo-*délire* of nonsense and the dangerous *délire* of depth. For Deleuze, there are in fact four types of nonsense. The first two (represented by the esoteric word and the portmanteau word respectively) are tame and respectable: they make sense, in both senses of the phrase. But they belong to the surface, which is fragile, and each corresponds to a form of deeper nonsense, a dereliction of sense (Deleuze uses the phrase 'plongée de sens'). There are 'passion words', the sounds of which hurt and destroy, which Wolfson tries to neutralize by translation, and there are 'action words' in which sense is replaced by associations between sounds, a sort of active phonetic dissemination: Artaud's *cris*. This nonsense absorbs, devours everything: the whole structure disappears, the series are dissolved, no organization is left on which language can be built; the little girl plays with language and its amusing nonsense, the schizophrenic is delirious and no longer communicates.

So language emerges because sounds can be separated from bodies, abstracted into words expressing incorporeal events. The threat of the primary order shows that repression is involved in this process, that in Freudian terms the whole affair is an instance of sublimation. Deleuze in fact holds a version of the theory of the sexual origin of language (perhaps to the 'bow-wow' and 'pooh-pooh' theories, we should add a 'come hither darling' theory, as J. B. S. Haldane once suggested). Apart from the fact that the three images of the philosopher and the three types of organization have an obvious analogue in a famous Freudian tripartition (the superego/ego/id series), he proceeds to account for language by means of a distinction between two types of surfaces: the *metaphysical* surface on which language (as abstract and separate from the body) develops, and the *physical* surface of the human body organized into erogenous zones, that is into series, by a paradoxical element, the phallus (this term is, of course, borrowed from Lacan). There is a link between the two surfaces: the physical announces the metaphysical, and sexual organization prefigures the organization of language. Language is, after all, an oral activity, and Deleuze, like most psychoanalysts, sees a link between eating and speaking, between oral aggressive drives and the acquisition of language. The wheel has come full circle: he started with a praise of simulacra (or phantasma in Greek); he ends with a theory of phantasies, the psychoanalytic version of the pure event.

Délire in Deleuze

Although the word '*délire*' hardly ever appears in *Logique du Sens*, although it is certainly not one of the concepts which the text explores, it can be seen as an important element of the Deleuzian system: the existence of *délire* is one of the reasons why sense must be distinguished from the other three dimensions of the propositions; and Deleuze's analysis of sense will now enable us to define and explain *délire*.

Deleuze's definition of a structure enables us to account for *délire* both as a threat to and as a substratum of the linguistic structure. The specific characteristic of Deleuzian structure is the dialectic of lack and excess which governs the relationship between the two series, the one signifying, the other signified. We saw in the last chapter that this was a central characteristic of Nonsense: too much signifies, and too little is signified; the abundance of words balances the lack of meaning. After all, *délire* is first characterized by logorrhea, an unceasing flow of words, indicating that communication is no longer possible.

This, however, is not sufficient: this kind of dialectic, in its most superficial sense (much words, little meaning), can be understood without the help of Deleuze's complicated construction. I shall now try to show that his analysis accounts for *délire* in a non-trivial way, that it explains connections between elements in my corpus which otherwise would remain odd or mysterious.

The first idea is that the dialectic of lack and excess enables us to situate *délire* among various forms of discourse. For there is something paradoxical in a delirious text: it appears to lack meaning (partly or utterly) and yet, somehow, it always means. Even if the reader fails to understand *what* it means, he is certain that the text means to mean. In other words, he is in the same situation as Alice reading *Jabberwocky*, when she exclaims 'somehow it seems to fill my head with ideas – only I don't exactly know what they are!' What Deleuze's conception of sense points out is that there is a similar uncertainty in all propositions, and that this is a specific dimension of every one of them. There is a point where meaning is not fixed, where it is still uncertain, where interpretation wavers, before signification, manifestation or designation – the tertiary ordering – indicate, from above, the right way.

But there are texts where the uncertainty is sustained. Sometimes the attitude is deliberate. There is a profound similarity between the author of logical paradoxes and the author of literary nonsense (Dodgson and

Carroll). Sometimes it is only provisional, as in enigmas, where signification or designation finally manage to fix meaning and reassure the reader: a text like Roussel's has to be explained, even if posthumously. He did mean something, and he provided a key to it. We all experience a certain feeling of relief. He is received back into the fold, no longer a lunatic, but one of us, though a slightly eccentric character, a poet. For there are two main ways of dealing with the dimension of sense. Either one recognizes it as constitutive, and abandons the intricacies of signification, the facilities of manifestation, the certainties of designation – this is the role of the poet, forever reminding us that sense and nonsense are inseparable, that the signifier has a proliferating life of its own, always in excess of the signified it is supposed to bear. Or, alternatively, one is caught in the hesitancy of paradox, unable to escape from the perpetual exchange between sense and nonsense, compelled to roam aimlessly on the surface, along the line that joins the series, and eventually to fall back into the depths of somatic drives. Here one occupies the position of the madman, and the text becomes *délire*, sense irretrievably caught up in nonsense. Of course, *délire* is here becoming all-embracing. It occurs, at least potentially, in any discourse, since there is sense in every proposition: this is precisely what Deleuze's conception of sense helps us to understand.

The second idea that a reading of Deleuze suggests is that the presence of serial processes or coined words in the corpus can at last be understood. The existence of couples of series, and the uncertain application of one series to the other, are central to Deleuze's conception of sense as produced by paradox (the paradoxical element, we recall, is stamped on the coined word). But these serial processes are also essential to, for instance, Roussel or Wolfson. Wolfson's brand of *délire* is characterized, among other things, by an obsession with foodstuffs and words (with foodstuffs as they are translated into words on the tin labels), and by a general process of translation whereby a series of English words is linked to a series of words in other languages. His is the serial *délire* of the translator who has gone beyond the pale. And even if Roussel's key provides an explanation of the events related in the novel (each of which belongs, in *Impressions d'Afrique*, to two series: the presentation on the stage, and the pseudo-explanation given later), the result is still unsatisfactory (from the point of view of signification), for it is produced by the association of two series of words, the two sentences which provide the pretext for Roussel's fiction.

We can now also understand the presence of coined or portmanteau words in our texts (Brisset's etymologies and Wolfson's translations amount to the production of coined words, if only indirectly). We know that they are normally present in *délire* since psychiatrists often define *délire* as discourse containing portmanteau words. Deleuze's conception of the paradoxes and uncertainties of sense explains their function in language. For a portmanteau word is the embodiment of the hesitation between sense and nonsense (it has no meaning, yet its component parts do, and it acquires meaning from its various contexts), between the word and its sense, between designation and expression (we remember that Deleuze makes a distinction between esoteric and portmanteau words). 'For the Snark was a Boojum, you know': the sentence has no signification (I cannot verify it, or draw inferences from it), its designation is void (in spite of the 'five unmistakable marks' that ought to enable me to recognize a Snark, should I meet one in the park), and its only manifestation is that it claims to a knowledge in me which I know I do not possess ('you know': how should I know that the Snark was indeed a Boojum?). And yet, of course it makes sense. Since this is the last line of the last fit I have had time to become acquainted with the absent Snark, and the sentence is clearly poetic because it cannot settle between sense and nonsense. The last line of this poem would provide a beautiful opening for a piece of fiction (perhaps the same piece of fiction – the first sentence of *Finnegan's Wake* is the continuation of the last).

This is all too abstract, so I shall consider the following sentence:

'Ugh ugh blugh blugh ugh blug blug'.

The term 'sentence' may be surprising, since the syntactic correctness of this string of words is not apparent. Yet the elements are separated by blanks (an indication for the cryptographer that they are indeed words), and by placing the string between inverted commas I have treated it as a sentence. I have no right to do this, though, for the text has no structure: it does not mean anything, has neither signification nor sense.

As it happens, I have been cheating. Instead of producing the amiable sounds myself, I have borrowed them, ready-made, from an article by Paul Ziff. He uses the 'sentence' to refute the celebrated theory of meaning put forward by Paul Grice. The point made by Ziff (he invents a specific context for the utterance, but any will do) is that even if the sentence can be given a non-natural meaning[15] there is still an important sense in which it has no meaning. Here we recognize the now familiar paradox: the utterance is both meaningful and meaningless.

The author's gesture is deliberate: he means nothing, and nothing is what he means to mean. So far, I have followed Deleuze in using the term 'paradox' in a loose and illicit manner, but in this case we encounter genuine classic instances of paradox. What is the status of the nothing that he means? ('I see nobody on the road,' said Alice. 'I only wish *I* had such eyes,' the king remarked in a fretful tone. 'To be able to see Nobody! And at such distance too!' *Through the Looking-Glass*, ch. 7.) And how can anyone, without logical contradiction, mean not to mean? I am not interested here, of course, in definite descriptions or the theory of types, and I am not certain that Russell's solutions apply in the case of sense. But Deleuze's conception of sense refers to the paradoxical origin of any proposition, to a moment, if we use a temporal metaphor, when signification has not yet been assigned, or, to use a spatial metaphor, to a place where the direction is not indicated: this, the specific locus of paradox within language, is where certain texts flourish, from nonsense to poetry, including *délire*.

To take the second kind of paradox ('I mean not to mean', 'I order you to disobey', 'I lie'): strictly speaking, one can consider that they are solved by the theory of logical types, by distinguishing levels of text, the framing and the framed. Yet, clearly, this does not work for the kinds of texts which are classified as literary, or for our delirious tradition. They resist the distinction, they deliberately blur the frontier, they organize a game of mirrors in which the question of who speaks, and at what level of signification, can never be satisfactorily answered. Perhaps the best illustration of the paradox of sense (where 'paradox' is again used in that vague and illicit way) is the literary or pictorial *abyme*, where author, reader and hero, or painter, spectator and object keep exchanging roles, as in Velazquez's *Las Meninas*. What the *abyme* illustrates is the impossibility of fixed interpretation, of deciding between sense and nonsense. Deleuze's text itself also provides an illustration of this hesitation: there is a strong element of *abyme* in it. His offhandedness appears to be deliberate; his constant jumping from subject to subject, from concept to concept, is a reflexive act: the philosopher's own brand of *délire* answers to the *délire* in the corpus. And this *abyme* deals with the paradox of sense: in philosophy, paradoxes appear only as problems to be solved. The philosopher cannot dwell forever in the neutrality of sense; he is inevitably trapped by the 'true sense' of signification: Deleuze more than anyone else, with his obsessive use of tripartitions, his methodical and irresistible progress. Schizophrenics throw themselves under the wheels of the philosophical Juggernaut. They

110

are duly crushed, philosophically explained; but somehow they survive, in the proliferation of the text, in its sometimes ludicrous or contradictory statements. In Deleuze there is not only a philosophical theory of sense, but also a literary practice.

But I have wandered from my text. I have failed to demonstrate that Deleuze's conception of sense illuminates its meaning, or lack of meaning. If the main aspect of a communicative utterance is the 'will to say' of its author, Ziff's text can be characterized by his will *not* to say anything. But can one maintain that the text is utterly senseless? In fact those meaningless sounds do produce an embryo of meaning: they can be pronounced (and so belong to an imaginary language) and are soon caught in symbolic conventions; ever since I started reading cartoons, I have associated the word 'ugh' with the conclusion of an unintelligible speech by a Red Indian chief. So the absence of intended meaning, the lack of a signified, is balanced by an excess of signifiers which in turn creates meaning. Since this is a chain of words, some meaning must be assigned to it by linguistic structure or convention, even if the utterance is intended to be nonsensical. In the excess of signifiers, language speaks on its own. Deleuze's conception enables us to understand this genesis of sense, the presence of *délire* as a necessary part of language.

Délire is the embodiment of the paradox of sense (the dialectic of excess and lack). It is also the mark of another dialectic: the abstraction of language from the human body, and the expression of the body in language. Deleuze's point is that the two dialectics are closely related, as is apparent in the movement of his text. I have mentioned that he starts with a discussion of simulacra, or phantasmata, and ends with an analysis of phantasies. This discussion provides a fascinating insight into the process of tradition-making, as well as into the relationship between words and the body. The spelling shows that he uses the distinction established by Susan Isaacs, a Kleinian psychoanalyst, between conscious fantasy (day-dreaming or fiction) and unconscious phantasy (the pre-verbal psychic expression of somatic drives). Deleuze quotes Isaacs's article, but distorts it, by inserting it into the philosophical tradition of his own making (he assimilates phantasy to the Stoic *lekton*). Basing himself on an article by Laplanche and Pontalis, he places phantasies within language. For him, a phantasy has three characteristics: *a* it is a pure event, neither imaginary nor real, neither external nor internal, neither active nor passive; *b* it is an 'acosmic singularity', and

111

therefore does not presuppose a phantasizing ego; and *c* it has a verbal existence, but only as nonsense or paradox: it is best expressed (here Deleuze draws on an article by Irigaray) by a verb in the infinitive: there is no indication of subject and object, of tense, aspect or mood; the phrase retains the plastic quality characteristic of sense.

As we can see, this theory establishes an analogy between phantasy and sense, and also between language and the body (according to Isaacs, phantasy is the point where psyche and soma meet). The complicity is not only between sense and nonsense, but also between words and bodies: the primary order, the secondary organization and the tertiary ordering are three aspects of the same process.

And this is where the text ends, in the last of the Deleuzian tripartitions, in literature, not philosophy. The thirty-fourth and last series ('On primary order and secondary organization') contains a distinction between satire, humour and irony. It is the literary equivalent of the three images of philosophy (Platonic, Stoic and pre-Socratic), the three structural modes of meaning and language (primary order, etc.), and, of course, the spatial metaphor which governs the whole text (depth, surface, height). Satire is concerned with the depth of the primary order, it deals with insults and obscenities, and regresses to oral aggressive sex, to excrement and food: it is the art of regression, and Swift, the famous satirist, is also the author of the infamous poems to Stella. But irony is the art of heights: its game of equivocation and metaphor is controlled by an all-mastering subject; it is a form of domination where the subject is placed in the elevated position of a God. Humour, however, forces the subject to creep along the ground, on the surface: not going down to the satirical incoherence of depth, where objects are dismembered, but clinging to the discrete absurdity of surfaces, where sense rules over the serious game of paradoxes, and negation no longer denies but only confuses: the place where Alice can no longer say whether meaning what one says and saying what one means are two different acts, where time has stopped and little girls forget their names. The classic philosophical concept of irony is overthrown with Platonism and its heights: it gives way to humour, the uncertain art of surfaces. But this point of arrival also symbolizes the movement of the text (philosophy, psychiatry, literature) and locates *délire* within literature (as the result of a philosophical/psychiatric progress), somewhere *between* satire and humour, as that which threatens to disrupt those merely literary concepts, and gives them philosophical depth.

Conclusion

With Deleuze, you always start in philosophy and end in literature: the critic as much as the text. For Deleuze is not like any other philosopher: a critique of *Logique du Sens* can only take the form of a reader's response, of fascination and resistance, not objective judgement. The only adequate instrument for an assessment of Deleuze is pastiche.

Indeed, if one tries to raise objections to Deleuze's text, one hesitates between two attitudes: either downright dismissal, in the manner of that famous review of *Lyrical Ballads*, beginning 'this won't do'; or resignation, since the text is impossible to refute. There is no point in constructing an anti-Deleuzian argument which would disprove his theory of sense: it would immediately be adopted, adapted, and caught in the web of the Deleuzian tripartitions. We might complain at the length of his theoretical leaps, the ludicrousness of some of his arguments, and the off-handedness of his method: his extensive use of punning (as in the case of *sens*), his disquisitions on alcoholism, his abrupt transition from astrology to Leibniz, and his peculiar association of common sense with agriculture ('common sense is agricultural; it cannot be separated from the problem of enclosures. . .' *Logique du Sens*, p. 93).

But this would be too facile: the off-handedness is part of a strategy, which involves more than purely philosophical risks (there is something of the madman and the guerrilla in a philosopher who deals with surfaces). In an interview with Claire Parnet,[16] Deleuze expressed his irritation at objections. He was ready to grant his opponents anything, provided he could get on to other things (there is a conception of philosophical argument in this: not competition, rhetorical struggle, where points are made and won, but co-operation, where several people move along together). He has adopted Jean Luc Godard's motto: 'not ideas that are just, just ideas'. His own version of it might be: 'errors rather than stupidity'. Better far the mistakes of philosophical *délire* than the stupidities of common sense.

Yet, in *Logique du Sens*, Deleuze does not quite reach this position: it is present in the text as a tendency, which creates a tension, to me the main source of the fascination of the book. A theory of sense is presented, which can be assessed, attacked, and applied. But evaluation is made difficult by the author's literary posture: a discussion which starts with concepts often ends in metaphor (the ludicrousness is sometimes due to this). The theory of sense, for instance, based on a conceptual quadripartition (signification, manifestation, designation, sense), ends with a metaphorical system (height, depth, surface): concepts borrowed from other fields are made to fit into the metaphor.

Deleuze denies that he makes use of metaphors. He certainly belongs to the metaphorical tradition in philosophy (he wrote books on both Nietszche and Bergson), but he attacks the artificiality of metaphor, he refuses the implicit comparison, and therefore the displacement, which metaphors contain: he claims to use terms *literally*.

One of the difficulties involved in understanding the meaning of Deleuze's key terms, like 'surface', is that the reader has to thread his way through a complex network of metaphors, philosophical ('metaphysical surface') or literary (the soft surface of the human body, the captivating surface of the mirror, the mysterious surface of dormant water). The text proliferates poetically, through networks of images: Deleuze rejects the metaphor of the tree (ordered, binary growth, with an origin – the root – and a centre – the trunk – a metaphor used by linguistics, as in Chomsky's trees) and prefers the rhizome, with its unordered, multi-directional development. This attitude belongs to a philosophical tradition: philosophy no longer works through rational distinctions (as it still did in *Logique du Sens*), but through textual proliferation. It becomes, to put it in a deliberately exaggerated manner, the spontaneous overflow of powerful feeling.

One might say that, in *Logique du Sens*, Deleuze is turning into a Romantic philosopher, abandoning the classicism of the historian of philosophy and finding his own critical way by crossing the frontier with literature in style, content and general attitude. Of course, Deleuze's Romanticism is, at best, odd. In the broadest possible terms, one can describe Romantic theory and practice as based on a contrast between poetry, or the language of emotion and subjectivity, and science, or the language of rational argument and objectivity. The general tendency in philosophy has been to claim a place, at least an ancillary one, among the sciences, and to disdain the status of art. Deleuze mentioning his dislike of Descartes goes against this trend: he takes philosophy back to literature, blurs the frontier between feeling and reason, and adopts a conception of sense and language where *délire* and expressive style are central.

Romantic themes abound in Deleuze's work. There is the Stoic interest in the growth of living organisms, as opposed to the Aristotelian division into classes, and numerous images strongly reminiscent of Herder's conception of 'vegetable genius' (a frequent theme among German Romantics). The imagery of flight as opposed to stasis and structure (one recalls Deleuze's admiration for Anglo-American literature, from Lowry to Kerouac), of 'devenir' and geographic progression as opposed to chronology and historical analysis of origins indicates an anarchic vein in Deleuze, which can also be found in libertarian Romantics. His main theme, of course, is that of the madman and the child: the schizophrenic and the little girl are Romantic characters, one this side of common sense, the other beyond it, but both endowed, in their innocence, with powers of vision. A third character must be added: the poet who translates their vision into intimations of immortality, or inspired ravings. In Deleuze his part is played by the philosopher, concerned with the paradoxes and ambiguities of sense rather than with objective truth. Deleuze's is a Romanticism of sense rather than of manifestation (of expression), in which the author is replaced by the *délire* of impersonal or collective discourse.

Délire, then, is the point where philosophy meets literature, where the language of rationality is absorbed by the language of expression, and where Deleuze's philosophical culture and literary leanings merge to produce a text. Small wonder, then, that the text should be *en abyme*, that the philosophy of *délire* should give way to *délire* as a form of philosophy.

Notes

1 *Twelfth Night* III, 1.
2 cf. K. K. Ruthven, *Myth* (Methuen 1976).
3 According to the bow-wow theory, language originated in the imitation of natural sounds: the first words were onomatopoeias. The pooh-pooh theory claims that language has emerged progressively from emotive sounds, the spontaneous expression of the subject's feelings. For the yo-he-ho theory, man is a social animal, and language has its source in the songs that accompanied communal physical effort.
4 Conversely, he refuses to be made the source of an orthodoxy: he has always refused (the difference with Lacan is flagrant) to become a master, hence his insistence on collective work, and, in his later period, his sharing of authorship with Guattari.
5 There is an element of provocation in Deleuze's use (and abuse) of Carroll: the naïve Carrollian (including the present author) will hardly recognize his beloved text, and will think – with reason – that the philosophical onus which Carroll's texts are made to bear is crushing them. But, hopefully, he will in the end be grateful for some new insights.
6 It is *nowhere*, and can only 'stand' if it is personified, i.e. if the event becomes fiction.

7   From this discussion it might appear that what Deleuze is talking about is not *events* but *facts*. In 'Facts and Events' (*Linguistics and Philosophy* (Ithaca: Cornell University Press 1967)), Zeno Vendler makes a systematic distinction between facts and events, based on a linguistic difference between two kinds of nominalization. Deleuze's use of the term 'event' goes back to the Stoic distinction between objects and events, which is also linguistically based – in this case on the difference between nouns and verbs. Thus, the Stoic 'event' may be taken to include both facts and events as analysed by Vendler.

8   The term 'attribute', like 'expression', is clearly derived from Spinoza.

9   Sextus Empiricus, quoted in B. Mates, *Stoic Logic*.

10 We notice that each half of the series is made up of *events*, each represented linguistically by a verb (to fail to see, to hide, to steal), the agents or patients of which vary (as in phantasies, cf. the article by Freud discussed in Chapter 2). This is where the plot makes sense: from the repetition of events there emerges a structure of meaning.

11 This is partly why I translate 'sens' as 'sense', not 'meaning'; the main reason, of course, is that what is usually called the theory of meaning is concerned with signification rather than sense.

12 This contrast is also used by structuralism: Lévi-Strauss opposes the irreversible time of diachrony, of history, to the reversible time of synchrony, of myth.

13 Deleuze is to be praised for having penetrated this enigma.

14 The words 'primary' and 'secondary' have obvious Freudian connotations: for Freud primary processes are opposed to secondary processes as the unconscious is opposed to consciousness and the pre-conscious, or the pleasure principle to the reality principle.

15 Grice opposes 'natural' to 'non-natural' meaning, as in the two following sentences: *a* 'natural': 'these spots mean measles'; *b* 'non-natural': 'when Deleuze uses the word "series", he means two parallel sets of elements joined by a frontier'. The purpose of his article is to provide a satisfactory definition of non-natural meaning; ' "A means (non-naturally) something by x" is roughly equivalent to "A intended the utterance of x to produce this particular effect in an audience by means of the recognition of this intention".'

16 G. Deleuze, C. Parnet, *Dialogues* (Paris: Flammarion 1977).

Further reading

A few of Deleuze's early works (i.e. up to *Anti-Oedipus*) are available in English: *Proust and Signs* (New York: G. Braziller 1972); *Masochism* (Faber 1971), and *Nietzsche and Philosophy*, tr. H. Tomlinson (Athlone Press 1983). A short fragment of *Logique du Sens* is translated in J. V. Harrari (ed.), *Textual Strategies* (Methuen 1980) (Cornell University Press 1979), which also contains a note on Deleuze.

There has so far been little critical commentary on Deleuze, but see M. Cressole, *Deleuze* (Paris: Editions Universitaires 1973). On *Logique du Sens*, see M. Foucault, 'Theatrum Philosophicum', in *Critique*, **282** (Paris 1970) (tr. in *Language, Counter-Memory, Practice* (Ithaca: Cornell University Press 1977)). On Deleuze and Wolfson, see J. Mehlman, 'Portnoy in Paris', *Diacritics*, **2**: no. 4 (Johns Hopkins University Press 1972). On *Nietzsche and Philosophy*, see the review by Richard Rorty, 'Unsoundness in perspective', in *The Times Literary Supplement*, (17 June 1983), p. 619. A number of *L'Arc*, no. 49 (Paris 1972) (2nd, enlarged, edn, 1980) is devoted to Deleuze. The most enlightening information is to be gathered from Deleuze himself in his *Dialogues* (with Claire Parnet) (Paris: Flammarion 1977).

On Stoic logic, see Benson Mates, *Stoic Logic* (University of California Press 1961). Deleuze relies heavily on Emile Brehier, *La théorie des incorporels dans l'ancien stoicisme* (Paris: Picard 1908). H. P. Grice's article, 'Meaning', and P. Ziff's reply, 'On H. P. Grice's account of meaning' can be found in D. Steinberg and L. Jakobovits, *Semantics* (Cambridge University Press 1971).

On the notion of *abyme*, with special reference to Velazquez's *Las Meninas*, see L. Dällenbach, *Le récit spéculaire, essai sur la mise en abyme* (Paris: Seuil 1977); and of course the opening pages of M. Foucault's *Les Mots et Les Choses* (Paris: Gallimard 1966) (tr. *The Order of Things* (New York: Pantheon 1971)).

On fantasy and phantasy, see Susan Isaacs, 'The nature and function of phantasy', *International Journal of Psychoanalysis*, **XXIX** (1948), pp. 73–97. The article by Laplanche and Pontalis mentioned in the same section is 'Fantasme originaire, fantasme des origines et origine du fantasme', *Les Temps Modernes*, **215** (Paris 1964). The article by Irigaray is 'Du fantasme et du verbe', *L'Arc*, **34** (Paris 1968).

4
The psychoanalysis of délire

Introduction

The chamber walls were dark all round, –
And to his book he turned again;
The light had left the lonely taper,
And formed itself upon the paper
Into large letters – bright and plain!

The godly book was in his hand –
And, on the page, more black than coal,
Appeared, set forth in strange array,
A word *which to his dying day*
Perplexed the good man's gentle soul.

The ghostly word, thus plainly seen,
Did never from his lips depart;
But he has said, poor gentle wight!
It brought full many a sin to light
Out of the bottom of his heart.

It is not necessary to imagine, like Wordsworth in *Peter Bell*, that 'dread spirits' are 'playing with soul and sense', to feel the power of the word: it is not merely a power to inform, but also to form and to deform, to shape and to destroy, to set free and to imprison. In the Jewish legend of the Golem the creature comes to life when a passage from the Talmud is inserted into its mouth; it reverts to the immobility of clay when the word is withdrawn. But sometimes the word is not withdrawn, it remains within the mind, thus perplexing the good man's gentle soul: this is the experience of verbal hallucination, where language tortures the subject and induces delirium. The ghostly word which can never from his lips depart, characterizes the delirious psychotic: in turn, it produces another set of words, no less ghostly, the words of theory, of the analyst. We shall now explore the aspect of our tradition which is concerned with the power of the word as a source of hallucination and *délire* – where it will appear that the analysis of *délire* is related to the question of metaphor, of fiction and interpretation, of the letter and its inscription.

The first task is to distinguish this aspect of the tradition from the one with which I dealt in the last chapter. Several figures have emerged so far in our analysis of *délire*: the little girl whose recitations go wrong and who can no longer say whether she is Alice or Mabel; the 'schizophrenic', possessed by language and trying to turn his dependence into mastery; the poet, whose *délire* is an instrument of insight; and the philosopher, who casts himself into all three roles. Another is waiting among the props, eager to strut upon the stage and utter his gibberish: the analyst.

These characters can act in two types of play: either a comedy, an optimistic story of integration, according to the classic definition of the genre, or a tragedy, a heroic story of exclusion. In the previous chapter, the philosopher played the part of the stage-manager of a comedy: characters shared *délire* as a common matrix for all language and meaning. In this chapter, the psychoanalyst will produce a tragedy, where a sharp distinction is maintained between the delirium of the psychotic patient and the theorizing of the psychiatrist. *Délire*, even if it is revealed as containing a nucleus of truth and as having the same structure as a theory, remains a symptom. Consequently, a new character will appear, to utter this *délire* which is delirium: the paranoiac.

The distinction is somewhat forced: one should not take the psychoanalytic account of *délire*, which I will now develop, as a form of reduction or repression. *Délire* is a symptom which needs to be explained, but not morally condemned or patronizingly lamented. Nor is it necessarily conceived as a disease to be cured – it is rather treated as a defence, as the patient's own attempt to cure himself (as in the case of Wolfson), an attempt which involves important insights into the illness and contains an element of truth. A truth, not hidden as in the case of neurosis, but explicitly stated and almost theorized: this is how Lacan described Schreber's *délire*. And yet *délire* must be clearly distinguished from normal language. It can be defined as a series of divergences from reasonable speech, the main one being the use of coined words. And because of these differences the delirious patient is, in a way, excluded from the communicating community – one of Lacan's maxims is that the madman is no poet. Poetry is a reordering of experience, a new

119

experience of language and of the world, whereas delirium is mere repetition, in which the subject is possessed by language.

From the very beginning we are faced, in the psychoanalytic account of *délire*, with a contradiction: *délire* is both delirium in the medical sense, a non-creative and repetitive flow of words, and a medium for truthful insights, a form of theory. This, of course, raises questions about truth itself (what is truth, if *délire* can contain an element of it?) and about language (what is language, if its least controlled form is closest to its most controlled, the discourse of science, or theory?). But it is also, perhaps, the first opportunity for us to study *délire* without inverted commas. *Délire* is no longer a metaphor, a tag which we attach to literary or semi-literary texts, but an object of study, already constructed and delimited in that model of positive science, Kraepelin's textbook of psychiatry. And perhaps this will also enable us to reconsider the nature of metaphor itself, in its relation to *délire*.

Delirium: Schreber

In the psychoanalytic tradition, some texts stand apart. They are constantly re-analysed, and a reinterpretation of them seems to be a necessary part of the education of psychoanalysts, the written equivalent of the didactic analysis. Freud's case-histories are the best examples of such texts, and the analysis of Schreber's *Memoirs* plays a special role among them.

There are two reasons, I think, why this case of delirium has given rise to so many cases of the *délire* of interpretation. The first is that in this case we have a written document, which provides an objective basis for interpretation. Usually, the patient's words do not get outside the analyst's consulting-room, except as interpreted by the analyst: consequently, the analyst remains sole master of his case. Schreber's text is one of the rare cases in psychoanalytic literature where a new analyst has access to exactly the same material as Freud, and can pit his wits against the master's. And the limitations of the text, its enigmatic character (we have little means of knowing more about Schreber than he tells us, and essential biographic details are still missing) inevitably elicit interpretations and encourage the *délire* of theory. Not that Freud's disciples have taken undue advantage of this opportunity to compete with the master: most reappraisals of Schreber are extremely respectful, sometimes to the point of piety. And this is due to the second reason for Schreber's celebrity in psychoanalytic circles: the 1911 study is a landmark in the development of Freud's conception of psychosis. The link between paranoia and homosexuality, the importance of narcissism and projection have been important elements of Freudian theory ever since, and analysts have rarely tried to challenge them.

I shall follow the path of pious recollection by examining two readings of Schreber's text, by Freud and by Lacan. And I shall treat Schreber's text as an instance of *délire*, and the two analyses as linguistic or literary analyses. In other words, my reading of the text will be determined by the tradition I have been exploring, based on the idea that psychoanalysis deals, among other things, with the workings of language, and with its literary use in fiction.

Memoirs of my Nervous Illness, by Daniel Paul Schreber, is a forbidding book, with its long subtitle ('Under which conditions can a person suspected of being mentally alienated be kept in a mental institution against his express wishes?'), its two series of addenda and its legal appendixes, including the report of the psychiatric expert and the judgement which finally set Schreber free (a landmark in the history of psychiatry). From the very beginning the reader is aware of at least two contradictions. The first holds between the contents of the book, which are undeniably delirious, and its form, or rather the genre to which it belongs: it is not, properly speaking, an autobiography, not only because it only deals with the period of the author's illness, but also, and mainly, because its purpose is to plead for Schreber's release. It is a defence in the legal rather than the psychological sense. Who would have thought that delirium and legal argument could coexist in the same text, or rather (since it is a characteristic of paranoia that normal processes of thought are not impaired, so that paranoid delirium has a striking plausibility) that delirium could be the content of an entirely serious legal discussion, an effective one, for the defence was successful, and Schreber was set free? In fact Schreber harmoniously weaves two strands of discourse into his text: the mythopoetic (his religious *délire*) and the positive (the discourse of judicial proof and scientific psychiatry). For, apart from us, there are two types of readers who are addressed in the text: his former colleagues, the judges who are to hear the case, and Kraepelin, whose textbook he quotes several times (acknowledging its general value and pleading, in his own case, an exception to the rule). Schreber fully accepts the contradiction. He knows that what he writes is unbelievable and will be taken as evidence of his insanity: but he maintains that it is true and asserts his firm desire for truth, and the accuracy of his observations. Like Brisset, he knows that he is writing poetic science, a contradiction, but one he is determined to maintain.

For there is a striking mixture of honesty and calculation in Schreber: and he is caught, as far as the strategy of his writing is concerned, in another, more formidable, contradiction. He is pleading for his release, and needs to convince his readers: his must be a strategy of verisimilitude (this is why he needs the authority, in the etymological sense, of Kraepelin). But at the same time he wants to state the truth, and to communicate the cosmology which has been revealed to him. So he has to work out a compromise, like Wolfson or Brisset. This is nowhere more apparent than in the case of the screams. We learn from the report of Dr Weber, the head of the clinic where he was kept, that one of his symptoms was a continuous urge to scream, which was why he was kept apart from other patients. At first, Schreber denies the existence of his screams, or at least the necessity for his isolation (p. 197); a few pages later, he indirectly acknowledges their reality by explaining them away as 'miracles' (his breathing organs are manipulated by God so that he is compelled to scream – p. 205); five chapters later, the existence of the screams is mentioned as a proof of the truth of his account and the authenticity of his experience (p. 273). This type of logic would have delighted Carroll: it is the symptom of a literary strategy, whereby a writer, caught between the need to express and the necessity to conform, finds a compromise between the two incompatible urges. The ending of *Jane Eyre*, where the heroine finds conventional happiness in marriage with a slightly damaged Rochester, but where her physical passion for him finds expression in her superiority and domination over him because of his blindness, is a good instance of such a strategy. The true locus for *délire* is literary fiction. Even medical delirium finds expression through fiction (the paranoid woman whose case is discussed in Lacan's doctoral thesis was also the author of a novel of some merit, on which Lacan's analysis is partly based): fiction is the type of discourse in which the relation between language and truth is viewed in non-positivistic terms (where truth is distinguished from verisimilitude), where sincerity and certainty can coexist with coherence and agreement (or adequation), where the language of poetry is interwoven with the language of science. Perhaps we have a new definition of *délire* here: *délire* as strategy (the delirious aspect of the text being due to the surface traces of the strategy), as compromise between the compulsion to express (truth as inner certainty) and the necessity to communicate (truth as agreement between perception and object). This contradiction pervades Schreber's text.

But, for the reader who, having read the interpretations of the text, is placed in the position of a would-be analyst, there is a third contradiction: Schreber's narrative revolves around an absent centre, the third chapter, withdrawn from publication because deemed unsuitable (presumably by his relatives). In it Schreber dealt with members of his family, probably including his father. And this is precisely the information which, for a psychoanalyst, is vital to a full understanding of the case: one can understand the difficulty of Freud's task, and the satisfaction he derived from its completion. All the interpretations are attempts at recreating the third chapter (and the best of all would be the one which, like Pierre Menard's *Don Quixote* in Borges, reproduced Schreber's missing text word for word) and reconstructing the absent father (he is hardly ever mentioned in the rest of the text). But, on the other hand, the task is banal: it is familiar to every reader of fiction, who is always called on to close the gaps left open in his text by the author. Perhaps the only difference between Schreber and a novelist is one of social position, not one of strategy or control over one's text: doubt is cast on Schreber's mastery over the myths he composes by the fact that he was certified as insane, so that the open character of his text (the inconsistencies, the gaps, the threads left dangling) can be interpreted as symptoms of *délire*, not as a rhetorical ploy, a way of opening a space for the reader's participation in the process, while carefully monitoring his reading. But this is only an external, perhaps an irrelevant, difference. In many ways Schreber is a good novelist.

Here is a brief account of the facts, before we turn to Schreber's fictions. Schreber was a high-court judge in Germany, the son of a famous doctor who specialized in physical training and hygiene and was the author of several textbooks on indoor gymnastics and child care. He was married but was disappointed in his desire to have children. In 1884 he stood unsuccessfully as a Liberal candidate for the Reichstag and immediately succumbed to his first nervous illness, which was treated in the university clinic in Leipzig by Professor Flechsig. After six months he was discharged. In 1893, at the age of 51, he was appointed President of the Senate of the Supreme Court in Saxony, a position of great eminence, and an extraordinary promotion for one so (relatively) young: five months later, he was again admitted to the university clinic at

Leipzig. He remained in psychiatric care until 1902, when the appeal court at Dresden ordered his release. In 1903, he published his memoirs. In 1907, he suffered a relapse, and had to go back to a mental home, where he remained until his death in 1911, the year when Freud published his interpretation (Freud, when he wrote, knew neither of Schreber's death nor of his last illness).

Some of the facts appear in the *Memoirs*, which concentrate on the second illness, its immediate causes and the subsequent internment. But they are caught in an extremely complex fiction. Like the writer of an autobiography, Schreber starts with his antecedents. But he goes much further back, or beyond, than Tristram Shandy, who started with the moment of his conception. Schreber's first chapter deals with God and immortality, his second with the crisis in the kingdom of God caused by Schreber's illness. A whole cosmology is produced to account for Schreber's present position: if this is fiction, the correct comparison will perhaps not be the bourgeois novel, but the epic. There is in fact a Miltonic ring in the story of a glorious God (conceived as rays, like the rays of the sun: in fact, he *is* the sun), who is also a dual God in the Manichean tradition (the superior God, Ormuzd, is opposed to the inferior God, Ariman) and a curiously imperfect and vulnerable one (the rays of God, which are also its nerves, always risk being fatally attracted to the nerves in a human body, which carry the soul; 'the human soul is contained in the nerves of the body': this is the opening sentence of the *Memoirs*). There is even a serpent. Flechsig, the main persecutor, has appropriated certain rays of God for his own use, and has attempted 'soul murder' on Schreber. But this is because Schreber is Christ, the new Messiah, whose nerves can attract God and regenerate humanity. So a Miltonic struggle takes place in which Schreber wages a losing battle against Flechsig, and also against God: 'miracles' or 'wonders' (the German word he uses is *Wunder*) are performed against him. But in the end he accepts God's will and experiences redemption. He must not die to save the world (indeed, he *cannot* die) but he must experience 'unmanning', the resorption of his male sexual organs, the transformation of his body into a woman's body, so that he can bear the new human race which will replace condemned humanity (indeed for a while Schreber was convinced that everybody was dead, and that he saw around him only pale images of men, 'fleeting-improvised-men', as he called them). At first, his virility resisted, but after a while he recognized his mission, though still accusing God of perfidiousness, and protesting against the miracles constantly performed on his person: voices, ghosts, compulsive thought and action, strange growths and miraculous birds or wasps which tease him or talk to him.

Contrary to appearances, the interest of Schreber's text does not lie in his delirious cosmology: he is only a little more imaginative than Joanna Southcott. Psychiatrists have often remarked how predictable paranoid delirium is. The sense of a mission, the unanswerable logic of persecution and miracles, the certainty of being the sole survivor of a disaster, are common enough symptoms. But Schreber's talent, like Brisset's, is philological. His work contains not only the usual coinages and delirious misuse of words, but also an embryo of analysis (no doubt due to his rhetorical position: the burden of proof was on him). Schreber is not a professed philologist like Wolfson, but rather, like Carroll, a practitioner. In both cases, practice precedes theory.

Schreber, as we have seen, is beset by verbal hallucinations. Although his enemies conjure up ghosts to distract him (sometimes rather ludicrous ones, like a grand piano), they are mostly manifested through voices, inside his head (alien souls penetrate his mind, sometimes in droves: 'on one occasion 240 Benedictine monks under the leadership of a Father whose name sounded like Starkiewicz suddenly moved into my head', Schreber, p. 49), or through talking creatures, like the garrulous birds. Schreber is fully aware of the peculiarities of this hallucinated language. He carefully distinguishes the normal speech of human communication from the nerve speech, produced by the vibration of nerves during the process of nerve connection (an electrical metaphor) which enables a soul to be 'plugged' into another soul, and so to invade it or be absorbed by it. Nerve speech is compared to inner discourse and to dreams. It is silent, escaping the mastery of the speaking subject, and sometimes his consciousness. It is the language of possession, used by divine nerves to meddle with the human soul. It is language working on its own account, beyond or before consciousness.

Nor is this Schreber's only insight into the semiotic structure of his hallucinations. The voices talk to him in a special language, the *Grundsprache*, the language of origins, a sort of archaic German characterized by 'euphemisms', i.e. inversion of meaning (thus 'reward' is used for 'punishment', 'poison' for 'food', Schreber, p. 13). This is reminiscent not only of Freud's theory of the opposed meanings of primitive words, but also of the use of inversion in the paranoid formulas which he finds at work in Schreber's discourse: the *Grundsprache*, which ignores negation, is the language of the unconscious, the unconscious as language.[1]

Perhaps the most impressive of Schreber's intuitions about language concerns its relation to the body. The many wonders that affect his body (he is given a new heart, his stomach is taken away, and his lungs are eaten up by a worm) are always accompanied by exclaiming voices, and his mouth is a prime target for the aggressive miracles: 'why don't you say it aloud?' scream the voices whenever he is eating, in order to force him to confuse the two oral activities, and to speak with his mouth full. But the link is not only external (the voice being an accompaniment for the act). Language is directly connected with the body; nerve speech, as its name indicates, is language embodied. 'It seems to lie in the nature of rays that they *must* speak as soon as they are in motion' (Schreber, p. 130): the vibration of the rays or nerves *is* speech. And as it is also the cause of voluptuous sensations, there is a concordance between grammar and physical pleasure: 'whenever expressed in a grammatically complete sentence, the rays would be led straight to me, and entering my body (. . .) temporarily increase its soul voluptuousness' (Schreber, p. 219).

So, if grammar is a source of physical pleasure, ungrammatical language, mere noise, is the main source of pain (two of Schreber's symptoms are his sensitivity to noises around him and a compulsive urge to scream): the persecution of which he is a victim takes the form of a dereliction of grammar. Voices attack him either by incessant repetition of cacophonic fragments, meaningless sentences with omitted words and syllables, or by the ironic use of heroic formulas, in which Schreber is hailed as 'prince of Hell' (Schreber, p. 162). The heroic formulas are grammatical, but they overshoot the mark, they are loaded with too much meaning, and are, therefore, the obverse of jingles.

It is the omission of words, and what Schreber calls the 'grammatically defective forms' which is important: it characterizes the working of the hostile rays which attack him all the time. The rays, says Schreber (p. 48, n. 26), have acquired the habit of not uttering the words which are not absolutely necessary to the meaning of the sentence. And this practice has given rise to exorbitant excess, so that sentences are hardly ever complete: 'Why don't you say it . . .?' say the rays, meaning 'Why don't you say it aloud?'. Here, as Schreber recognizes, the deleted word is not semantically trivial, and cannot be guessed. But this is part of the rays' strategy. It enables them to insult him (the answer to that

126

question is imposed on him by the rays: 'no doubt because I'm a fool') and to compel him to complete their sentences (the 'interruption system', or 'system-of-not-finishing-a-sentence' consists of elliptical questions or pseudo-questions, like 'Why then?' or 'Why because?', which compel him to find causes for every one of his sensations or thoughts (Schreber, p. 216)). Most importantly, it prevents the voluptuous attraction of the divine rays by Schreber's nerves which could occur if the sentences were complete and grammatical.

Schreber resembles Wolfson in many ways. Like him, he is aware of the noxious power of words, and he adopts the same defences. For instance, he defeats the painful aggression of the rays' formulas by *converting* them: 'In earlier years my nerves simply had to think on, to answer questions, to complete broken-off sentences, etc. Only later was I gradually able to accustom my nerves to ignoring the stimulation which forced them to think on, by simply repeating the words and phrases and then turning them into not-thinking-of-anything thoughts. I have done that for a long time now with conjunctions and adverbs which would need a full clause for their completion.' (Schreber, p. 220). The main conversion is not unlike one of Wolfson's devices: it consists in the slow repetition of the phrase, so that it loses its aggressive force. The voices are hoist with their own petard: Schreber's slow repetition counteracts their insistent garrulousness. Indeed, Schreber's tactic consists mainly in inverting his opponent's tricks. Thus the miraculous birds with their unceasing chatter do not understand their own words: the only relation they are aware of is homophony, not homonymy or synonymy. So, if Schreber utters words phonetically similar to those they tease him with, they are dumbfounded, and miss their cues. And Schreber gives examples of such homophonies (like Wolfson's, his rules are not very strict): 'Santiago' for 'Carthago', 'Chinesenthum' for 'Jesus-Christum', etc. (p. 210). By using poetic tricks, that is by working on the material of words, on the signifiers, Schreber, like Wolfson, defeats his aggressors and reaches an ecstatic communion with God, based on *metrical* communication. God's nerves and his communicate by vibrating rhythmically, and his vibration is the physiological equivalent of metrical language (p. 137, n. 64).

So Schreber's text shows us, once again, that *délire* is not merely an abnormal form of discourse: it is also a metalinguistic activity. This is why Schreber, like Roussel or Carroll, is a novelist. Not because he invents wondrous tales (as we have seen, there is a certain repetitiveness and banality in wonderlands), but because he develops linguistic strategies. His struggle with God occurs first through language, then in language, and finally about language.[2] And this is why Carroll, the teller of tales, has so many strange insights into psychotic processes: he is consciously playing with words. And Nonsense there is in Schreber, too. He dreams that he goes into the depths of the earth in a lift or a train compartment (p. 74); one of the ghosts he sees gradually disappears like the Cheshire Cat (p. 103); and like Alice he recites poetry because meter, as we have seen, has a prophylactic value and can keep the voices at bay (p. 224). Indeed, nonsense is the main characteristic of the voices' strategy, and one of the formulas constantly repeated is 'all nonsense cancels itself out' (p. 182). The formula must have struck Schreber, for he mentions it twice in the addenda, and attempts to explain it: the very exaggeration of nonsensical utterances, he claims, defeats their purpose and destroys them (Schreber is no longer painfully affected by them) (p. 312). And he adds a historical explanation: nonsense may triumph for a while, but it will always disappear in the end, and reason will return, even if it takes an eternity (Schreber can wait that long: he is no longer dependent on time; it is eternity that depends on him, p. 331). In this Manichean struggle between nonsense and reason, nonsense is the instrument of the ultimate victory of reason (as Satan is nothing but a tool in the hands of God). The structure of Schreber's *délire* is based on this reversal, whereby linguistic madness produces reason. Perhaps, in spite of Lacan, Schreber is a poet after all, the type of poet described by Harold Bloom, who is overridden by the anxiety of influence and fights against an overbearing predecessor: his story is one of linguistic *askesis*, his *délire* nothing but an exaggerated form of misprision. Memoirs of my nervous illness, or how I learnt to answer back to God.

The *délire* of interpretation: Freud

Schreber's *Memoirs* were invented (in the archaeological sense of the term)[3] by Jung, who was trying to force upon Freud his theory of *dementia praecox*. Freud resisted and countered with a theory of paranoia.[4]

Freud's interpretation is based on two conspicuous elements in Schreber's *délire* – the fantasy of his transformation into a woman, and his privileged relation with God – and on the necessity of finding a genetic connection between them. The immediate cause of Schreber's illness was the frustration he must have felt at not having children (the Schreber 'line' is mentioned in the *Memoirs*): but, according to Freud, the deeper cause is the resurfacing of a repressed homosexual attraction towards his father or his elder brother (hence his 'unmanning'), followed by a feeling of guilt which was projected first on to Flechsig, and then on to God. There is a form of compensation in this: since Schreber has to accept his homosexual tendencies, he justifies them by the delirious construction which places him in the centre of the universe. Paranoia, therefore, is characterized by latent homosexuality, megalomania, persecution delirium, and a regression to narcissism, defined as the moment when the ego unifies the objects of its sexual instincts, and chooses its own body as the first object of its desire. *Délire*, then, is a form of defence: the paranoiac reconstructs the world through his fiction, so as to continue living in it.

Towards the end of his analysis, Freud offered a tentative prognosis. What enabled Schreber to come to terms with his homosexual fantasies and to reach a sort of cure, was that in the last years of his father's life, his relations with him had been unclouded. The prognosis turned out to be wrong, but the major intuition on which it was based, that Schreber's condition was due to his relation with his father, has been substantiated: Freud's disciples have demonstrated their detective talents by debunking the image of the good doctor Schreber, the philanthropist and founder of Schreber's gardens (horticultural plots for the German working class). A post-Freudian or antipsychiatric reading of his works reveals a sadistic meddler whose main concern was to imprison children in a set of physical and mental constraints. The plates in Dr Schreber's books show rather gruesome pieces of apparatus, like the 'Geradhalter', the bar fixed on to the table where the child is doing his homework, which prevents him from adopting a slouched posture. The child in Dr Schreber's system is taught through constraint, frustration or discomfort (one case quoted in Dr Schreber's *Kallipädie* (1858) possibly concerns the future paranoiac himself: he tells of a serious illness which affected one of his children, aged one and a half; the cure involved the complete subjection of the child to his father, which, the father says, saved the child's life). Of course, the interpretation of Schreber's symptoms receives new light from these relations about his family background: many of the miracles performed against his body by God or Flechsig can be traced to deeds done to him by his father. Thus the miracle of cold (Schreber, p. 171), whereby the blood withdraws from the extremities of the limbs causing a sensation of intense cold, can be explained by the father's insistence on cold ablutions from the age of six months onwards (Schreber himself says the miracle did not disturb him greatly as from his early infancy he had been used to enduring heat and cold).[5] It is often said that it takes three generations to produce a psychotic: perhaps Dr Schreber was so efficient that he was able to skip one.

Freud's analysis is not restricted to the contents of Schreber's *délire*. It also deals with its structure and the semiotic operations that take place within it. This is understandable: the question of the sign lies at the heart of paranoia. We all live in a world of signs, but for the paranoiac everything is a sign, and signs take on a new importance and urgency. Persecution delirium only exaggerates processes of interpretation (like deciphering indirect speech-acts, or threading one's way through mazes of conversational implications) which occur all the time in our minds. There is lucidity in paranoia: analysts have often noticed that the jealous paranoiac rightly interprets signs of which his or her mate is not even aware. Freud discovers this kind of lucidity in Schreber, and he uses it to analyse the sign-work, analogous to the dream-work, that is present in *délire*. One of the first interpretations he gives, in the first part of his paper (which is supposed to be a description of the case, not an interpretation of it), is an instance of condensation. The identification of heavenly bliss and sexual pleasure in Schreber is explained by the association of the two senses of the German word 'selig': 'departed' or 'late' (as in 'the late Dr Schreber') and 'sensually happy'. In other words, Schreber's *délire* is in this case not to be explained by childhood associations but by language at work, by metaphor. The interesting point here is that the condensation is *linguistic*: it is not (or only marginally) due to the patient's personal history (as when an element of the dream condenses several episodes in the patient's life simply because they happen to have occurred to *him*), but it exploits a possibility created by the linguistic system (and is, therefore, very similar to jokes).

The interpretation given in the second and third part of Freud's paper also deals with semiotic operations: mainly those of inversion and projection, the unconscious analogues of grammatical negation. Indeed, the second part ('attempts at interpretation') begins with an instance of (Freudian) negation which Freud immediately tries to protect from the reader's resistance – an indication that negation is also at work in his text, and that he attributes great importance to the example.[6] He gives his definition of negation (or denial, cf. ch. 2) and then proceeds to illustrate it with the case of the talking birds, who repeat meaningless sentences and are easily taken in by homophony. Freud interprets them as girls: often compared to geese, 'girls are supposed to be endowed with brains no bigger than birds', and have a tendency to repeat, parrot-like, what they have been taught. Now, it is not immediately obvious how this constitutes an example of denial, unless one interprets the notion as a form of metaphor. What has occurred is in fact a displacement: the girls are transformed into birds, using a system of metaphors provided by language; the displaced element – girls – is still recoverable in two ways: the dead metaphors can be interpreted, and the girls are still mentioned as secondary elements, since Schreber gives the birds the names of girls. This process of displacement, together with the return of the displaced element, is in fact comparable to what happens in denial, where the denied element is recoverable either by de-transforming the surface proposition or because it is present somewhere in the immediate context. The whole process is a semiotic one, which involves metaphor on two levels: *a* the whole process of displacement can be interpreted as one big metaphor; *b* the process works through a system of dead metaphors present in the German language. No wonder then that the birds should be taken in by cases of homophony, where the difference between 'Santiago' and 'Carthago' ceases to be relevant: the displacement in content (from girls to birds) is represented in the text by the displacement of homophony (a poetic displacement authorized by rhyme – but we know that nerves speak in metrical language).

Inversion and displacement, then, structure Schreber's *délire* (the affect is inverted when Schreber's love for Flechsig turns to the conviction that he is persecuted by him; and, of course, there is displacement of affect from Schreber's father to Flechsig and to God). But these processes are semiotic or based on language. At the heart of paranoid delirium there is a linguistic nucleus, a fantasy: 'loving a man'.[7] Freud classifies the various types of paranoia according to the various ways of negating this basic proposition: 'I (a man) love him (a man)'. In *persecution delirium*, the verb is negated ('I do not love him, I hate him') and then, through projection, the subject and verb are inverted (another form of negation): 'he hates me'. The surface formula is 'I hate him because he persecutes me'. In the *delirium of erotomania*, the object is negated: 'it is not him I love, it is her'; again, projection reverses subject and object, giving 'she loves me'; the surface formula is 'it is not him I love but her, because she loves me'. In *jealousy* the delirious formula negates the subject: 'I do not love men', *she* (my wife) does'. Last, but not least, comes megalo-mania (which is also present in the other three forms). There, the proposi-tion is negated as a whole: 'I do not love anybody, I only love myself'.

The interest of this analysis is that it somehow de-metaphoricizes the word 'transformation', as I have used it in discussing the transformations of the basic fantasy. Nowadays, the term has precise meaning in linguistics. Usually, talking of transformations in the context of fantasies would be metaphorical: the unwarranted importation of a concept from another field, in order to give a specious air of scientific vigour to one's analysis. But Freud (who did not himself talk of transformations) is much closer to modern linguistics: Freud the linguist may turn out to be at least as important as Freud the psychologist. The operations at work in his analysis all have precise linguistic equivalents: noun phrase negation (megalomania), sentence negation (persecution, first phase), active/passive transformation (persecution, second phase), topicalization and focus (erotomania and jealousy). Chomskyan linguists always yearn for a psychological basis for their theories, and Freud may well have provided it by showing the link between the psychological processes of negation, projection and condensation, and a number of important linguistic transformations.[8] If *délire* is to be analysed as a work of reconstruction, Freud's interpretation demonstrates that the reconstruction is linguistic. Schreber may not be able to impart new experience to his readers and, unlike the poet, his use of metaphor may not be truly creative, but he evinces the same yearning for metaphor, and the same command of rhetoric as his more successful rivals. But, of course, the word 'command' is inadequate, since the delirious linguistic 'work' is unconscious. Truth is reduced to the nucleus, the true insight is hidden in the midst of the delirious revelation: the paranoiac, as an unsuccessful poet, needs a psychoanalyst to interpret his words.

But a nucleus of truth there is: Freud was aware of the importance of his analysis, and claimed to share the intuition with Schreber. The unconscious formulas of fantasy are equated to the propositions in Schreber's *Grundsprache*, identified as the language of the unconscious. This is what the patient and the analyst have in common: they share insights into the depths of language. The parallelism between the euphemistic element in the *Grundsprache* and Freud's theory of the opposed meanings of primitive words appears to be more than a coincidence. This explains the celebrated last page of Freud's essay, where he admits a 'coincidence' which 'may damage his theory in the eyes of the readers':

Schreber's divine rays, a combination of nerves and sperm, are nothing but the image (projected on to the external world) of the Freudian libido, and they make his *délire* 'strangely concordant with [Freud's] theory'. The patient's delirium has the same structure as the analysis: the term '*délire*' subsumes them both.

Psychosis and discourse: Lacan

One of Lacan's early seminars (held in 1955 and published in 1981) deals with the question of psychosis, largely through a commentary on Freud's analysis of Schreber. The question is important to Lacan, first because he wants to prove that, contrary to the usual opinion, psychoanalysis can deal with psychosis, and second because it extends his own early work on paranoia (his doctoral thesis and the articles he wrote in his surrealist period). But his analysis, like Freud's, hinges on a conception of language: Schreber's *délire* casts light on the workings of normal language; it is, he says 'surprisingly similar to the structure of verbal exchange' (Lacan, p. 376); conversely, psychoanalysis is defined as 'the science of language as inhabited by the subject'. 'In a Freudian perspective, man is nothing but the subject caught in and tortured by language' (Lacan, p. 276). As with Freud, *délire* appears as the double of theory. And its topic is discourse. The analysis of *délire* enables us to understand how discourse functions, just as the study of the structure and function of discourse helps account for *délire*. The only difference between Schreber and Freud is that the former is 'a martyr of the unconscious' (Lacan, p. 149), who bears witness but has no access to the true meaning of his testimony, and therefore cannot share it in normal discourse. A parallel structure, then. Lacan claims to find a dialectical structure of excess and lack in Schreber's text: he contrasts Schreber's *Grundsprache* with the empty language of the garrulous birds. There are two poles in delirious discourse: the language of intuition, which gives a feeling of ineffable understanding, but where excess of meaning prevents communication; and the empty formula, the jingle, where the sheer lack of meaning precludes all sharing. In the first case, meaning is there, but the subject understands it *too* well, and consequently he cannot share it with others, so that his meaning eventually eludes him; in the second, discourse comes to him from others (if only through projection) and he fails to understand it because he has not been given the key. But this,

Lacan argues, illustrates the structure of normal discourse. His famous formula (typically enigmatic) is that 'the subject receives his message from the other in an inverted form'. In the context of the seminar on Schreber, the maxim ceases to be enigmatic: Schreber's main symptom is the verbal hallucinations in which (through projection) his own discourse comes back to him from a fantasized other and persecutes him; and the linguistic operations in Freud's analysis (the passive transformation, for instance) function in the same way.

So for Lacan there are two exemplary forms of discourse. The first he calls *fides*, 'the word that is given', a mixture of testimony or appeal and performative utterance. The example he gives is the sentence 'you are my wife', which obviously gives *you* a place as well as *me*, and is an attempt to involve you, to elicit from you the answer 'I am your wife' and so to get my message back from you in a linguistically inverted form. The second is the *lie*, words used to take me in. The possibility that you may be lying assures me that you are a subject in your own right. It is not lying itself which is important, but my hesitation, the fact that I cannot tell whether you are lying or not. Lacan's example is a famous Jewish joke (also quoted by Freud): the first Jew truthfully says to the other that he is going to Cracow. This makes his friend angry: 'you liar, I know perfectly well you're going to Cracow; so why do you tell me you're going there to make me believe you're going to Lemberg?'. As we can see, this structure is parallel to the one discovered in *délire*: in *fides*, meaning is fully apprehended, and discourse is an attempt to communicate it, to make the other accept and endorse it; in lying, meaning becomes uncertain, because the other may be deceiving me. In the first case, communication is due to an excess of meaning (the meaning which I possess is too much for me, I must compel the other to share it); in the second, it depends on the possibility of its absence (Do you really mean what you say? I am compelled to fish for clues, to elicit responses so that I can interpret the signs). Founding words and deceiving words are the two poles in the structure of discourse.

Admittedly, this goes back a long way before Freud, to the religious tradition of revelation (I receive my message directly from God and bear testimony to His word), and to the philosophical tradition of methodical doubt (Lacan pays tribute to Descartes's evil demon – a necessary stage, he says, in all philosophical argument). But this is only an elaboration of Schreber's intuition: bearing witness to God's revelation, in the knowledge that God is always playing tricks with him. Lacan's reading of Freud grafts a philosophical tradition on to Freudian orthodoxy. His insistence on the philosophical concept of the subject is a good instance of this. And his theory of the subject is based on his theory of discourse. Just as there are two types of *délire* and two poles of discourse, so there is a division within the subject, between two 'others', one with and one without a capital 'O'. The subject, as we saw in Chapter 2, is not unified, it is a locus, where at least three characters dwell: the ego and two 'others'. So Lacan moves from the psychological concept of the ego to the philosophical concept of the subject. Far from being a centre (of consciousness, for instance), the ego is defined as alienated, and determined by the other. The first ego, which emerges out of the original '*corps morcelé*' (where the subject is only an incoherent bundle of desires and part objects) is the *alter ego*. The centre of the subject lies in the other, and the object of the subject's desire, is the object of the other's desire: jealousy and rivalry are the fundamental forms of relationship.[9] But communication can only work if the struggle between the other and the ego (the mirror image of the other) is transcended: there must be rules, a pact, a compromise; if communication is going to work, the mirror relationship must be broken by the intervention of a third party, the Other, exactly as in the Freudian analysis of jokes. For Freud a joke may be a substitute for the indecorous advances that A (a man) would like to make to B (a woman). Enter C (usually another man) and a joke replaces the lechery: words are bandied about, circulated, exchanged. But they are not addressed to B: A uses them to make C laugh at B. C ceases to be an intruder, and becomes arbiter or master of the situation. So there are two 'others': the mirror image of the ego, and the absolute or absent Other, who is the one we always address because he makes the rules (he *is* the rules). The other, we know all too well; the Other, we recognize but do not know (Lacan plays on the two French words '*connaître*' and '*reconnaître*'): father, Flechsig or God are mere images or substitutes for this essentially abstract creature. He will soon receive a description: the 'name of the father', which stresses its symbolic character – not a person, but a signifier.

This Lacanian analysis of the subject precedes the one cited in Chapter 2 (the figure on p. 62). It is the foundation on which Lacan's concept of the signifier (and therefore his theory of psychosis) is based: the function of the elusive Other is to guarantee the possibility of meaning, by underwriting the rules governing signifiers. Lacan uses Saussure's concept of signifiers in a broad sense: he takes it to refer to linguistic elements of all levels in as far as they are part of the linguistic system.

Thus, words (which for Saussure are signs, combinations of signifiers and signified) are considered as signifiers in so far as they are caught up in the linguistic chain, in the relations of syntax. For Lacan, unlike Saussure, signifiers are contrasted with signs. Signs refer to absent objects – Man Friday's footprint in the sand announces his presence on the island. Signifiers, however, do not refer to objects but to the chain of language. They do refer, but to other signifiers. They are elements in a semiotic system. This is why Lacan's example of a signifier (Lacan, p. 188) is only apparently bizarre. Day and night, he says, are perhaps the first signifiers ('language begins with the opposition between day and night' – a mythical statement, as are all assertions about the origin of language); the distinction between them is not given by nature (the transitions of dawn and dusk are too gradual), it must be established by a semiotic decision which creates a pair of distinctive units, exactly as a given language divides the spectrum into colours which are not natural but semiotic in origin (any student of linguistics knows that the Welsh do not classify colours in the same way as the English).

The rule of the signifier distinguishes humans from animals: humans are possessed by the symbolic law, inhabited by language (this is why the experience of possession in *délire* is crucial). Our psychic reality is interwoven with signifiers, in other words it (the unconscious) is a text. A sense of reality (the acceptance of the reality principle) implies the subject's integration in the signifying system. The murder of the father, the Oedipus complex and the threat of castration are myths evolved by Freud to describe the process whereby the subject is caught up by the signifier. There are, therefore, according to Lacan, basic signifiers, without which no world of human signification can be built: the phallus, as signifier of the difference of the sexes, is one. Psychosis occurs when those basic signifiers disappear, when the relation between the subject and the signifier is perturbed. The normal process of access to subjectivity is described through a sewing metaphor, the 'upholstery buttons' or '*points de capiton*':[10] the subject attaches significance (it anchors itself, to use another metaphor) to certain signifiers; these signifiers, like upholstery buttons, pin down the floating mass of signification, by attaching it to the system of signifiers; if they fail, the correspondence is no longer achieved, and words no longer carry meaning (or each word carries the whole of meaning) and communication, or intersubjectivity, fails. Psychosis is caused by a hiatus in the chain of basic signifiers: in the case of Schreber, Lacan improves on Freud's analysis by declaring that the missing signifier is 'being a father', the basic signifier which constitutes a man (and he insists on the fact that the realization that one is a father goes beyond the biological fact: it presupposes a certain cultural level, an organization of signifiers).

This cataclysmic absence has two consequences. The first is hallucination: the primordial male signifier, because it has not been accepted by the subject, because it has been the object of the aggravated form of repression which Lacan calls 'forclusion' (his translation of the Freudian term *Verwerfung*), reappears in the outside world in the form of hallucinations, of Flechsig, or God, or voices. And this is why the hallucinations are mainly verbal: the loss of a fundamental signifier is compensated for (according to the dialectic of excess and lack) by frantic signifying activity (of dissociation, of the breaking down of signifying chains), by a profusion of meaningless or over-meaningful words. *Délire* is both the result of this disruption and the means of recovery: hence its fundamental ambiguity. On the one hand we have the logical system of the paranoiac, where normal processes of thought are taken to extreme conclusions; on the other hand, this logical construction, in itself delirious, is always threatened by even more delirious outbursts, of coined words, meaningless jingles, or logorrhea.

This gives us an idea of the structure of psychosis (the loss of a founding signifier and the attempt at recovery). It also points to the rhetorical element which we have already noted in *délire*. For the signifier works according to the laws of rhetoric or dream-work. To illustrate this, I shall borrow an example from Niederland, on this occasion an unwittingly Lacanian analyst, who shows that the displacement from Schreber's father to Flechsig and God, as well as the various fictitious figures he introduces (Flechsig's ancestors) are related through their names: He presents this relationship in the following manner:

REALITY (real names)   DELIRIUM (Schreber's names)

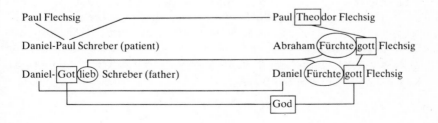

From this it is apparent that Daniel-Paul Schreber contains in his own person (in his name) both his father and Flechsig, and that the signifier 'Gott' circulates under different forms, both in delirium and in reality. The rejected 'name of the father' does indeed return in the form of hallucinations: it actually creates characters (novelists like Dickens often use the same technique more consciously in their onomastic creations).[11] The names 'Gotlieb' or 'Theodor' (God-beloved and God's gift) and 'Fürchtegott' (God-fearing) are good illustrations of the main operation of *délire* as analysed by Freud in terms of negation or inversion. Signifiers obey the poetic laws of language, and their arrangement is governed by syntax; the relations between signifiers are either metaphorical or syntactic. Thus, in his discussion of 'points de capiton', Lacan stresses the retrospective effect of syntactic conclusion: we do not understand a sentence until we know we have reached the end; its meaning remains in suspense until the closure (the 'sentences within sentences' considered in Chapter 2, above, depend on this rule.)[12] Hence the importance of interrupted sentences in Schreber's delirium; Lacan shows that the interruptions occur before significant words and demonstrates the elusiveness of meaning, its dependence on the organization of signifiers. 'What did the Caspian sea?', as Reginald exclaims in one of Saki's stories, to the utter bewilderment of the vicar's wife. Retroactive interpretation, figures of speech, plays on words and rebuses[13] (as in the case of the French paranoiac who placed a broken hoop on the doorstep of his supposed enemy – a hoop is *un cerceau* in French – and the message was: 'c'est ainsi que je *sers* les *sots*'; my enemy is an idiot, and this is how I treat idiots) – such is the poetics of *délire*, the (not so) free play of the signifier which has become detached from signification.

From Lacan's interpretation of Schreber, we ought perhaps to retain the idea of the two functions of *délire*: disruption of the signifying system and reconstruction. Here again we find the dialectic of excess and lack: the disruptive *délire* which is a symptom of the patient's illness manifests the lack of the coherence which makes meaning possible, whereas the reconstruction of a whole cosmos as much as of syntax (the pompous style of the paranoiac; his taste – not restricted to Schreber – for the language of law, metaphysics or science) evinces an excess of coherence which again precludes meaning.

138

Metaphor

> *As other men, so I myself do muse,*
> *Why in this sort I wrest invention so:*
> *And why these* giddy metaphors *I use,*
> *Leaving the path the greater part do go;*
> *I will resolve you:* I am lunatic![14]

This is not Lacan's description of his own style. But is it one of Schreber's insights into the metaphoric nature of *délire*? The definition of *délire* given in the last section, through an opposition between drifting and structuring signifiers might make us think that such is the case: metaphor might be the rhetorical name for the drifting language of madness. But there is an element of common sense even in the most visionary psychoanalyst: Lacan, whose contrast between poets and madmen I have already mentioned, has noticed that paranoid *délire* is in fact short of metaphors (Lacan, p. 247). He pays great attention to metaphor (two of his seminars are devoted to a line by Victor Hugo, 'Sa gerbe n'était pas avare ni haineuse'), but only as a feature of normal discourse. So the tables are turned; it is the structured signifier of normal discourse which works metaphorically, not the drifting discourse of madness.

The same applies to Nonsense, a form which is related to 'high literature' through the negative operation of parody. The language of Tennyson or Wordsworth may be highly metaphoric: not so that of Lear and Carroll. Even Lear's most Romantic elegies, like *The Dong with a Luminous Nose* or *The Courtship of the Yonghi-Bonghi-Bò* are remarkably short on metaphors: the rare survivors are clichés, obviously parodic (such as the simile 'as the sea my love is deep'). Carroll is no better: there is a fine vein of matter-of-factness in his poetry, as when the star of the nursery song, up above the world so high, becomes a bat:

> *Twinkle, twinkle, little bat!*
> *How I wonder what you're at!*
> *Up above the sky you fly,*
> *Like a tea-tray in the sky.*

We can also quote this famous description of the Romantic seaside:

> *The sea was wet as wet could be,*
> *The sands were dry as dry.*
> *You could not see a cloud, because*
> *No cloud was in the sky.*

How can you expect metaphors from a poet so resolutely down to earth? Why is the poet so wary of metaphor? And why does he, instead, insist on syntactic correctness? (Nonsense texts never dissolve into gibberish, even when, like 'Jabberwocky', they are made up of coined words.)

I have already stated that Nonsense is a meaning-preserving activity: its implicit goal is to save meaning by maintaining the correspondence between signifier and signified which communication requires. Nonsense may fiddle with the upholstery buttons, but only to check that they are sewn on firmly and in their proper places. But, of course, this is an idealized view of language: meaning shifts around, and metaphor is the name of the process by which it does so. It is a threat to orderly language, and allows for the proliferation of meaning. First, there is no limit to the number of metaphors for any given idea, or, to use I. A. Richard's terms, to the number of vehicles for a given tenor. Second, metaphor is one of the more dubious indirect speech acts: it is a sort of rhetorical double-bind, which states one thing but requires you to understand something different. Hence the literalness of the schizophrenic patient who clings to what is said and avoids metaphors because, unless they have died and frozen into cliché, they are ultimately undecidable. What is unacceptable is the unregulated, and therefore unruly, creativeness of metaphor. This is why Nonsense remains close to the language of common sense, on the safe (or rather the inadequate) side of literalness or matter-of-factness. In so doing, of course, it loses meaning: it goes from a potential excess of meaning (through the proliferation of metaphors) to nonsense, a lack of meaning (in Deleuzian terms, common sense is a limitation of sense, on which it imposes the 'right' direction).

In order to counteract metaphor Nonsense employs a double strategy. It goes beyond metaphor, with the portmanteau word, or it stays on the safe side, in matter-of-factness. One way of destroying a metaphor is to push its undecidableness to the limit: since a portmanteau word is a coinage, one will never know whether it is metaphorical or not. 'Twas brillig, and the slithy toves did gyre and gimble on the wabe': we shall never know if 'slithy' is an appropriate epithet for a tove, if the tove's movements of gyring and gimbling are directly descriptive or delightfully metaphoric. Coinages are metaphors gone berserk. On the other hand, down-to-earth words (mostly about food: the grossly material against the spiritual), failed puns or boring poems all prevent metaphors from occurring. Tautology is the best form of anti-metaphor: simple repetition prevents shift of meaning,[15] and Nonsense shows a strong relish for analytic truths.

This commits us to the somewhat paradoxical idea that Nonsense and *délire* are not instances of language made free but of language maximally constrained. *Délire* appears as impoverished language, incapable of the metaphoric creativity of normal (not to mention literary) discourse. So it would appear that delirium is not only repetitive in content, but also stereotyped in style. The paradox is only apparent, for this is a familiar experience for the psychiatrist: a certain stiltedness of expression, combined with great inventiveness in imagination and interpretation characterizes the paranoiac. But this also commits us to the view that language is in essence metaphoric (that metaphor is not an added ornament) – a position already adumbrated above in Chapter 2.

This view, which is certainly held by Lacan, derives from an extremely influential article by Jakobson, 'Two aspects of language and two types of aphasic disturbances.' The core of this article is a distinction between two types of aphasia, or loss of speech, corresponding to the linguistic distinction between syntagm and paradigm. There are, for Jakobson, aphasias of similarity, and aphasias of contiguity. If similarity is impaired, the patient continues to form syntactically correct sentences, but he loses his grasp on the individual word: he experiences difficulty in naming objects, loses command of metalanguage and no longer understands metaphors; instead, he uses metonymy (thus, when asked to name a fork, he will answer not with a metaphoric replacement, but with the word 'knife', obtained through metonymic association). On the other hand, if contiguity is impaired, the patient no longer makes whole sentences: word order becomes chaotic, grammatical relations (concord, for instance) disappear, together with grammatical words like conjunctions or prepositions. But the patient retains a command of metaphor: when asked to define the word 'hut', he will not answer 'has burned', or 'is a poor little house' (metonymic association through syntactic contiguity) but with metaphors – 'palace' for instance, or 'rabbit hole'. From this rather pat distinction (much contested since), Jakobson drew the conclusion that metaphor and metonymy are two poles, or two processes in language, which are at work everywhere in language. From then on, the article becomes prophetic and Jakobson lets himself be carried away by his concepts.[16] The distinction is said to have relevance in aesthetics, enabling him, for instance, to contrast Cubism (which is metonymic: the object becomes a series of synecdoches, where each fragment stands for the whole) with Surrealism (which is metaphoric), or to separate the metaphoric Romantics and Symbolists from the metonymic Realists (Anna Karenina is described through metonymic details: her handbag, her clothes, etc.). Jakobson even produces a little known nineteenth-century Russian novelist, Gleb Ivanovitch Uspensky, whose literary style was characterized by an abundance of metonymy, and who suffered from a Jekyll and Hyde dissociation: his first two names had become two different persons, the virtuous Gleb and the nefarious Ivanovitch. This, we are told, is an instance of similarity impairment, for the two different symbols can no longer be used for the same referent; it is also a case of private delirium turned literary; and lastly, it is an example of Schreber-like insight: 'Ivanovitch' contains the name of the father. Widening his analysis, Jakobson concludes that the two processes appear in all symbolic organizations, for instance in the dream-work: for him, displacement is metonymic, but condensation is an instance of synecdoche, and identification or symbolism is metaphoric. Lacan simplifies this by contrasting metaphoric condensation with metonymic displacement.

Thus metaphor and metonymy become the names not of two figures of speech among scores of others but of the two fundamental semiotic processes. (It is debatable of course whether there are only two: negation or inversion surely deserve to be classed with them.) And one can draw two sorts of inferences from this position. The first concerns language: meaning is not fixed, but appears retroactively as the result of various metaphoric shifts, a conception which Lacan develops through the concept of the 'bar' (in Saussure's formula $\frac{S}{s}$, the bar expresses not only a link, but also a separation) and the 'point de capiton' (a broadly similar conception of meaning is to be found in I. A. Richard's *Philosophy of Rhetoric*).[17] The second concerns non-linguistic mental processes, like dreams, which also appear to be governed by syntactic operations. If metaphor is the generic name for the semiotic processes which create meaning and which are realized in language both as figures of speech and as syntactic relations, we must expect to find equivalents in dreams not only for the rhetorical devices (condensation and displacement) but also for the syntactic rules. Hence one must question Freud's statement that the unconscious knows no negation: his own analysis of the Schreber case shows the existence of psychological negation. A Lacanian psychoanalyst, Mustafa Safouan, shows in his book on dreams that the dream-work has a syntax, parallel to that of language: linguistic–conceptual relations like determination, negation, causality or modality are expressed in dreams through 'syntactic' rules, which govern the relations between images in dreams (succession, composition, inversion).

But psychoanalysts, even Lacanian ones, are interested not in language *per se*, but in its effects on the subject, especially on the human body as experienced by the subject. There are two ways of considering this: either you hold that the signifier has precedence, i.e. that metaphor produces meaning, and that the signifier forms and informs the subject, or you search for the origin of language and metaphor in the sexual activity of the human body. Ernest Jones adopts the second position when he explains symbolism as eroded comparison and metaphor. If one pursues this line of argument to the end, one will find that the ultimate source of metaphor is the human body, and end by adopting a sexual theory of the origin of language (this is the 'come hither darling' theory mentioned earlier). According to the Swedish philologist Sperber, language was first used to attract the attention of the sexual partner, and originally man was nothing but a talking peacock. The sounds were then used metaphorically for working: the only way for man to resign himself to the wearing task was to regard it as an equivalent for the sexual act. It is metaphors which make us work, and metaphors of a particular kind: tools are metaphors for the male organ, materials represent the female organ, and all activities symbolize the sexual act.[18]

Sperber's theory may be linguistically ludicrous (and also blatantly male-chauvinist), but, like every true *délire*, it is based on stubborn facts. Take the way sexual words, which are subject to a form of taboo, work in our language. They have several interesting characteristics: first, since they ought not to be spoken, they multiply (they have more synonyms than other kinds of words); second, though specialized, they often derive from the most general words (the French word 'foutre' comes from the verb 'faire'); third, and probably most important, their tenor can transfer metaphorically to any other word: given the right context, any word in the language can replace the words of sex (the inevitable consequence of verbal taboo is innuendo). The following text appears to be based on a recurring cricketing metaphor (it is taken from Pinter's *No Man's Land*): 'How beautiful she was, how tender and true. Tell me with what speed she swung in the air, with what velocity she came off the wicket, whether she was responsive to finger spin, whether you could bowl a shooter with her, or an offbreak with a legbreak action. In other words, did she google?' It is easy to see how the metaphor becomes sexual. The expectation is clearly established in the first sentence; words denoting parts of the human body (like 'finger') establish a common semantic field – common to sex and all activities in which human beings are involved; the passage from the woman to the cricket ball is helped by the chauvinist practice whereby a car or a boat become endearingly female (although cricketers would be unlikely to refer to the ball as 'she'); so that in the end the word 'google' is de-semanticized, and becomes a coined word referring to an unspecified sexual act (the exact interpretation is left to the readers' fantasies, their natural gift for metaphor). We come back to Freud's idea that portmanteau words are made up of fragments of repressed sexual words. Or we could turn the idea the other way round, and maintain that the most innocent coined word will end up acquiring sexual meaning. This is the case of the French word 'choubinette', invented by French POWs in the German camp at Schubin, to designate the tin stove on which they cooked their rations; in the closed world of the camp, it was possible for a linguist (himself a POW) to follow its semantic development: it soon designated all sorts of stoves; then a portable one, a pipe (through metaphor); then (through metonymy) a head, and eventually, again through metonymy, the female sexual organs.[19]

What I have suggested so far is that the human body is the ultimate source of metaphor (in the broadest sense), and that language has a metaphoric origin. But one can go even further in that direction, and state that the place in the human body where language is produced, the vocal organs, is itself treated as a metaphor (or a synecdoche) of the entire body; in other words, sounds metaphorically represent instinctual drives. The Hungarian phonetician, Ivan Fónagy, has made this point by starting from the fact, of which any language user is aware, that there are phonetic metaphors. Language is arbitrary: we do not normally pay any attention to the metaphoric quality of the sounds we use in normal communication. Nevertheless, if asked, we tend to have surprisingly similar opinions as to which sound is light and which dark, which sad and which happy, which sweet and which sour. For instance, 80 per cent of those asked say that /m/ is sweeter than /k/. Of course, this may only be arbitrariness at one remove, due to language-specific associations. And sometimes it is the case: thus, although French and Hungarian children think that /i/ is sweeter than /u/, English children think the contrary, probably because the word 'bitter' contains /i/. But in a great number of cases the preference does not seem to be caused by linguistic associations: according to Fónagy, it is caused by body associations; sounds somehow 'represent' instinctual drives – which, we may recall, Freud described as lying 'on the borderline between psyche and soma'.

But what exactly is meant by this 'representation'? Fónagy shows that beneath the normal semiotic use of sounds, unconscious vocal gestures persist: a phoneme, after all, is an ideal sound, a target, the realization of which in speech may vary considerably. Indeed words are often recognized even where the sound produced would normally correspond to a different phoneme (thus the Hungarian word 'igen', meaning 'yes', uttered under strong emotion, is actually pronounced with initial [e], but correctly interpreted as /i/, not /e/). This is another instance of the crossing of a frontier where the transgressed rule is preserved even when it is denied. So the speaking subject, though he conforms to the arbitrary rules of the system, nevertheless expresses emotion (not always conscious) through his 'vocal style'. When the expression is unconscious, and instinctual drives are expressed through phonetic distortion, what cannot be reached by the conscious control of the system can be reached through metaphor: like jokes, metaphors involve regression to the pre-verbal stage, to the archaic strata of the ego.[20] This is why dead metaphors often rightly interpret vocal gestures which remain unconscious to us as we are making them. In English as well as in French, one speaks of 'a strangled cry'. This in fact corresponds to a physical reality (the passage of air through the glotta is made difficult by the contraction of the muscles); and it expresses hatred, a desire to strangle: the body mimics the goal of the emotion. Furthermore, metaphor is not only a privileged means of access to the expression of instinct by the body, it is also in the body itself: the vocal organs serve as an analogue of the whole body. In a way we have always known this and the lips have always been taken to represent other lips in the body (one of Baudelaire's more scandalous poems 'A celle qui est trop gaie', is based on this metaphor, and the erotic significance of the pouting mouth for which Brigitte Bardot was famous is also connected with this). Fónagy, however, goes further: the constriction of the glotta, by analogy with the constriction of the other sphincter, expresses anal drives; velar consonants and vowels should, if this is true, be used frequently by toddlers, especially for words associated with anal functions. Fónagy (p. 90) states that such is the case, and quotes the French word 'caca' as an example. Or, again, the use of 'open' vowels (this is itself a striking metaphor) expresses a displacement of libido from the genital to the vocal organs: hence the 'vulgarity' of open vowels, the disapproval of yawning in public, and the erotic significance of the lips.

It is easy to take Fónagy to ridiculous extremes (as when Julia Kristeva[21] claims that the anal drive is expressed by 'open posterior vowels'), but his views are based on a wealth of evidence and a rather down to earth attitude to the workings of metaphor in everyday language. This discussion of metaphor, however, is taking us off course, into the problem of the origin of language (a phylogenetic question) and the development of language in the ego (its ontogenetic counterpart). We must now return from the metaphoric to the literal and consider how the system creates the subject, and imposes itself on the human body.

The letter

I have already had occasion to mention the concept of 'the letter',[22] put forward by Serge Leclaire: the human body, as experienced by the subject, is a series of erogenous zones, each bearing an inscription, a letter. We enter the world of Kafka's *In the Penal Colony* where the sentence is actually inscribed on the condemned man's body by a complex machine, the pride and glory of the officer in charge of it: what he is especially proud of is the elaborate tracery of the letters his machine draws on (and into) the skin. But is 'the letter' any more than material for a parable?

Leclaire starts with the question of sexual pleasure. The fulfilment of a physical need, obtained by the baby with the help of another person, normally its mother, leaves a trace in its memory: when the need (in Freudian orthodoxy conceived through a metaphor of energy – tension and appeasement) recurs, so does a hallucinatory trace of the first experience. Pleasure is linked to the difference between the object that fulfils the need, and the trace, in the memory, of the lost (mythical) first object: the object is similar, but the satisfaction is different. The satisfaction we obtain is not what we seek and the pleasure we experience is that of the straining towards a goal – the repetition of the original fulfilment – which we never reach. Pleasure is a tension, a hesitation, and an ultimate failure. It is measured by the difference between the fantasized (the remembered) and the actual. It is also caused by the presence of another (as we saw in the mirror stage). For the primary

146

THE PSYCHOANALYSIS OF DÉLIRE

pleasure is given by the other, who not only guarantees that it has taken place, but plays an active part in it.

Leclaire describes this process in a series of metaphors. An erogenous zone develops around a scar, a dimple, any part of the body where there is a physical difference (a distance) between two lips. When the other (the mother), caresses a dimple on the baby's body with her finger, this both marks the distance between the two lips and effaces it. This is the physical side of the process of inscription which constitutes erogenous zones.[23] So letters initially have a material–physical sense: they are actually traced on the surface of the child's body. But this is a parable. The letter has never had any real existence, and is by definition a lost object of satisfaction, the unattainable goal of desire, and therefore an abstraction. This is why the use of the term 'letter' is more than a metaphor. For a letter, as a linguistic element, also possesses this quality of abstraction: it is the mark for an absent object, defined by differential significance. It is both there, in the erogenous zone, as a trace, and distinct from it, detachable from the body on which it is inscribed. It is this abstract quality which allows it to persist. This expresses the elusive aspect of the inscription (a Stoic or Deleuzian event), and permits the repetition in which pleasure (or displeasure) is experienced. The term that links the two aspects of the letter is 'different'. From the physical point of view there is a distance between the two lips of the wound or dimple, and a temporal difference between primary satisfaction and present (unsatisfactory) fulfilment. On the ideal side, difference is what transforms the parts into elements of a system. The letter, then, is both material and abstract, physical and ideal. It is the first element in the system which, according to Leclaire, constitutes the unconscious.

The second element is the object. Desire is produced by the illusion of a missing primary object – marked and disguised by the letter.[24] So desire finds objects to replace the lost one; they recall (similarity) and fail to equal (difference) the primary experience of satisfaction. For whereas letters maintain difference, objects hide it or temporarily efface it. Between two lips, the difference can never be abolished, but the distance between the mouth and the object which satisfies desire can be reduced and even annulled (Psychanalyser, p. 80). This is why the object is in itself indifferent. Anything can become an object of desire: it is not a 'thing', but a function.

The third term in the system is the subject itself. It is the instance which bears the 'eclipse' of pleasure: the repeated attempt at full

147

satisfaction, and the repeated failure; a pulse, a permanent oscillation, between the assertion of the primary distance and the temporary erasure. The three correlative functions (letter, object, subject) form the nucleus of the unconscious, a frail, unstable structure, always threatened (by psychosis), which tries to gain stability by producing a conscious structure (consciousness is an effect of the unconscious, the surface has this unstable depth). And the terms of consciousness promise more solidity: signs (conscious equivalents of letters), conscious objects and the controlling ego.

But as well as being both material and abstract, letters have another important characteristic: they are collective. There is a collective store of letters (the linguistic system) and this is what allows communication between subjects, and interpretation. The letter, then, must also be taken literally. Leclaire shows the importance of letters of the alphabet for particular unconscious processes. He quotes the role of the Roman number V in the Wolf-Man's unconscious, and Freud's interpretation of it (*Psychanalyser*, pp. 90–1). The figure, which plays the enigmatic part of a formula or cypher, is first isolated in the dream image of a butterfly flapping its wings; the patient associates this with a woman standing with her legs apart, and Freud reminds us that the fifth hour of the day was for the Wolf-Man the time for depression. But the associations go much further; the figure is the formula, or letter (like the combination of a safe) for the opening movement which is so important in the patient's nightmares: the sudden opening of the window in the dream of the wolves is an example of this. So this formula works not only as content (the number five) but as letter, a particular shape on the paper: it is twice present in the first letter of the word 'wolf', it is also twice present in the sketch the patient produces to illustrate his dream, as the wolf's ears ∧∧ (and whereas six or seven wolves are mentioned in the dream, only five figure in the sketch); and the dream expresses the traditional fear of being eaten by a wolf (as in *Little Red Riding-Hood*), whose jaws can be represented by a capital V on its side: < . Leclaire also notes that many associations concern openings of the body.

Of course, a 'letter' in this specialized sense does not always have to be a letter of the alphabet: for instance, a word may function as a letter. In many dreams, there is a key-word, around which the whole dream revolves. Often it is a coined word: it is then apparent that it functions like a cypher. Leclaire is particularly good at analysing coinages as unconscious or secret names (one is reminded of the secret name of

Eliot's cats, the name that no human research can discover, but that the cat himself knows, and will never confess, or of numerous magical practices concerning names) providing the key to the subject's unconscious. This secret name is in itself meaningless ('effanineffable', as Eliot puts it), but it makes sense, gives meaning to the productions of the patient's unconscious: thus it resembles Deleuze's paradoxical element.

How relevant is all this to the language of psychosis? First, Leclaire's structure (letters, objects of desire, subject; signs, surface or conscious objects, ego) describes the origin of sense in nonsense in terms which are by now familiar to us: at the bottom of it all there is a coined word, a paradoxical element, a secret name, a formula, a cypher, a primary signifier. The coined word, the piece of nonsense, is deeply related to the subject's body (it turns a human body into a particular subject's body, and appears on its surface), but it only makes sense if it is abstracted from the body, assimilated into the shared linguistic system. (Eliot's cats may carefully hide their secret names, but they acquire a public name, otherwise their caterwauling would be in vain.) But, second, Leclaire also shows that the unconscious infrastructure is fragile: it breaks up if the process of abstraction fails to take place (if the letter is rejected through Lacanian forclusion). The language of madness is characterized by the fact that it cannot abstract letters from bodies. Hence many of the symptoms of *délire*. The first is a tendency to take words literally, i.e. to confuse them with bodies; thus a schizophrenic, accused of 'getting drowned in a glass of water' (a French phrase equivalent to 'making a mountain out of a mole hill') will refuse to drink water out of a glass (Leclaire, *Les mots du psychotique*, p. 129). Second, there is the multiplication of coined words, false names, to compensate for the absence of the primary letter (hence the multiplication of the cat's names in Eliot's poem). Third, there is the proliferation of signs, due to the same original lack: for the psychotic, everything becomes a sign, every object is enigmatic and mysterious, if not threatening. The word of signs has to be organized by the letter if it is to be mastered by the subject: failing this, the subject falls into *délire*, and becomes prey to the disorderly multitude of signs. Fourth, there is hallucination: signs are taken for wonders (a good description of Schreber's *délire*). The missing letters are inscribed on a hallucinatory body, where they function like a machine for vicarious pleasure, which persecutes and threatens to destroy the patient's body, bereft of its libido. This is why Schreber's hallucinatory bodies or nerves always threaten him, taking away parts of his body, clinging to him like tapeworms, feeding parasitically on his pleasure. *Délire* is the verbal equivalent of visual hallucinations: it reconstructs what was disrupted by the failure of the letter. But it is always doomed to frustration, if not failure, for it also expresses a primary disruption (hence the painful experience of possession, when my delirious words are turned against me). We are back again to the dialectic of excess and lack which rules the linguistic structure of *délire*. And metaphor is now seen as siding with order: the drift of meaning which it produces is the condition for the orderly functioning of the structure. It is the necessary compromise between the subject who appropriates the linguistic system and attempts to control it, and the system which always escapes from the subject. This is why Nonsense is at once so close to *délire* and yet so far away. By claiming to aim at the subject's total control of language, it misses the compromise of metaphor, and threatens to end in communicative failure, in *délire*, where there is no subject to master the system. As a result, the system also fails, since no subject can carry it: it only rattles and jabbers in wild unmeaning rhymes. The risk run by the Nonsense writer is real. This is why Carroll is so timid and hesitant compared with Artaud. He has to recreate a controlling subject which he starts by dismissing when he renounces metaphor. So, far from being an addition to communicative language, an ornament, figures of rhetoric embody the very conditions of possibility of language. I shall leave the last word to Coleridge, and to his rather shrewd comment on the psychological origin of meter (the important word is 'hold in check'): '[The origin of meter] I would trace to the balance in the mind effected by that spontaneous effort which strives to hold in check the workings of passion. It might easily be explained likewise in what manner this salutary antagonism is assisted by the very state, which it counteracts; and how this balance of antagonists became organised into metre by a supervening act of the will and judgement, consciously and for the foreseen purpose of pleasure.'[25] Lacan was right to assert that the madman is no poet: a poem a day keeps psychosis away.[26]

Fiction

In this chapter, I have frequently made a comparison with fiction. Patients and analysts have been busy writing novels and interpreting them: every psychotic is a Lawrence in search of his Leavis, every analyst a Boswell with too many Johnsons. I shall now attempt to develop the metaphor.

The comparison is obvious, and has often occurred to psychiatrists. The paranoiac is doubly concerned with plots: the plot he supposes is being prepared against him, and the plot he writes himself. So the term 'novel' is frequently used by psychoanalysts to describe their patients' imaginings. One can even reverse the comparison: Marthe Robert has developed a theory of the origins of the novel where it is derived from family romances in the Freudian sense (and the fabrication of a family romance is a classic symptom of paranoid delirium). Indeed, the catalogues of symptoms in pre-Freudian studies of paranoia abound in references to literary techniques: lexical creativity (coinages), a taste for verse, 'orgies of metaphors' (a point which contradicts Lacan's analysis of paranoia), verbal puzzles and cryptograms, all these are prominent in the symptomatology of 'délire d'interprétation' in Sérieux and Capgras, or of the 'mattoid's' delirium in Tanzi.[27] And a similar comparison can be used for analysts: they build their interpretations on flimsy and fragile material, their relation to truth is not certain, and they can be carried away by their interpretations like literary critics. Indeed the paranoiacs of classic psychiatric studies seem to have a lot in common with the serious novelists, as popularly imagined: an extreme dedication to their work, to which they sacrifice their private life and all hopes of material advancement; great talents for imagination and fancy; a strong sense of mission ard of distance from the *vulgum pecus*, together with a becoming diffidence (which sometimes coexists with a taste for endless litigation). Paranoiacs are the élite of lunatic asylums, says Tanzi, and the pictures he gives of them resemble portraits of Balzac.

If the psychotic is highly creative in his delirium, he needs an equally creative critic to interpret his work – like Freud in relation to Schreber, as Freud was well aware. If we take the comparison further, we may have to acknowledge that all theory is structured like *délire*. The first step is to recognize that *délire* is a form of communication: you engage in *délire for* someone, and though most *délires* appear before the patient has reached a mental home, the psychiatric relationship can nurture them. In Schreber's case, for instance, the delirious comments are addressed to Flechsig (as the introductory letter shows), and there was little sign of *délire* before he was admitted to the clinic. François Roustang has shown that psychoanalytic dialogue tends to produce *délire*: in the course of analysis, the patient 'lets himself go', his discourse breaches the bounds of common sense and control by the ego, he 'unspeaks' (Roustang coins the word 'déparler'). He is on the verge of delirium. The only reason why he remains in control (and this accounts for the risks attendant on an incorrect analytic intervention, which may provoke *délire* and psychotic episodes) is that another person is present, who understands him, and who guarantees that his speech is not delirious. The analyst is a 'garde-fou', and analysis is a controlled form of the 'délire à deux' which numerous psychiatrists have described.

But what about the analyst, and the risks he takes? How can he tell that his own interpretation is not itself a form of *délire*? He needs a control (the word is used in a technical sense to describe an experienced analyst supervising his younger colleagues): he must become a disciple. Roustang seems to have found the atmosphere of Lacan's *Ecole Freudienne* (with its recurrent purges and schisms) somewhat oppressive, and was led to reflect on the master–disciple relationship. His book deals largely with Freud's relations with his disciples, which were far from cloudless, as clearly appeared in the case of Tausk. The disciple is in a relationship of persistent transference with his master: this is the equivalent to a failure of analysis, since the ultimate aim of analysis is the dissolution of the transference and the consequent liberation of the patient. So the disciple tries to produce theory in his own right, and is 'spoken' by his master: an experience of possession which gives his discourse the same structure as the psychotic's. Theory is the *délire* which one manages to impose on others (the master's *délire* is imposed on the disciple); it is a shared, and therefore socially successful, *délire*, closely resembling the types of delirium which one finds in paranoid and schizophrenic cases. Like paranoia, it is logical, rigorous, internally coherent and based on inferences; it attempts a global interpretation, and if it fails, the way out is to fall back on schizophrenic discourse, a form of tinkering, *bricolage*, contenting oneself with accounts of limited fields, with fragmentary constructions which do not aim at universal explanatory power. This is in fact the strategy which Roustang notices in Freud's theoretical dealings with Jung (p. 73): it is a strategy of *délire*, outwitting the opponent's *délire* and substituting one's own.

The comparison is slightly facile, and I have presented an exaggerated version of Roustang's ideas. Nevertheless, it raises problems about the relation between interpretation (psychoanalytic construction) and science, between fiction and truth. What conception of truth am I to hold if my interpretation is always on the verge of *délire*? (The analyst, or the literary critic for that matter, is always threatened with 'interpretation delirium', to use a category from classical psychiatry.) Freud was fully aware of this; in his article on 'Constructions in Analysis', he describes the patient's delirium as equivalent to the constructions made by the analyst in the course of treatment. There are two ways of dealing with this: either one dismisses psychoanalysis as unscientific, or one concedes that it may enable us to understand things about science which science itself cannot reach, namely that it is *délire* made conscious and denied, and that science is born not of reason, but of desire and *délire*, like fiction and interpretation. This does not undermine science, but it does tell us something about psychoanalytic conceptions of truth.

If I hold that there is an element of desire in scientific discovery, I cannot maintain a conception of truth as agreement (between perception and object). A new term appears in my discourse: certainty.[28] There is no criterion of truth other than the subject's desire and his certainty (a certainty often concealed behind his doubt). Two conclusions can be drawn from this. There is a constructive relation between truth and lying; truth is to be recovered from the subject's lies, hesitations and symptoms. And the truth that psychoanalysis is concerned with is psychic truth, not historical or material truth: it is best reached through myth (this is why *Totem and Taboo* has a relationship to truth, although not the usual one in anthropology), through construction. This construction can be materially incorrect and yet true: truth is not in the statement, but in the effect produced on the patient. The construction obtained in the analytic process may be purely mythical (in the same way as *Moses and Monotheism*, as an account of the origins of religion), and yet produce a liberating effect on the subject.

We are on dangerous ground here, that of a theory of truth as effectiveness. But we must not assume that the effect is all that matters: the reconstruction, even if it is mythical, plays on symptoms, slips of the tongue, and dream elements. Its building bricks are the basic signifiers of the subject's unconscious. It therefore functions like a puzzle. The reconstructed picture may have nothing to do with the original but it must be made of the same pieces. This is why the metaphor of the novel is so important: I may recognize myself in a novel, even if the story is entirely different from mine.[29] The analyst's novel somehow enables the patient to find the truth about himself. But what of the paranoiac's novel? It is also a construction, and in a way it may be successful (enabling

Schreber, for instance, to come to terms with his latent homosexuality). The analyst will always be able to find an element of truth in it. At the same time, it is also a symptom of disruption, it is diseased – and is always in danger of giving way to the other side of *délire*, the disorganized *délire* of jabbering and gibberish, the outcome of which is silence. It may enable the subject to recognize the truth about his own desire, but it does not produce an effect of truth.

It is necessary to distinguish here between 'reality' and 'the real'. The reality in which the subject lives is constructed by him, but it is only a myth, a substitute for the missing original truth, for the lost primary experience, or trauma, which alone is 'real'. The real is what lies permanently beyond the subject's grasp, and therefore cannot be defined except negatively, as nothingness, as death or (as we saw in Chapter 2) as the impossible. *Reality* is a construction: it is the work of symbolic and imaginary processes. But the construction (like the linguist's construction of *langue*) is based on the irreducible and inexplicable fact of *the real*, which merely *is*, over which we have no control, and of which we have no knowledge. At this point, the ghost of the Kantian thing-in-itself flits about the stage, uttering dismal howls. Or is the phantom Heidegerrian? The Lacanian 'real' seems to provide an answer to the famous opening question in Heidegger's *Introduction to Metaphysics*: 'Why are there beings rather than nothing?'[30]

The construction of reality is fragile: an encounter with the real (either a moment of insight or a traumatic experience) can destroy it and produce *délire*. What cannot be symbolically constructed is rejected through forclusion. It remains in the real and reappears in destructive hallucination. But an encounter with the real is also the aim of the process of repetition, an always foiled attempt: there is also a *délire* of repetition, or rather of its failure, which has the same relation to the viable repetition of normal behaviour as farce has to tragedy (the well known conception of historical repetition in the Hegel–Marx tradition). This is a good definition of interpretative *délire*, the *délire* of reconstruction: it is an unhistorical repetition, a failed myth, which turns the comedy of historical repetition, of successful myth, into tragedy. Schreber was only a failed Joan of Arc: and I am sure that, at the back of his mind, he knew it.

Conclusion

I started this chapter with a paradox: how can *délire* be at the same time delirium and insight, at once the most uncontrolled type of fiction and an expression of truth? And I am concluding with a contradiction: *délire* as a form of speech has two fundamental roles – it testifies to a disruption of discourse, and it is an attempt at reconstruction.

This chapter has also dealt with a more or less systematic comparison between *délire* and theory: a whole tradition has stemmed from Freud's acknowledgement of Schreber's powers (Roustang is only one instance). A specular relationship seems to exist between the paranoiac and his analyst. This parallelism has deconstructive value. But the insistence on science might make us miss the proper point of comparison, which is literature. *Délire* is a special form of discourse: it is concerned with language, and it is naturally metalinguistic in the same way as literature; it implies a practice of language which is close to its theory.

I have also been exploring the relationship between language and the human body in two ways: inscription, or the formative effect of the signifier on the body; and abstraction, or the origin of language in the body. The two conceptions are not necessarily opposed, for inscription is complemented by abstraction (the 'letter' is inscribed because it can be abstracted). Nevertheless, they function as opposed terms, the second of which is embodied in various myths of the origin of language, which seem to have held a particular fascination for linguists of all descriptions, and not only for Brisset (one could mention the Marrist heresy in Soviet linguistics): this compulsive repetition of the myths suggests that they have the same function as the Freudian anthropological myth – to contain in their *délire* a nucleus of truth (the inscription of language on the body).

But it is also time to assess briefly the psychoanalytic side of the tradition of *délire*, to underline its ambiguity, so that we can understand the critique by Deleuze which will be considered in the next chapter. The main aspect of this tradition is law and order: the subject, although no longer central and masterful, is still a structure; its function is to be captured by the law of language, its liberty to accept linguistic necessity. *Délire* is therefore a false experience of freedom, the stale substitute for a failure in the expression of desire; it is not creative, but always limited and circular. It is not even an attempt at liberation, only the symptom of a failure to conform to the Law, the only possible form of freedom. There is no possibility of breaking away from the Law and its structure (the dialectic of lack and excess, the precedence of the signifier and the related access to culture), from the vicious circle of metaphor (the production of meaning) and interpretation (the consumption of meaning).

155

An obvious criticism of Freud concerns the outrageous power of interpretation he claims to possess: the delirious productions of the patient are reduced by swift and accurate interpretation. The interpreter is a reductive poet; he produces diagnostic metaphors. Wondrous talking birds flit about: 'haha', quoth he gleefully, 'they are merely girls'; the Wolf-Man dreams of wolves, little Hans of a horse: they are merely their respective fathers.

Another road is conceivable, another side of the tradition, where the subject (the term will soon disappear) is no longer the prisoner of linguistic structure, where *délire* and desire are intertwined, where the proliferation of language will always defeat the interpreting talent of the analyst, where metaphors are liberating and not reductive. We shall now venture on it, but not on our own: Deleuze and Guattari are already there.

Notes

1 This apparent pre-Freudian awareness is not due to the hindsight of the post-Freudian reader: the same recognition of negation or inversion, as a characteristic not only of psychotic, but also everyday language, can be found in Perceval, another famous literary 'madman'.

2 Schreber's linguistic relations with God go through three stages. At first, they struggle *through* language: the medium is more or less transparent, affects are communicated through the instrument of words. But soon the instrument obtrudes: a sort of arms race develops, in which the linguistic weapons are more prominent than the affects they are supposed to carry. The nerves are reduced to their speech, hallucinations are increasingly verbal, the archaic language becomes pervasive: the struggle goes on *in* language. Finally, it occurs *about* language: the objective is linguistic gain or loss, an efficient conversion, a successful metrical vibration; Schreber becomes both poet and philologist.

3 An archaeologist 'invents', in the etymological sense, a find, by bringing to light something already existing but hitherto unknown.

4 I shall avoid defining this term: it has a long and confused history, like most psychiatric terms. Its modern uses derive from the work by Kraepelin, and Freud used it much more broadly. It is not certain that clinical psychiatry would classify Schreber as a paranoiac: Kraepelin or Tanzi insist on the rarity of hallucinations in paranoia proper, which distinguishes paranoid delirium from the delirium of *dementia praecox*. So from the point of view of psychiatry, Jung was perhaps closer to the mark than Freud.

5 The example is borrowed from Niederland, 'The "miracled-up" world of Schreber's childhood'.

6 Freud describes his interpretation of the talking birds as obvious, but immediately follows this by a paragraph on the absence of ch. 3 from Schreber's *Memoirs*, and the consequent uncertainty of interpretations.

7 A fantasy, for Freud, is not only a scene, it is also a sentence, cf. the article 'A child is being beaten', discussed in Chapter 2, above.

8   This suggestion, however, is not in line with the latest developments in Chomskyan theory, where the more 'natural' and intuitive transformations (like the passive transformation) are abandoned in favour of more universal movements and constraints.
9   Lacan is here directly influenced by the Hegelian 'dialectic of master and slave', as interpreted by Kojève.
10 I borrow the English term from John Forrester's review of Lacan's *Séminaire III*.
11 It is well known that Dickens often chooses significant names for his characters (onomastics is the science that studies names): thus in *Bleak House* the house of Dedlock is close to extinction, George Rouncewell an honest character, unlike Mr Krook and Mr Vholes.
12 Shakespeare's Sonnet 104, quoted in Chapter 2, is a striking instance of such retrospective reading; the word 'turned' has to be reanalysed when the next line is read; meaning is disclosed retrospectively, from the end of the sentence backwards.
13 Rebuses are not limited to delirium or games (picture-puzzles: cf. Roussel): they are used by certain ideographic or pictographic writing systems (like Egyptian hieroglyphs). The ways of the signifier are legion.
14 From a sonnet by Drayton, quoted by Coleridge in *Biographia Literaria*, ch. XIX.
15 This corresponds to the layman's view of language: the linguist might suggest that no two utterances are ever the same even if the second reduplicates the first. There may be no such thing as tautology in ordinary language, as Miss Brodie knew in her prime, when she passed judgement on girl-guides: 'For those who like that sort of thing, that is the sort of thing they like.'
16 This should not be taken as a criticism: a linguist's greatest insights often come when he goes beyond the limits of common sense or of his own system, and risks drifting into nonsense or *délire*. There are, as we know, two sides to Saussure: Jakobson is more circumspect, but he too engages in flights of imagination.
17 He took a broad view of the metaphoric process: for him, the psychic analogue of metaphor is transference in the psychoanalytic sense.
18 This account is based on Safouan's discussion of Sperber.
19 cf. P. Guiraud, *L'Argot* (Paris: PUF 1956), pp. 79–81.
20 The term seems to imply a rather outdated Darwinistic conception of the evolution of the human mind from a pre-verbal to a verbal stage: it assumes that the history of the individual repeats the history of the species (hence the so-called 'archaic strata' of the ego). Such a conception, which is implicit in Fónagy, is questionable, to say the least.
21 cf. *La Révolution du Langage Poétique* (Paris: Seuil 1974), p. 225. However, it must be noted that in this case our sense of the ludicrous is based precisely on the kind of metaphor that Fónagy describes: in 'posterior', the vocal organ is treated as a synecdoche for the whole body.
22 Although the term 'letter' has a relationship with letters of the alphabet and letters in the post (cf. Lacan's seminar on *The Purloined Letter*, in *Ecrits*), Leclaire uses it to designate a *concept*: hence I shall use the phrase 'the letter', with definite article, where one might expect 'letters' in the plural.
23 The central metaphor is that of an original *wound*, which leave a trace, a *scar*, inscribed (for ever) on the surface of the body. Leclaire here goes back to the etymological sense of 'trauma': a wound.
24 The primary experience is an *event*: as such it is original in both senses, both foundational and irretrievable; it cannot be repeated. Repetition can only be achieved if desire is transferred to a substitute, an *object*. This condemns desire to constant failure. But the transference is possible only because letters, in their primary inscription, also have an ideal – a linguistic –

side: they can be repeated. The linguistic system, by constituting objects, gives a kind of permanence to the subject's desires.

25 *Biographia Literaria*, ch. XVIII (Everyman's Library, p. 196).

26 Leclaire's account may seem far-fetched. It goes against the grain of common sense, especially in its total separation of human from animal desire. But we must recognize two great qualities in Leclaire's analysis. First, it provides a solution to what has emerged as our main problem, the problem of *abstraction*, that is of the relationship between sounds as materially produced by organs of the body, and sense as the immaterial entity transmitted in human communication. Second – and this is where Leclaire has to leave the realm of common sense – it defines desires as specifically human, as fundamentally different from animal need. According to this conception, which is central to Lacanian psychoanalysis, there is no such thing as 'animal desire': man is no naked ape.

27 'Mattoid', from the Italian *'matto'*, 'mad', is a term coined by Lombroso, the criminologist, to describe border line cases where the subject, though clearly eccentric, manages to remain outside the asylum gates.

28 A predictable Hegelian move: we enter the idealist dialectic of knowledge and certainty which pervades the *Phenomenology of Mind*. Indeed, the truth obtained is not mere psychological illumination (where reality is undistinguishable from hallucination): it is the truth of the subject's desire, which means that it must be (re)constructed and that it is dependent on the intervention of the other.

29 At worst, this is another paranoid symptom: the ability to project my *délire* on to any story whatever. The patient whom Lacan studies in his doctoral thesis, herself a novelist as we have seen, was convinced that a contemporary author of bestselling novels wrote mainly about her, although, of course, she could only point to the most irrelevant details in support of her theory.

30 cf. J. C. Milner, *Les Noms Indistincts*. The reference goes back to Leibniz, whose *A Resume of Metaphysics* (*c.* 1697) begins with the following sentence: 'There is a reason in Nature why something should exist rather than nothing.' cf. Leibniz, *Philosophical Writings* (Everyman's Library 1934), pp. 145–8.

Further reading

1 Schreber's memoir is available in D. P. Schreber, *Memoirs of my Nervous Illness*, translated, with an introduction and a discussion, by I. Macalpine and R. A. Hunter (Dawson 1955). Page numbers in this section refer to the German edition, which are given in the English translation.

Schreber refers extensively to Kraepelin's textbook (English translation, *Lectures on Clinical Psychology*, New York: Hayner 1969). Lacan's doctoral thesis is *De la Psychose paranoiaque dans ses rapports avec la personnalité* (Paris 1932) (Paris: Seuil 1975).

Perceval, the Victorian 'lunatic', first published his autobiography in 1838. Large extracts have been republished in G. Bateson (ed.), *Perceval's Narrative* (Stanford: Stanford University Press 1961).

Harold Bloom's theory of literary influence can be found in his *The Anxiety of Influence* (New York: Oxford University Press 1973); and *A Map of Misreading* (New York: Oxford University Press 1975).

2 Freud's analysis of Schreber is in the *Pelican Freud Library*, vol. 9 (Penguin 1979); and in the *Standard Edition*, vol. XII. Articles on Schreber are legion. I have used the biographical material unearthed by W. G. Niederland, 'Schreber: father and son', *The Psychoanalytic Quarterly* (1959); 'Schreber's father', *Journal of the American Psychoanalytical Association*, **8** (1960); and 'The "miracled-up" world of Schreber's childhood', *Psychoanalytic Study of the Child*, **14** (1959). On Schreber's father, see the book by Morton Schatzman, *Soul Murder* (Allen Lane 1973).

On the psychoanalytic concept of projection, see Sami-Ali, *De la Projection* (Paris: Payot 1970).

3 Lacan's analysis of Schreber is in *Séminaire III: les psychoses* (Paris: Seuil 1981), reviewed by John Forrester in *The Times Literary Supplement* (1 October, 1982), p. 1079.

On the conception of the subject in contemporary French philosophy, see the articles by Althusser, Kristeva and Lacan mentioned in Chapter 2. See also Alain Badiou, *Theorie du Sujet* (Paris: Seuil 1983).

On the Freudian analysis of jokes, cf. Todorov, 'Freud sur l'énonciation' *Langages*, **17** (Paris 1970); and 'La rhétorique de Freud', in *Théories du Symbole* (Paris: Seuil 1977).

Niederland's article on names in Schreber is 'Three Notes on the Schreber Case', *The Psychoanalytical Quarterly*, **20** (1951), pp. 579–91.

4 Jakobson's analysis of metaphor and metonymy is in 'Two aspects of language and two types of aphasic disturbances', in *Selected Writings*, vol. 2 (The Hague: Mouton 1971), pp. 239–60.

On metaphor in general the reader may wish to consult I. A. Richards, *The Philosophy of Rhetoric* (Oxford University Press 1936); G. Lakoff and M. Johnson, *Metaphors we live by* (Chicago: University of Chicago Press 1980); and A. Ortony (ed.), *Metaphor and Thought* (Cambridge University Press 1979), which contains an extensive bibliography.

Sperber's sexual theory of the origin of language is in 'Uber den Einfluss sexueller Momente auf die Entstehung der Sprache', *Imago*, I (1912), pp. 405–54. Safouan's discussion in *L'Inconscient et son Scribe* (Paris: Seuil 1982) deals with rhetoric from a psychoanalytic point of view and with dreams. Ivan Fónagy's articles are collected in *La Vive Voix* (Paris: Payot 1983).

5 My discussion of 'the letter' is based on two texts by Serge Leclaire: *Psychanalyser* (Paris: Seuil 1968); and 'Les mots du psychotique', *Change*, **12** (Paris 1972). Freud's analysis of the Wolf-Man is in *Pelican Freud Library*, vol. 9, (Penguin 1979); and *Standard Edition*, vol. XVII.

6 Marthe Robert's analysis of family romance can be found in *Roman des Origines et Origine du Roman* (Paris: Grasset 1972) (tr. *Origins of the novel*, (Harvester Press 1980)). The psychiatrists mentioned in this section are Serieux and Capgras (*Folies Raisonnantes,* 1909), and Tanzi (*Trattato delle Malattie Mentali*, 1904). Excerpts from both works will be found in *Classiques de la Paranoia, Analytica* **30** (Paris: Navarin 1983).

François Roustang is the author of *Un Destin si Funeste* (Paris: Minuit 1976). On the relationship between Freud and Tausk, see Paul Roazen, *Brother animal: the story of Freud and Tausk* (London 1970). Freud's article, 'Constructions in Analysis' is in the *Standard Edition*, vol. XXIII. On the relationship between desire and interpretation and the psychoanalytic conception of truth, see S. Cottet, *Freud et le Désir du Psychanalyste* (Paris: Navarin 1983). On the difference between reality and 'the real', cf. J. C. Milner, *Les Noms Indistincts* (Paris: Seuil 1983).

5

Beyond délire

Two conceptions of *délire*

Man is a shop of rules: a well-truss'd pack
Whose every parcel underwrites a law.

George Herbert is a Lacanian poet – or should I say that Lacan is a religious psychoanalyst? The conception of *délire* expounded in the last chapter treated man as a shop of linguistic rules, whose every parcel underwrites a syntactic law. Sometimes the pack comes untrussed: *délire* is both a symptom of this dereliction and a defence against it. We might call this a structural conception of *délire*, where *délire* is a linguistic activity dominated by the law – a displaced use of the rules of normal language (with serious consequences, the main one being the exclusion of the delirious speaker). So, on the one hand, there are no metaphors in delirious speech, and, on the other, *délire* as a whole is an instance of the metaphoric process: everything in delirious utterances can and must be interpreted. The law which governs *délire* is semiotic; it gives *délire* its distinctive structure (the dialectic of excess and lack) and produces a mirror-effect: the paranoiac's delirium is faithfully reflected in the *délire* of the interpreting analyst. *Délire* is both close to theory and distant from it; this relation is mediated by their common opposition to a third type of discourse – poetry.

But a positive account is also possible, as has already been suggested in Chapter 3. This side of our tradition insists on the non-signifying and a-syntactic aspects of delirious speech, and treats it as a flow of words and affects. It is in accord with classical psychiatrists like Tanzi, who saw 'orgies of metaphors' in *délire*. Reading or hearing *délire* is no longer an attempt at interpretation, it is an involvement in the flow of words, where the willing audience swims with the current, and allows itself to be carried away by the metaphors. Instead of a linguistic system, we have the unreliable and unpredictable workings of poetic language: not a pack of rules, a system, but a strange growth, a machine with a dynamic of its own. *Délire* is made up of metaphors, and yet nothing in it is metaphorical: it must all be taken literally. As a consequence, frontiers are blurred, and *délire* reigns everywhere. At best, we shall be able to distinguish between the *delirium delirans* of the philosopher and the *delirium deliratum* of the patient. But we might as well invert those terms, for as they stand they still give the philosopher mastery over the madman. The disappearance of frontiers precludes interpretation and prevents reconstruction. And so we soon find ourselves beyond *délire*: it disappears in the current of desire. Something is produced: affects, sounds, gestures and various bodily expressions, words. And something, not someone, produces it: let us call it libido, or desire. '*Ça parle*': in the new version of this celebrated formula there is no exclusion, no difference between the philosopher and the madman, Artaud and Spinoza. And it is a strange sort of philosophy which can travel so far, and take such risks.

To understand the contrast between these two conceptions of *délire*, we can reconsider the two metaphors mentioned in Chapter 3: the tree and the rhizome, the one structured around a centre and working through binary oppositions, the other proliferating in all directions, by accretion, not separation or opposition, without plan or order. If we take all this literally, we shall see that Chomsky's structural 'trees' are hardly metaphoric (or, in other words, that they use the aptest metaphor, for according to Jakobson binary oppositions are natural to and constitutive of language). A tree has a binary structure and so has *délire* in so far as it conforms to linguistic law. But a rhizome has no centre, no structure: neither has *délire* if it consists in a flow of words and/or libido (Schreber's 'nerves', part semen, part sunrays). In this case, the structural analysis of language is unable to account for *délire*: the only possible analysis is *pragmatic*, through a theory of speech acts, of non-verbal communication, of non-systematic uses of speech and non-communicative functions of language.

The two conceptions of *délire* imply two different attitudes to metaphor. In the structural version (which I shall call *Oedipal*), metaphor is all important; it is absent from *délire*, but it is an essential aspect of the workings of language: interpretation, symbolism, representation, all have something to do with the metaphoric process. In the delirious conception of *délire*, in contrast, metaphor has no place, although it is omnipresent. Deleuze and Guattari, with their astonishing gift for metaphor, keep insisting that their terms are *not* to be taken metaphorically: the unconscious *is* a machine, the body politic *is* a body. For the very word 'metaphor', and the implied contrast between the figurative and the literal, presuppose a distinction between the uttering subject and the grammatical subject ('sujet d'énonciation' and 'sujet d'énoncé'), which is questioned by the delirious conception of *délire*. Deleuze and Guattari quote Kafka: 'metaphors are one of the reasons why I despair of literature'.[1] Not metaphor, they say, but metamorphosis: words are things, and are involved in events or acts; they mix with other objects and affect them. The universe of *délire* may be wildly imaginative: it is also painfully literal. There are no longer any clear frontiers between words and things.

This idea of literalness is easily understood within a conception of language where *délire* is considered as a malfunction. But this repudiation of metaphor by philosophers whose whole work is based on the stystematic development of a few metaphors sounds remarkably like Freudian denial. When Deleuze and Guattari assert that the unconscious is, literally, a machine, are they doing anything but making an exaggerated and illicit use of what Lakoff and Johnson call a 'structural metaphor'[2] (in this case the 'mind is a machine' metaphor; 'I'm a little *rusty* as I start this chapter, my mind just won't work today')? The exact status of the copula is a little uncertain, and once more we seem to have strayed beyond the bounds of common sense.

As a first approach to a rather obscure conception of *délire* (the delirious conception), we can follow Deleuze and Guattari in distinguishing two forms of thought. There is a central tradition of philosophy, to which both the critical approach of Descartes and Kant, and the systematic one of Aristotle and Hegel belong. It is based on three assumptions: the power of truth, the foundational role of myth (e.g. the Cave), and the juridical contract between reason and language. *Imperium, muthos, logos*: the model of philosophy is Truth, Justice and Law. This is the dominant tradition of common sense, of public and official thought (the Hegelian philosopher, as civil servant, being its true representative). It is governed by two universal concepts – Totality (as the foundation of Being) and the Subject.[3] But there is another tradition, subordinate but persistent; that of antinomian thought (outside the main tradition, and beyond the control of the subject): its heroes are philosophers like Nietzsche or Kirkegaard, or poets like Artaud and Kleist; its form is not argumentative and logical, but aphoristic; its main characteristic is not *muthos* or *logos*, but *pathos* – personal involvement, the experience of suffering; not so much a foundation as a foundering. For them, there is no Totality, and there is no Subject to grasp it, only a collection of fragments, particles, and flows of desire. And since there is no *logos*, there is no control over language. The main linguistic experience is one of *délire*; except that there is no longer any *délire*, since this presupposes two poles of language, one delirious, the other rational. Because it is omnipresent, *délire*, like metaphor, has disappeared.

I am not offering this contrast between rational and delirious thought as a serious picture of the history of philosophy. Nor do Deleuze and Guattari (they present it as an illustration of the opposition between the State and what they call the 'war-machine'). But it does illustrate the two aspects of our tradition: the semiotic structure, and the flow of words, *délire* as symptom and as poetry. And it is also a point of entry into *Capitalism and Schizophrenia*, a series of instructions for its use. It provides both an *abyme* of the text (Deleuze and Guattari belong to the tradition of antinomian thought) and an illustration of its method (its sweeping generality, the vast scope of the critique). But the main point of the illustration is that it adumbrates a theory of *délire*, or rather depicts the movement of the delirious theory of *délire*: from pervasiveness (this corresponds to vol. 1: *Anti-Oedipus*) to dissolution (in vol. 2: *Mille Plateaux*).

I have been carried away by my argument. I have failed to begin at the beginning, and must retrace my steps. As the astute reader will have guessed, this chapter is devoted to the second, or delirious, conception of *délire*. It deals with the later works of Gilles Deleuze, in which he teamed up with Felix Guattari: *Anti-Oedipe* (1972), *Kafka* (1975), *Mille Plateaux* (1980).[4] I have also used two volumes of essays by Guattari, *La Révolution Moléculaire* (1977, 1980) and *L'Inconscient Machinique* (1979), both of which express positions shared by Deleuze. (There is more to this collaboration than mere convenience or mimicry – to every Marx an Engels shall be granted. The refusal of individual authorship is itself a philosophical position, the beginning of a reflection on language which culminates in *Mille Plateaux*.)

The corpus is impressive: in the space of nine years, they have produced 1500 published pages. The scope of the inquiry is astonishing: they move freely from philosophy to literature, from psychiatry to anthropology, from biology to archaeology and linguistics, from geography to mathematics. And their ambition is not modest. As the title indicates, and in spite of repeated statements about the impossibility of the task, they have set out to offer a solution to the problem which haunted French philosophy in the late 1960s and 1970s: how to combine Marxism and psychoanalysis. The 'and' in *Capitalism and Schizophrenia* indicates the claim that such articulation can be found. And this is only the subtitle: the title of the first volume indicates that the first – and necessary – step is a *critique* (perhaps a reference to Marx, in the shape of an inverse symmetry: *Anti*-Oedipus, or *Capitalism* and Schizophrenia; Das *Kapital*, or a *Critique* of Political Economy). But the title of the second volume, borrowed from Bateson,[5] marks a change: there will not be a single logical construction, moving relentlessly from the abstract to the concrete, but many partially independent modules; not a tree, but a rhizome, with not one, but a thousand points of entry.

This does not make my task easy. I cannot explore all the plateaux: the ascent is tiring, there are no guides, and there is a constant danger of avalanches. So I shall climb the plateau of *délire*, and discuss the theory of *délire* in *Anti-Oedipus*. In order to understand this, which is a point of arrival, not of departure, I shall have to go back to the three critiques which form the nucleus of *Capitalisme et Schizophrénie*: those of Freud, of Marx and of Saussure.

Délire in Anti-Oedipus

In *Logique du Sens*, as we saw, *délire* is important but implicit: it is the surface effect of the indirection which is present in all manifestations of language (Deleuze calls this 'sense'). *Délire* is everywhere (potentially, there is *délire* in every utterance, in so far as it has sense), and it is particularly evident in the literary corpus (Artaud, Wolfson) which is the main object of the book's critical attention. In *Anti-Oedipus*, the situation has changed: instead of being an implicit foundation, *délire* has become a concept. The term appears on many pages, it is defined, it is the object of critical elaboration. The existence of delirious discourse is the basis for a critique of the Oedipus complex, but the study of *délire* is only a starting point. Other, more important objects appear: society, history; not merely the schizophrenic, but also capitalism.

Thus, we find explicit theses on *délire* in *Anti-Oedipus*. The starting point is the same as in Lacan: the very existence of *délire* raises problems about Freudianism. There is a nucleus of truth in *délire*: but it cannot be reached by a process of separation (the gold from the dross), of sifting or extracting; it rather lies in the disappearance of all separation, in the erasing of frontiers. The first comment one can make about *délire* is that the truth about it cannot be grasped from the outside: it requires a degree of involvement and renunciation on the part of the philosopher. He must abandon his normal processes of thought, proceed by paradox (Deleuze and Guattari talk of the 'bright black truth' of *délire* – *Anti-Oedipus*, p. 9), he must become delirious.

But becoming schizoid does not mean abandoning logic, it means adopting another point of view – not the logic of identity and the exclusion of incompatibles, A is A, A is not B, but the point of view of paradox: A is B, society *is* a body, man *is* a machine. There is a coherence in *délire*; and it revolves around three theses.

The first is that *délire* is the linguistic manifestation of desire. There are two aspects to this. *Délire* is an effect, produced by the machinery of desire; it is the outward manifestation of desire; its rejection of linguistic and social rules is the direct expression of the fundamental freedom of desire. But *délire* is also secondary, a translation into language of the workings of 'desiring machines': perhaps a necessary translation (desire is the victim of Oedipal repression, and can only find expression in *délire*), but also a potential betrayal. So that *délire* appears in two inseparable forms: it is the free expression of desire, and it is its betrayal, precisely because it is an expression, something which is extruded from desire and therefore exterior to it.

The second thesis is that *délire* is not an individual affair. Our natural tendency (this is particularly apparent if we talk of *délire* in terms of fiction) is to refer the delirious productions to an individual author. We may have noted the repetitive character of the paranoiac's delirium, yet we hailed Schreber's genius. At worst, we give the paranoiac's name to a case-history; at best, we turn him into a *poète maudit*. *Anti-Oedipus*, however, stresses the collective nature of *délire*, even if it is produced by an individual patient, and its *social* character. For the dominant tendency (particularly in psychoanalysis) is to privatize *délire*: the process may be universal (like the Oedipus complex), but it is of interest only as enabling particular individuals to come to terms with themselves. Against this trend, Deleuze and Guattari have implicitly adopted one of the slogans of the French far left in the 1970s: '*le personnel est politique*'; personal problems are directly political. By this one must understand not only that the personal problems which all of us encounter in our everyday life (sexual problems, for instance) have direct political significance, but also that they do not have to be mediated by or discarded for collective political positions. The traditional attitude of the Marxist left has been to protect itself from *délire* as from a danger. The political activist who becomes delirious is hurried to a clinic, to the tune of the embarrassed comments of his comrades (this is what happened in 1969 to the general secretary of the French Communist Party, Waldeck-Rochet; any connection between his illness and the invasion of Czechoslovakia was stoutly denied). Or again, Marxist critics carefully separate the Sexpol period in Reich from the delirious orgone period, during which, as is well known, he was mad, i.e. no longer (politically) conscious. Conservatives are apt to equate radicalism with madness, and some psychoanalysts still hold to a version of this fallacy.[6]

Deleuze and Guattari have gone in the opposite direction. In support of their thesis, they point to the political and historical content in the delirium of schizophrenic or paranoid patients. The *délire* of a West Indian patient expresses his relation to the white majority and his experience of the Algerian war.[7] Even Schreber's *délire*, to take a more familiar example, is full of historical and political notations: the unsuccessful parliamentary candidate has views on the Germans as a chosen people, threatened by Jews; and in one of his metamorphoses, he becomes a virgin from Alsace fighting against the French or a Mongol prince. *Délire* has political, social and racial meanings, independent of the individual subject. Conversely, politics and political parties can produce *délire*. This does not mean that all fascists are paranoiacs; but it does mean that there is a mass-psychology of fascism, and that political organizations which ignore the connection between society and the unconscious are only digging their own graves (this is very much what Reich was saying to the German left when he wrote his book).[8] Nor is the connection one of form and content: for Deleuze and Guattari the origin of *délire* is historical, political, racial (*Anti-Oedipus*, p. 326); or again 'la libido délire l'histoire' (*Anti-Oedipus*, p. 422) (with its use of '*délire*' as a transitive verb, this is untranslatable: but it is presenting *délire* as a process operating on history.)

By this Deleuze and Guattari mean that certain barriers must disappear. There is no separation between the personal and the social: libido and politics interpenetrate. First, one finds politics in psychiatry. This is an important theme in French culture, in part attributable to the existence of a mass Marxist party, which for a long time exerted an influence on French intellectuals: every human action or expression is, in a sense, political; there is no space reserved for purely private concerns. Or rather, to avoid the danger of turning a rich and important political and cultural movement, the French Communist Party, into a simplified version of the Totalitarian Organization pictured in Orwell's *1984*, there is a separation between what is relevant – the public or political sphere – and what is unimportant, the private sphere. There is a political side to psychiatry, embodied in legislation, ideological theses and forms of struggle and *délire* itself is a form of political expression, as the history of ranting shows: against political or psychological repression, the exaggerated reaction of *délire* carries with it both the political contents of a revolt and its violence. But even in the sanest and most common-sensical acts, like standing for parliament, desire rules, as appears in the case of Schreber.

One could easily caricature this, as the view that all true revolutionaries are schizoid and that mental asylums are the red bases of the future (certain versions of anti-psychiatry in the 1970s were not far from this position); or, on the other hand, that prospective politicians ought to be psychoanalysed, for even Mrs Thatcher is ruled by libido. But such a version misses the main point: there is no separation between the individual and the collective (this is what breaks down the barrier between libido and politics). There is no individual subject, or rather subjects are just surface effects. Both the political and the psychological field are permeated by the same form of energy, libido, which has effects both political (the class struggle) and individual (*délire*). The only difference is one of scale, between 'molar' and 'molecular': a theme to which we shall return.

This removes another separation: that between the rational and the delirious. Since both are produced by the same libido, the truth in *délire* is as important as the same commodity when contained in rational discourse. 'Au fond de la société, le délire' (*Anti-Oedipus*, p. 427): at the basis of society lies *délire*. If libido is the energy of the collective unconscious, and *délire* is the direct product of libido, then it stands in the same relation to society and the individual that Deleuzian sense has to the proposition: an element of indirection, a necessary precondition, but not a foundation. In that sense, the *délire* of libido rules history; in that sense also the origin of *délire* (as we know it in the surface productions of poets and madmen) is political, historical, racial, for the contents of the collective libido are directly 'invested' in the historical field. Note the economic metaphor: this is a study of capitalism, and the Freudian concept ('*investissement*' is the French term for the Freudian concept of

Besetzung, which is known in English as 'cathexis') must be taken literally. Libido and history presuppose each other: *délire* is the outward form of this relation. (There are therefore two *délires*: deep *délire*, the precondition of all human expression; and surface *délire*, the direct, but limited expression of the first; exactly as, according to Deleuze, there are two types of nonsense, the nonsense of depth, present in all propositions, and the surface nonsense of explicitly nonsensical texts.)

Before explaining my third thesis about *délire*, I must stop and reflect on the type of analysis I have given so far. The first point is the coherence of *délire*: a coherence based on paradox, on the abolition of distinctions, on renunciation of the identity principle. A is not A, society is the individual. By doing this Deleuze and Guattari do more than take their metaphors literally. They abandon the methods of science as we know it. For a science is founded by separating the relevant from the irrelevant. If I want language to become the object of scientific analysis, I must give up hope of accounting for certain aspects of it, I must separate *langue* from *parole*. Of course, the subsequent history of the science will mainly consist in reintroducing parts of *parole* into *langue*: nevertheless, the separation will always exclude certain aspects of the object. (Even if there appears a separate science of *parole*, pragmatics for instance, it too will exclude from the scope of science certain aspects of language use.) Deleuze and Guattari reject this approach, or rather invert it: instead of excluding, they include; they give back to the act of comprehending its etymological meaning. They do not abandon all distinctions ('molar'/'molecular'; 'paranoid'/'schizophrenic' for example); but these are means not of separation but of accretion: they do not sever, they contain or constrict. Nor is this position so far from common sense as one might suppose. In *Metaphors we live by*, Lakoff and Johnson develop an *experiential* account of truth, in which metaphor is one of the necessary paths to truth and not a deceitful ornament. Deleuze and Guattari merely take us one step further, by taking metaphors literally.

The logic of separation is at the core of interpretation, as Freud, a positive scientist, understood it. Thus, Schreber's historical or political delirium is either discarded as irrelevant or reinterpreted so as to be relevant: not a German virgin fighting against the French, but a son resisting his homosexual attraction to his father. By refusing the separation on which such reduction is based, Deleuze and Guattari attempt to take into account the richness of *délire*. The ways of libido are innumerable, and great is its creativity; on the other hand, interpretation

168

is predictable and banal. It is not Schreber, but Freud, who is repetitive. Before he has even started, we know what he is bound to come up with: castration, the phallus and the Oedipus complex. The Oedipus complex is a mincing-machine (one of our authors' best-known maxims). Better trust the richness of *délire* than the poverty of the analyst.

This has consequences for the type of philosophy Deleuze and Guattari practise. In Chapter 4, I quoted a critic's view of the dryness of Deleuze's *Logic of Sense*. There, philosophy was a specialized subject, with problems of its own, and Deleuze refused to pay any attention to contemporary fads. But if the biscuit was dry then, it is now rich and moist. Both the personal and the political intrude: Deleuze and Guattari have adopted – and with a vengeance – the aim often ascribed to Hegel when he wrote the *Phenomenology of Mind*, of combining uncompromising philosophy with problems of daily life. So the -isms (Marxism, etc.) are back. Philosophy once more receives the broad definition which is characteristic of French contemporary culture. But the main novelty is that we have left for good what was so far a tradition centred on language. Although *délire* is still an important concept (perhaps more so than ever) it is no longer only analysed as an instance of language; it is an effect of much wider processes, the origins and consequences of which go far beyond language, and whose nature is not semiotic. Language will be firmly put in its place (or rather the empire of Saussarian linguistics will be contested) and a 'non-signifying semiotics' (gestures, facial expressions) will be sketched: libido has replaced semiosis.[9]

I can now state the third thesis on *délire* in *Anti-Oedipus*. It is the most important, and it follows from the first two. It distinguishes two types of *délire*, corresponding to two main forms of society: the revolutionary and the fascistic, the schizophrenic and the paranoid. Two things must be noted here. First, a psychiatric distinction[10] is being assimilated to a politico-historical distinction. Second, it is also being asked to carry a moral value: the description of the 'method' as 'schizo-analysis' indicates that the schizophrenic pole is the positive one. But this is not an arbitrary value-judgement. In social terms, the contrast is between authoritarian and libertarian organizations: on the one hand States, with their insistence on centralized power (see the work of Immanuel Wallerstein),[11] and their hierarchical separations between States and between classes; on the other hand, looser organizations of smaller groups, without territorial limits, without hierarchy. The best example of the latter is a society of nomads, whose main value is not authority (which implies stability and order) but flight. The metaphor can be taken historically: on the paranoid view, history has a beginning – each society has its foundation myth – and above all an ineluctable end, an apocalypse (be it the bloody apocalypse of the end of the Third Reich, or the classless society of Marxism). Schizophrenic history, in contrast, starts in the middle: there is no Kermodian sense of an ending,[12] only the flight of time, a vector, but one for which the customary terms of beginning and end are irrelevant. Time flies off in all directions. And the metaphor is also a psychiatric one. Desire can be structured, as in paranoia, with its insistence on interpretation, signs, verisimilitude and legal rights; or alternatively it can follow the uncertain paths of flight, where there is no frontier because there is no goal: this is the case in schizophrenia, where the law is subverted, the structure of language dissolved, the family uprooted, and the Name of the Father drowned in the names of history. In fact, the description of *délire* given in the first two of these applies to the *délire* of schizophrenia, the only real *délire* (the other form only repeats what Deleuze and Guattari call the 'dirty little secret': it never leaves the limits of the family).

There is an incipient contradiction here: *délire* is both the whole (the effect of the 'investment' of libido in the body politic), and a special part of this whole, a particular 'position' (in the sense Melanie Klein gave to this term): the schizophrenic. How can *délire* be at both poles and at only one of them? The situation is familiar in linguistics, where an 'unmarked' element in a pair refers both to the class and to one of its subsets (e.g. 'a dog' means both 'any dog, male or female', and, when opposed to 'a bitch', 'a male dog'). *Délire* is the unmarked term in the pair '*délire*' vs 'language'. It refers both to any linguistic activity (and indeed, as we have seen, its field is even broader than that), and to a specialized use of delirious language, the *délire* of the schizoid, to which another *délire*, paranoia, is opposed (the bitch is also a dog). What is notable here is that the unmarked/marked opposition has been reversed. Normally, we would expect 'language' to be the unmarked term. The delirious patient uses language, he *talks*. If I want to be specific, I shall indicate that he does not talk 'normal language', but *délire*. In Deleuze and Guattari, *délire* comes first: I may later specify that this *délire* is in fact paranoid, that it has the appearance of what is usually called normal language. But we must remember that this is a philosophical thesis: it does not simply state that we are all delirious, and that the schizoid is better (more lucid, more revolutionary) than most of us; what it states is that at the root of all our speech there is a non-semiotic flow of desire, which we do not control (as individual subjects) and which pervades society (and the State) as well as individuals. If we have so little mastery of our utterance (if we are produced not only by the unconscious but by a social unconscious – the Freudian personal unconscious is the last refuge of any philosophy of the subject, of the individual soul), then what we utter is *délire*, even when we say what we mean (we may mean, but we never master).

By giving a summary of the three theses, we can produce a theory of *délire*, perhaps the main thread around which the text of *Anti-Oedipus* is woven: 1 *délire* is desire, or rather delirious thought or language is the outward manifestation of desire and language is secondary to libido, only a surface effect; 2 this is because libido, and therefore *délire*, is primarily social, i.e. racial, political and historical; the political and personal fields coincide; 3 but there are two poles to *délire*; the real *délire* of schizophrenia, centred on flight and the reactionary *délire* of paranoia (based on the authoritarian structure of the hierarchic State).

Even if we refuse to yield to any sense of an ending, we have arrived somewhere: this is a point of arrival, a construction, a theory. We must retrace our steps, for many questions remain: what is the nature of that libido, both psychic and social? How can politics be ruled by desire? And where does desire come from? How does it appear? Not least, we have failed to settle the question of metaphor: is the theory based on a structural metaphor (a coherent network of metaphors), or must we, as Deleuze and Guattari insist, take it all literally? If we must retrace our steps, let us do it in an orderly fashion, and start from the beginning.

The starting point: desiring machines

If you take yourself for a Marx or a Freud, and you hope to create a whole new science, the question of the starting point will be both important and difficult for you. In many cases, the starting point will be a distinction, which separates the relevant from the irrelevant. *Das Kapital* begins with the distinction between use value and exchange value; Saussurian linguistics, logically if not chronologically, with the opposition between *langue* and *parole*. But Deleuze and Guattari, as we have seen, do not practise this logic of separation: they unite, they do not divide (an apt political metaphor). And what they unite is Marxism and psychoanalysis. If you look for the fundamental concepts of both theories, you may come to the conclusion that what Freud is writing about is libido, or desire; and, less predictably but not illogically, you may conclude that the fundamental specificity of Marx is that he has adopted the point of view of production (as opposed to circulation), and that his analysis of capitalism as a mode of production places a couple of actors in the centre of the picture: man (whose labour is the only source of value), and machines (the presence of which is necessary for capitalism to emerge). Desire, production, machine: these three concepts are Deleuze and Guattari's starting point. And since their logic is not one of opposition, their opening gambit – a bold move – is to unite desire and machine: a new creature is born, the desiring machine.

It is a moving moment. Let us read the first paragraph of *Anti-Oedipus*:

It is at work everywhere, functioning smoothly at times, at other times in fits and starts. It breathes, it heats, it eats. It shits and fucks. What a mistake to have ever said *the* id. Everywhere *it* is machines – real ones, not figurative ones: machines driving other machines, machines being driven by other machines, with all the necessary couplings and connections. An organ-machine is plugged into an energy-source-machine: the one produces a flow that the other interrupts. The breast is a machine that produces milk, and the mouth a machine coupled to it. The mouth of the anorexic wavers between several functions: its possessor is uncertain as to whether it is an eating-machine, an anal machine, a talking-machine, or a breathing-machine (asthma attacks). Hence we are all handymen: each with his little machines. For every organ-machine, an energy-machine: all the time, flows and interruptions. Judge Schreber has sunbeams in his ass. *A solar anus.* And rest assured that it works: Judge Schreber feels something, produces something, and is capable of explaining the process theoretically. Something is produced: the effects of a machine, not mere metaphors.

An effect is produced, a stylistic one, and it is not due to metaphor, but to an invigorating directness of language: this is why I have quoted the first paragraph in full. Hegel's programme is at last being carried out: not only are everyday problems considered (anorexia, for instance, which has a special fascination for Deleuze), but the language of everyday life is being used. Once we have overcome the cultural shock and understood the strategy (if we want to overcome the dominant form of thought, we must begin by destroying it stylistically, by taking the risk of *délire*: this is the language of conscious schizophrenia), we will realize that the text achieves what the first page of a philosophical critique usually sets out to do: it destroys (it produces a target for criticism, the Freudian topic of ego, superego and id) and reconstructs (it provides a certain number of concepts which it will use as building-blocks: 'machine', 'flow', 'break').[13] It also comments on what is happening: the last word of the paragraph is 'metaphor', and twice in the course of those few lines the authors insist that the concept 'machine' be taken literally, not metaphorically.

What, then, is a machine? First, what it is in daily life: a machine is a machine is a machine; it produces effects. Second, it is also defined by contrast with what it is not, in spite of the logic of unification (everything, especially the human body, is a machine – the old opposition between machine and man disappears); a machine is not a structure.[14] What a structure is, we learnt in Chapter 4: it consists of two heterogenous series, one signifying, the other signified; of elements which acquire value through opposition; of a paradoxical element which regulates the whole, and so makes sense of it. This definition has two consequences: first, the point of view of structure is one of *representation* (each movement of the 'empty square' along the structure produces a 'state of the structure', an image of it); and second, this representation is meant as a representation for a *subject*. If the structure produces anything, it is the idea of a totality and the idea of a subject, who appropriates and masters the totality. The point of view of machines, on the other hand, is – predictably – one of production; and what they produce is not a subject. This is a philosophical thesis (machine vs structure); it is also a psychological one. The psychological structure lies at the core of the subject; what we call the ego is the result of a structuring process, and it structures our thoughts, our actions, our words (*délire* is loss of structure). The psychological machine, on the other hand, is unstructured: it produces affects, drives, a flow of libido; it is unconscious (but unlike the Freudian unconscious, at least as described by Leclaire, it is not an unconscious subject). A machine produces flows of energy, of matter; another machine, coupled with the first, segments the flow, codifies it, and uses it as a mark on a body, on a territory. If this sounds too abstract, we need only think of a domestic cat roaming round the back garden: she uses a flow of excrement to mark her territory; but by shutting it off, and so using it for a purpose other than the relief of a physiological need, she turns it into a series of signs: she 'codifies' it, and inscribes it on the body of the earth in order to establish oundaries, to leave her imprint. She ehaves like a machine; in fact, she *is* a machine, and she produces a territory. The philosophical thesis has become ethological.

But there is also a historical thesis at work here, a pro-Marxist one (as the psychological thesis was anti-Freudian): machines as we know them appeared in history, and society under capitalism is marked by the pervasiveness of machines, by the alienation of man to machine.

173

The thesis turns this historical triviality into a philosophical position. The usual conception of machines considers them as extensions of human organs or faculties: it is hardly a metaphor to talk of a 'mechanical arm', and the logical (and historical) development goes from the hand to the tool and then the machine. Deleuze and Guattari reverse that order: machines are no longer man's tools, it is man who is an appendix to them. One could think of a violinist who, instead of mastering his instrument, is mastered by it,[15] as the patient is possessed by *délire*. Art and literature have long been haunted by this inversion (one can think of Čapek and his robots, or of Chaplin). Deleuze and Guattari make philosophical use of a deep seated obsession. And this is in fact how unification finds its logic: if, through a *historical* process, the relations of man and machine have changed, it is conceivable that, instead of the machine being humanized, man has been 'machinized'. Man's dependence on machines has been internalized, machines are inside man's mind: his desire is machine produced; in a sense the organization of man's desire is that of a machine. The historical is psychological is philosophical. Let us remember, then, the organization of a machine: production, not representation; two machines instead of two series; a flow of matter or energy and its cutting and coding; unconscious collective production, not individual subjects.

But the machines of *Anti-Oedipus* are *desiring* machines. A strange phrase, a contradiction in terms if we fail to recall that the distinction between man and nature has been blurred: 'the human essence of nature and the natural essence of man are identical in nature *qua* production or industry' (*Anti-Oedipus*, p. 10).[16] The first consequence of this has already been spelt out: desire works through machinery. But the converse is also true: there is no machinery which is not inhabited by desire (the most obvious instance is, naturally, literary: the execution machine in Kafka's *Penal Colony*). So the production of desire ('la production désirante') is the fundamental category of schizo-analysis. There are flows, of commodities, of money (capital is a machine: psychoanalysis has already shown that the flow of money is heavily invested with libido), of concepts (the conceptual machinery of logic), of bodily fluids, of words. These flows are segmented, coded and decoded. Schizo-analysis is the science of segmentation (from the Greek verb *schizein*, to cleave). It is hardly analysis, though (this is a relic of the Freudian origin of the critique): a synthesis, rather. As we have seen, the logic of Deleuze and Guattari's task is not one of separation, or distinction (etymologically, 'analysis' means 'solution' and 'dissolution'), but of production, of synthesis: putting things together, like a machine. Even segmentation is not analysis: it is only another aspect of the continuous flow, the production of elements (part objects, if what is segmented is a flow of body fluids or fantasies) for synthesis. And syntheses there are: both in the world of machines and in the world of philosophy. (The first chapter of *Anti-Oedipus* deals with yet another Deleuzian tripartition, the three syntheses of connection, disjunction and conjunction, linked to the three fundamental processes of production, distribution and consumption, and to the three flows of desire, *libido*, marks and signs, *numen*, and pleasure and pain, *voluptas*: the world is still magically structured by a rule of three.)

The starting point, then, is critical in the two senses of the term: it rejects one tradition (it is anti-Freudian), and accepts another (it claims to be broadly Marxist: 'desiring machine' is the fundamental category of 'materialist' psychiatry). The development of this critique leads Deleuze and Guattari to follow Wittgenstein's advice, and kick away the ladder; the term 'desiring machine', with its possible drift towards the perverse machinery of sadism or masochism (a matter of particular interest to Deleuze), with the reductive conception of sexuality it implicitly carries with it, has had to be abandoned; it no longer appears in *Mille Plateaux*. Before we kick the ladder away ourselves, let us climb three more steps, and deal with the three critiques already mentioned.

A critique of interpretation

Deleuze and Guattari's rejection of Oedipus is a rejection of interpretation and structure. The critique of interpretation is simple. Since the Oedipus complex is supposed to be universal, the results of any interpretation are known in advance; the richness of the patient's productions (his dreams, his delirious discourse, his insights) is reduced to ready-made explanations. Take Schreber, and the extraordinary variety of his *délire* (a whole new cosmology, a new mythology): behind it, there is always his father. Freud recognizes the predictable character of his interpretations. It is human sexuality, he says, which is predictable. Deleuze and Guattari turn this perverse argument on its head: human sexuality is rich and diverse (we all have our little machines), but the psychoanalyst's words are impoverished and banal. Psychiatrists, as we have seen, hold that *délire* is repetitive: but it is their paranoid *délire* of interpretation which is really repetitive. Freud is just a clairvoyant, predicting what he already knows. Hence Freudian interpretation is repression.

An example will show how this repression works. Deleuze and Guattari reread Freud's analysis of little Hans. The 5-year-old boy wants to go downstairs to sleep with his little girl-friend. For Freud, this desire is displaced: Hans cannot want a little girl, only his mother (and the little girl is duly 'interpreted'); Hans cannot want to leave the family: his desire to go away is interpreted in terms of the family; it must mean that Hans wants his girl-friend to be part of the family. Hans is duly forbidden by his father to cross the border, to leave the family territory. Psychoanalysis, when confronted with a dream, a fragment of *délire*, always reduces it by asking the question: 'what does it mean?'. But does it have to *mean* anything? Schizo-analysis adopts the point of view of production and asks another question, which does not dissolve desire: how does it work? What is the use of it? Thus Hans is not preoccupied with organs (and therefore afraid of castration), but with functions, with machines ('it' is used for weeing, etc.).

The second point of Deleuze and Guattari's critique – the critique of structure – is better known, and less original. It is a critique of the family, of what they call 'familialism': the imperialism of the Oedipal triangle, which imposes the structure of the nuclear family on multifarious desire. Deleuze and Guattari bring together several different critiques of psychoanalysis. From antipsychiatry they take the critique of the family, of the double-bind of the Oedipus complex (you can only 'resolve' it by reproducing it; you can only escape it by entering it). From Marxism comes a critique of the supposed universality of the Oedipus complex, which internalizes the historical structure of the family. From feminism comes a critique of the reduction of desire to the male sexual organs, of the patriarchal bias in the Oedipus complex. The Oedipus complex is a structure which produces an alienated subject. Since the structure has the form of a triangle, Deleuze and Guattari talk of the 'triangulation' by which the unconscious is imprisoned, *délire* controlled, and the subject tamed.

The next point concerns their conception of the lived body. In the last chapter, I presented two conceptions of the body: the pre-subjective 'corps morcelé', a bundle of drives and part objects, and the structured body of erogenous zones. The subject experiences his body as a structure of erogenous zones, and controls it as an organization, a system of organs.

This body, Deleuze and Guattari argue, is not the body of free desire, but the body of the Oedipal reduction. To the structure of organs and subject, they counterpose the desiring machine *par excellence*, the 'body without organs'. The phrase comes from Artaud, who disliked organs, wondered what their use was, and claimed to be able to do without them (as we saw, Schreber, too, claimed to be able to do without his stomach, 'miracled away' by God). And Deleuze and Guattari point to myths of a cosmic egg.[17] Each of us is doomed to try to 'make' our own body a body without organs: it is the place where our desire becomes materialized by being inscribed. In a way, we are in the same world as Leclaire's – the fantasized body is conceived as a locus for inscription. But what is inscribed on the body without organs is not letters but unordered, unstructured lines, without beginning or end. Deleuze and Guattari call them 'lignes de fuite' (a term borrowed from the vocabulary of perspective, where it denotes the lines, real or imaginary, which converge on the vanishing-point, to create a sense of depth). The phrase must be taken literally, as meaning the lines along which desire flows and by which the 'subject' takes flight; or rather not a subject but a singularity, an 'agencement', a temporary and unstable collocation of desire.[18] Hence Deleuze and Guattari's insistence on the theme of the appropriation and loss of territory.

The lines of one's flight may be inscribed either on the body without organs or else on a structure, on territorial lines, on boundaries: the precarious arrangement of a nomadic tribe versus the nation-State. This metaphor suggests, first, that the machine-like processes of desire consist in the inscription of flows, and the appropriation or loss of territory ('territorialization' or 'de-territorialization'); second, that this inscription can take two forms: the stable lines of a frontier which produce a subject (this is the paranoid inscription of triangulation), or the lines of flight on the body without organs (the schizophrenic inscription where desire is not reduced or repressed); or thirdly, that the image of a territory provides a link between the psychological and the social. The body politic is a body. It may or may not be hierarchically organized (the State or the nomadic tribe). It may or may not be familialized (paranoia or schizophrenia). In other words, the link between desire and politics, revolution in our unconscious and revolution out in the streets is that it is all concerned with a body, the body of the earth (territory in the etymological sense), the body politic (they call it 'socius', both the 'despotic body' and 'the body of capital'), or the body without organs.

The diagram below is one of two which Deleuze and Guattari use to illustrate the systematic opposition between paranoia and schizophrenia:

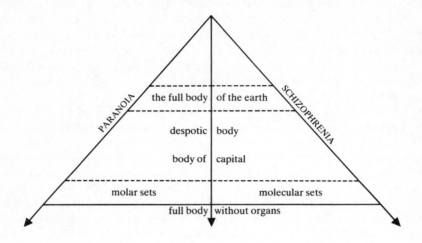

One of the standard criticisms of psychoanalysis (as also of Marxism) is the generality of its interpretations. Oedipal reduction prevents the psychoanalyst from capturing the singularity of an individual arrangement of desires, just as his global class analysis prevents the dogmatic Marxist from understanding the singularity of a concrete situation and the emotional involvement of the individuals concerned. Deleuze and Guattari's main point is that desire is singular. A machine, or rather an arrangement of machines, produces singularities; in this it is opposed to the general structure. By definition, a structure is what is common to all individuals of the same type: there is no structure of desire, we each have to discover our body without organs, and inscribe our lines of flight on it. If we fail to do this, we become alienated, structured, the victims of global, or molar, organization. The terms, borrowed from physics, are now clear: desire is molecular, an object for micro-politics; but structure and interpretation are molar, the objects of macro-political or macro-psychological study.

I shall close this critique of interpretation by adding two points. The first is that the critique rests on a systematic contrast between paranoia and schizophrenia, as the two poles of *délire*:

paranoia	vs	schizophrenia
structure	vs	machine
territoriality	vs	deterritorialization
hierarchic (the State)	vs	nomadic (the tribe)
molar	vs	molecular

The second takes the form of four propositions, summarizing Deleuze and Guattari's criticism of psychoanalysis.

1 Psychoanalysis imposes Lack, Culture and Law on the unconscious, thus structuring, reducing, and repressing desire. The unconscious, on the other hand, is productive: it produces desire, and threatens to smother the body politic with it; hence its revolutionary character, and the necessity for its repression by psychoanalysis, the watchdog of the modern State.

2 Psychoanalysis also hinders the production of discourse. For the unconscious produces not only desire, but also discourse, non-subjective, unstructured: 'collective arrangements of discourse' ('agencements collectifs d'énonciation'). Language flows, like desire, with desire: this might be the definition of the free *délire* of schizophrenia. But psychoanalysis structures this by interpretation: the primal repression is a separation between the uttering and the grammatical subject. This is the primary linguistic structure: one subject is the representation of the other; the process of interpretation can now reduce the one to the other; (you seem to be saying this, but at a deeper level you are really saying that; little Hans can never win, he is structured, caught between the two subjects).

3 Psychoanalysis is an interpretation-machine. It translates all the patient says into another language, reducing it to ready-made general propositions; it turns the patient into a subject in both senses of the term.

4 Psychoanalysis depends upon a particular form of power. Money changes hands (psychoanalysis is the only theory which says you have to spend money to make it work) and the patient submits to the analyst, the flow of libido being reduced to words and interpretations.

A critique of politics

Bunuel's film '*Belle de Jour*'[19] tells the story of a rich and beautiful doctor's wife, who suffers from frigidity, and has masochistic erotic dreams and fantasies which she acts out by becoming a part-time prostitute in a Paris brothel. Beyond the evident kinkiness of the film (an up-market version of 'Emmanuelle') one can perceive a contrast being drawn between affluence, culture and social success on the one hand, and on the other the primitive violence of passion. As Deleuze and Guattari would say, all *délire* is social and political, all desire is also a question of money and class (it is class membership and its outward signs which make the heroine a successful prostitute). A second point, slightly less obvious, is that beneath the veneer of moral values (love, kindness, consideration) there lies something deeper: the singularity of desire and its machinery. The heroine knows what is best and approves it, but chooses the worst, or, at least, follows the current of her desire. The third point is that fantasies are not enough: they are mere representations and desire is production. The film makes a careful distinction between fantasy and acting out. And the heroine's fantasies take the form of machinery at work, hence their pleasant absurdity. 'Let us write a letter', says Michel Piccoli to Catherine Deneuve in the middle of a crowded restaurant; so he smashes a wine-bottle, and they both disappear under the table, whose movements the camera now registers. What are they doing? 'They are writing a letter', says one of the spectators: a singular arrangement of desire, not at all the obvious thing. But the heroine also has to make her fantasies real. Deleuze and Guattari reject the Lacanian definition of the real as impossible. They invert it: 'in reality, everything becomes possible'[20] (*Anti-Oedipus*, p. 35). Reality is what my desire fabricates. We understand the hostility of the schizo-analyst towards fantasies: they always reduce production to representation, and turn life into a stage, on which the actors are always playing the same boring old Greek tragedy. They stifle desire. This is why the heroine has to act out, if she is going to escape Oedipal frigidity (an image of political as well as psychological repression). Except that the very term (used by Lacan) denotes a form of representation: 'out' suggests an 'in', something which the act will represent (and in the film, the fantasies precede the acting out). The dice are loaded: she will never escape her paranoia (the final scene of the film is a fantasy). The fourth point is that the heroine's actions are a form of flight, what the French call a 'fuite en avant', a headlong rush, without thought of the consequences (they are duly tragic). The moral grandeur of the heroine is that she remains true to the 'lignes de fuite' of her desire. Tragedy strikes when she retraces her steps and returns to the Oedipal order. The fifth point is that even in the course of the action, the heroine leads a double life. She goes on living a paranoid life of acceptance of the law (the social law of status and hierarchy, the moral law of kindness and love, and psychological law of the subservience of the body, the outcome of which is frigidity). She desires the repression of her desire and leads a life of innocence and purity (in white tennis clothes). But she also lives a schizophrenic life of acknowledged unmastered desire, as we have seen, where the goal of desire is the coupling of machines (of bodies as machines). One of her clients – this is typical of Bunuel's humour – is Oriental (he does not speak French) and insists on showing her a small black box from which a buzzing noise emerges. We never see what is in it. A sort of beetle? And what does he mean to do with it? Again, an individual collocation of desire, irreducible to the Oedipus complex.

This reminds us of the link between politics and desire (there is politics in desire, and desire in politics); but it is also an exercise in pastiche, showing Deleuze and Guattari's concepts at work on an (aesthetic) object. And this is what they want to achieve: to produce general concepts, but ones which do not immediately subsume singularities beneath general laws. For them, politics is everywhere, but not in the way orthodox Marxists would claim: not through a process of separation (this is class-interest and class-consciousness, that is desire; and only class-interest is relevant), not through global analysis (the mass interests of class rather than the particularity of desire in small groups). Like their critique of Freud, their critique of Marxism is directed against general interpretation (but it is not a criticism of Marx: *Anti-Oedipus* still displays deep piety about the founding father). There is a political thesis behind this: what is criticized is the process of generalization by which a class is elevated into an abstraction above its members, and the party becomes the representative of a class. This representation (again contrasted with revolutionary production) has contradictory results – it produces a bureaucracy (of party apparatchiks, of State functionaries, philosophers or psychiatrists) – but it also produces subjects, whereas revolutionary desire flows through small groups and produces collective action. In other words, it is not enough to fight fascism in the street: we must also fight it in our own heads, setting our revolutionary schizophrenia against our own fascist paranoia.

The question of fascism is important for Deleuze and Guattari. In a sense, it is easy to understand why: they found their only true precursor in Wilhelm Reich, and through him they rediscovered what classical

Marxist analysis ignored. There is a mass psychology of fascism: the masses are not betrayed into fascism by the shortcomings of the revolutionary party (the standard Trotskyist analysis); nor is fascism merely 'the openly terroristic dictatorship of the most reactionary, chauvinistic and imperialist circles of finance capitalism' (Stalin's famous definition). At first sight, Deleuze and Guattari do not offer a historical analysis, and their conception of fascism belongs to the political common sense of the left, where 'fascists' are seen simply as particularly vicious reactionaries. For them, the unconscious is a collective force, and fascism dwells in it as much as on the historical stage or in political parties. Consequently, a party which is consciously revolutionary may be unconsciously fascistic: here we have the beginning of an account of what is sometimes known as the 'Stalinist deviation'. There is molecular as well as molar fascism, in the paranoia that settles in desiring machines, in the daily behaviour of the comrade turned bureaucrat, of the revolutionary who is a male-chauvinist pig at home. This is where revolutionary Marxism lets in the cat of molecular fascism: in the generalization of interpretation and representation. If the analysis is made in molar terms, if collective agents (the bourgeoisie, the proletariat) emerge as the only subjects, then a process of representation (in the political sense) begins: the Party becomes the representative of the class, the Leader the sole representative of the party. Out of a collection of groups and fragmentary arrangements a Totality (the Party) and a Subject (the Leader) are extracted: this is the structure of fascism.

But this is a vicious circle. The argument has produced what it was trying to destroy: a generality – Fascism (and its structure). For there is no such single thing as Fascism. Only singular conjunctures, a multiplicity of partially intersecting fascisms (no Aristotelian definition through species, genus and difference is possible: only a map, where various lines suggest a rather fuzzy shape), a plurality of levels (individual, group or State fascism). Yet, when criticizing global analyses of Fascism, Deleuze and Guattari still use the term as a point of reference. This is a general difficulty of Marxist analysis: there is a need for global (molar) categories to make sense of the world; but there is also a need to destroy and dissolve them, to avoid the process of reduction which they necessarily involve.

Deleuze and Guattari escape from this theoretical double-bind by a critique of the Marxist notion of ideology. It is notorious that while Marxists may excel at global class analysis, they often fail to give a proper account of singular events or conjunctures, and of individual or small group productions or ideas. Some modern Marxists like Gramsci and Althusser have tried to overcome this failing by developing a theory of ideology, or of representation (even if, in its more refined analyses, e.g. in Althusser, it is a theory of the *production* of ideas by Ideological State Apparatuses). Deleuze and Guattari reject these attempts because they reject the standard distinction between the material sphere of economic production, or economic base, and the ideological sphere of superstructures. Instinctual drives are an integral part of the infrastructure; desire is at work in machines and is produced by them. This makes it clear that the concept of ideology is inadequate; it separates production from representation, and captures desire in its representative myths, whereas desire is really production, not tragedy or the Oedipal triangulation. In other words Deleuze and Guattari take the Marxian formula 'ideology is a material force' literally. For them, ideology is material (flows of desire, of words, of capital, of fluids), and it is a force (Euclidian geometry is a material force in the Greek city – *Dialogues*, p. 106), and it is consequently dissolved as a separate level of ideology or representation.

This casts light on the problem of metaphor. Deleuze and Guattari insist that we take their metaphors literally for the same reason that they reject the concept of ideology. Metaphor necessarily adopts the point of view of representation ('A is metaphorically B' implies that A is different from B). The point of view of production denies any such separation: desire is involved in the production of machines, bodies and social organization. The body politic, the *socius*, is not a metaphor: it is a form of the body without organs, embodied in the territory (the body of the earth), the despotic body (the despot and the hierarchical organization upon which he sits) and the body of capital. This attitude towards metaphor in *Anti-Oedipus* anticipates the third critique: the critique of structural linguistics in *Mille Plateaux*, from the point of view of language as a material force.

But we have now arrived at a historical thesis: Fascism is a historical phenomenon, it embodies a form of repression of desire, fascism, which is unhistorical, because it is present at all historical stages (exactly as Althusserian ideology, like the Freudian unconscious, 'has no history'). In other words, the critique of Marx is made from a Marxist standpoint: not that of the official Marxism of the Third International or its various heresies, but a revised and improved Marxism, in which desire at last plays its full part. This is perhaps the main Marxist thesis on which

Deleuze and Guattari base their work: desire is both collective and historical; there is a history of desire, of its violence and its repression, and this is the true history of the class struggle. And the relation of Deleuze and Guattari to Marxism is both ambitious and imitative. The founding fathers had a limited idea of the economy (for them, the base dealt mainly with the production of use-values), and their division of the course of history into stages identified with 'modes of production' reflects this narrow view. So Deleuze and Guattari offer a new periodization, intended to reflect the development of desire in history, its embodiment in three types of bodies and three versions of the treatment of flows: in other words in three 'social machines'.

The first is the 'territorial machine' which corresponds to the primitive organization of society. It inscribes on the body of the earth (the territory) the lines of genealogy and the organization of the tribe, with its hierarchy, its exchanges (of women), its constraints and taboos. The second is the 'despotic machine', which corresponds to the earliest form of the State. Flows are inscribed on the body politic: the lines of bureaucracy – the State apparatus – and also the geographic lines of big construction projects describe a pyramid at the top of which a despot is enthroned. The process of loss of territory ('de-territorialization') has started. The inscription of social organization takes place not on the earth (where boundaries are 'natural') but, in a more abstract manner, on the despot's body, as a symbolic representative of the whole social hierarchy.[22] The third machine is modern capitalism where flows are inscribed on an even more abstract, impersonal body: capital. Two elements meet in capitalist society, both produced by the disintegration of the despotic State: the de-territorialized worker, who is now free (to be exploited), and a 'decoded' flow of money, now free to purchase the worker's energy. The relation between flows, inscription of lines and bodies is described in terms of 'coding'. Flows are inscribed by simple coding (in primitive society), by over-coding (the strict hierarchy of the despotic State, where each element is assigned a stable place) and decoding (in modern society, where flows proliferate once more and freely merge).

It is easy to see not only the parallels with classical Marxism (this is still a theory of *stages*), but also the difference (the divisions are not defined by the development of the forces and relations of production, but by the economy of desire). And the same criticism can be made against this as against classical Marxist theory. Why so many stages and no more?

What is the concrete historical relevance of such sweeping generalities? I admit the force of the objections. Deleuze and Guattari seem to have admitted it in practice, for in *Mille Plateaux*, where the reference to Marxism is much less insistent, they seem to have abandoned this periodization. But their fascination with 'universal history' remains. *Mille Plateaux* (pp. 573–4) contains a theory of 'the three different forms of State' – archaic imperial States, where flows are over-coded, feudal monarchic States, where flows are already decoded, and modern States, where the decoding goes further – and a theory of the opposition between the State and nomadic war-machines.

But I am not so much concerned with versions of Marxism as with *délire*. The Marxist critique of Marxism casts a clearer light on their conception of *délire*. *Délire* is social, and it is a historical product. Despite their off-hand treatment of history, Deleuze and Guattari's position is profoundly historical. For them, the task is not to exclude or reduce *délire* (to a form of representation; by interpretation) but to assess its material force, its intervention in specific historical conjunctures. *Délire* cannot be analysed by semantic sciences (like philosophy or psychoanalysis), only by historical ones ('materialist psychology', history, politics: schizo-analysis). The question one asks *délire*, as we have seen, is not: 'what does it mean?', but 'what is its use, its impact, its force?', 'how is it produced?', 'how does it work?'. *Délire* does not mean, it acts: it does not carry with it its 'meaning' (reached after long analysis by the perspicacious theorist), but is the effect of a particular conjuncture, and produces effects on it. There is a politics of *délire*: and schizo-analysis provides its manifesto.

A critique of linguistics

One of the most striking features of *Mille Plateaux* is a new interest in technical aspects of language. This was a natural development. If their main objective was a critique of all the forms of theoretical imperialism that had dominated French philosophy in the 1960s and 1970s, a debunking of linguistics, that paragon of social sciences, was clearly required. And here again Deleuze and Guattari offer more than criticism: they intervene in the field of linguistics both from within (Hjelmslev and Labov against Saussure and Chomsky) and from without (the Marxist linguistic tradition of Vološinov-Bakhtin), and so produce an alternative theory. Their 'pragmatics' is to linguistics what schizo-analysis is to psychoanalysis, and it involves the same ambiguities. Their new conception of language marks the revival of the problematic of language within schizo-analysis, which turns out to be synonymous with pragmatics. What schizo-analysis deals with is signs, and organized systems of signs, or semiotics (in the plural).

Two of the plateaux are directly relevant here: number four ('The postulates of linguistics') and number five ('Some sign-regimes'). Deleuze and Guattari summarize the 'postulates' of linguistics as follows: 1 language is informative and communicative; 2 language is an autonomous object; 3 there are linguistic constants and universals; and 4 the object of scientific linguistics is the standard form of language, as opposed to dialects and idiolects. These postulates are indeed basic to structural linguistics, but they are developed from the point of view of separation which Deleuze and Guattari reject. They isolate the object of scientific study (*langue*, not *parole*; language, not the extralinguistic; standard English, not dialects) and they aim at the generalizations of science.

It is undeniable that the study of language confronts one with an initial choice. One may decide, for instance, that the main aspect of language is that it conveys information. But it is easy to see that there are uses of language in which no information is exchanged: *délire* is one example. In particular, it is easy to show that speaking is not only stating but also acting, and that communication can be an exercise of power. For Deleuze and Guattari the main thing about language is that it carries 'mots d'ordre'. This French phrase denotes not only slogans, but also their effects (in French a 'slogan' is what one shouts at a demonstration or reads on advertisements; a 'mot d'ordre' is what one receives from an acknowledged authority – a leader or a political party). The word 'ordre' conveys an idea of social hierarchy, of power ('ordre' as command), of organization (as in 'orderliness'). Every statement, even the most neutral and innocuous, carries a 'mot d'ordre'. This is, of course, obvious with imperatives or questions which require an answer, but it is also the case in statements. The Chomskyan linguist, J. R. Ross, once suggested that the deep structure of any sentence contains a performative, usually erased in the surface structure. Thus, the deep structure of 'the man hit the ball' would be 'I state that the man hit the ball'. A Deleuzian version of this would be: 'I order you to accept that the man hit the ball'. For even this innocuous sentence, as pronounced by the linguist, is a vehicle for relations of power; it carries with it the authority of the exemplum (the linguist's knowledge is a form of power), or of power relations within the classroom, if the utterer happens to be a lecturer (and it duly has effects on the audience: some note it down, and those who curse the stupidity of the example do so inwardly, and outwardly accept the authority of the teacher). Up to this point, Deleuze and Guattari are simply following J. L. Austin's distinction between force and sense, and between illocutionary and perlocutionary force. Their adhesion to pragmatics is, therefore, uncontroversial. But they take it one step further. For them, the power of language lies not only in the context of utterances or their contents: it lies in their grammatical form. Language is indeed fascistic: grammatical marks are marks of power; there is hierarchy in syntax (in the Chomskyan trees, for instance); and, of course, this is no mere metaphor.

It is the same with their critique of communication. Redundancy, they claim, is no mere instrument for counteracting noise, but a constitutive element of language: a statement is the redundant accompaniment of the act it accomplishes. Language is always redundant: there is no primary or direct expression, attributable to a subject (and therefore no communication between *subjects*), because there is no primary information, where language corresponds to something seen or felt outside it. Language always presupposes language, and there is no direct relation between an utterance and anything extralinguistic. There is no 'direct speech' (i.e. speech directly expressive of the subject's consciousness and of the world he is conscious of), only indirect speech, the translation of words already spoken. Discourse is a patchwork of already uttered discourses, a mosaic of references, allusions and quotations. Hence there is no individual act of utterance, and no uttering subject. *It* speaks, where 'it' is an unconscious machine, individual in its ordering but collective in its origins. Deleuze and Guattari call this an 'agencement collectif d'énonciation'. It produces both concrete utterances and the subjects who utter them. Our discourse is produced by a machine. We are part of its arrangement ('agencement') and therefore do not control it. We do not use language as a tool, but are just a few of its innumerable cogs. The central experience of language is one of possession, the true linguist is Son of Sam, the American chain-murderer, who acted under the command of ancestral voices, pro-phesying bloodbaths. And we must not suppose that language, and therefore its supreme embodiment, *délire*, is an individual phenomenon. Possession makes a subject of the utterer of *délire*, but it is a social phenomenon, and must be analysed as such. We are back to the 'mots d'ordre', and to their political illocutionary force.

The second fallacy of linguistics is its postulate of the autonomy of language. At the end of Chapter 2 we saw that this was how Jean-Claude Milner stated the principle of the arbitrary character of the sign. Deleuze and Guattari, however, return to the Stoic theory of the attribution of events or *lekta* to bodies: *lekta* do not 'refer to' or 'represent' bodies, but dwell on their surfaces, and emerge from their mixtures: the incorporeal act of cutting is both present and absent in the unholy mixture of knife and flesh. There are, therefore, machine-like arrangements, or mixtures, and collective orderings of utterances attributed to them. Deleuze and Guattari give the example of feudal society (termed 'l'arrangement féodal') (*Mille Plateaux*, pp. 112–13). The feudal system is first defined by a certain organization of bodies. The bodies of the sovereign, of the knights and of the villeins, male or female, enter into certain relations. They wear the signs of their rank, are clad in armour or cloth, and may or may not be entitled to ride a horse or to control of their own bodies (as in the feudal *jus primae noctis*). In other words a network of legal and political constraints regulates the interaction of bodies. We are already in language, which is inseparable from bodies and their mixtures: oaths, laws, blazons, and other collective orderings of utterance. There is no way of understanding these without reference to the acts which they perform and the bodies on which they act. And with their taste for sweeping generalities, Deleuze and Guattari conclude: 'all those things are combined in the Crusades' (St Bernard's 'mot d'ordre' had a very material force).

It is easy, therefore, to understand why the third postulate of linguistics – the existence of linguistic constants and universals – is also rejected. Against the universality sought by science, Deleuze and Guattari emphasize the singularity of linguistic events and the heterogeneity of language. Chomsky and most other scientific linguists aim at the identification of constants (rules of syntax, distinctive features, etc.); but Deleuze and Guattari support Labov in his insistence on the heterogeneity of language, and the multiplicity of dialects, modes of address, etc. They advocate the study of styles, not as individual creations, but as 'orderings of utterance', which create discordances within language, playing one language off against another. 'Style' is their name for the constitutive heterogeneity of language.

BEYOND *DÉLIRE*

If there is no homogeneity in language, there is no point in taking a 'standard' competence as the object of inquiry. Yet linguists typically dismiss dialects and idiolects, or consider them only as variations on the standard language. This is a reflection of linguistic colonialism (consider the fate of Celtic languages in Britain), and of struggles that take place around the dominant language, as in the case of Tess Durbeyfield, who spoke dialect at home and standard English at school. In opposition to all such reductions, Deleuze and Guattari insist on the variousness of idioms: you do not speak the same language to your boss, your beloved or your butcher. But they go further than this. Their study of Kafka (a Czech Jew writing in German) has convinced them that every discourse is permeated by the struggle between 'major' and 'minor' languages. This applies not only on the social level, but also within the individual. 'Major' and 'minor' do not denote types of languages (as Yiddish vs German in the case of Kafka) so much as functions of language. We are all bilingual in some part of our minds, and our (potential) creative use of language is due to this duality. The 'minor' operates within the 'major'. A minor language is subsidiary to a major language, but it attacks it and is a source of perpetual crisis: it questions its dominance and makes it relative. *Délire* is only the climax of this crisis, where the domination of the major language is on the verge of disintegrating: it is therefore part of the minor attempts against domination through language. Outcasts of language, unite! Women, workers, madmen, social, sexual and racial minorities contest the domination of 'rational' major languages. Artaud, Pasolini, Leroi Jones, Kafka draw the sting of the linguistic WASPs.

If the four postulates of linguistics define the structure of rational language, *délire* appears as its negation: it is neither informative nor communicative in a strict sense; it rejects the separation between language and the extralinguistic, between words and bodies; it is heterogeneous and cannot be accounted for through general rules (not a Chomskyan tree, rather a rhizome); and it is the embodiment of the struggle of minor languages within and against dominant ones. But since these postulates are fallacious, *délire* is also the truth of language, its basic form. Hence the study of language must take *délire* as its starting point, preferring *parole* to *langue*, pragmatics to syntax or phonology; and the name of the discipline will be schizo-analysis rather than linguistics. For even if it is all a matter of signs, if the metaphor of coding pervades the text, and semiotics replace economics as the main field of research, this does not

189

mean that language is still at the centre of the picture. There is a 'signifying semiotics' centred on language, but there are also non-signifying semiotics based on gestures, on music, dance, or again on numbers. *Délire* is everywhere: therefore it disappears as such, it is dissolved in the flow of language, for it *is* language. *Mille Plateaux* is indeed the last stage in this particular tradition: with it, it reaches its climax and its end.

Conclusion

It is even more difficult to assess *Anti-Oedipus* and *Mille Plateaux* than *Logique du Sens*. We must resist the facile pleasures of rejection, we must forget about the jargon, we must master the proliferating concepts and non-metaphoric metaphors. We must learn to follow Deleuze and Guattari through the maze of their encyclopedic reading, and listen patiently to their pronouncements about everything, tolerating their delight in shocking the bourgeois intellectual. We even have to forgive their dubious puns ('le pou est un poullulement', *Mille Plateaux*, p. 293), for we know they are all part of a stylistic strategy, that the linguistic means are adapted to the philosophical end.

In a review of *Anti-Oedipus*, René Girard notes the impossibility of global criticism. There is no point in saying that there is more madness than method, for the reproach will be triumphantly welcomed: after all, this is schizo-analysis rather than philosophy. This is probably why, after the first three pages, Girard proceeds to develop his own conception of mimetic desire. So *Anti-Oedipus* and *Mille Plateaux*, like *Logique du Sens*, are reflexive texts, where schizo-analysis is not only theorized but also practised. We are back to the question of genres: in this case the political essay and the picaresque novel.

First, politics. There is an extreme sense of urgency in Deleuze and Guattari's style, a sense of the seriousness of a political task. The philosopher becomes a militant, fighting for the liberation of desire, both inside and outside his text. The paranoid organization of *Anti-Oedipus*, with its regular progression (from negative, or critical, to positive tasks) gives way to the schizophrenic maze of *Mille Plateaux*, constructed around its own lines of flight, its own flows of desire, with their plateaux of intensity. The machine works: what it produces is arrangements of desire and *délire*. It may not mean anything, but its 'intervention', to use a

Leninist cliché, on the philosophical front, alters the situation. Deleuze and Guattari have made it yet more difficult to accept the unhistorical generalizations of psychoanalysis.[23] If we accept Barthes's definition of myth as the transformation of history into nature, then Deleuze and Guattari have exposed the myth of psychoanalysis, its transformation of the historical structure of the family into a natural order.

But their work is also a picaresque novel. The philosopher's line of flight takes them to strange places, and their Wonderland is as rich as Carroll's. We follow nomads on their trek through the desert; we see their war-machine capturing the State; the world is teeming with sources of danger and excitement, and every reader becomes Roderick Random discovering London. Nor are the wonders limited to the landscape described: the language, too, is worthy of that tradition. There is an extraordinary linguistic productivity in *Mille Plateaux* – coinages ('la visagéité)[24] or concepts ('la ritournelle') which even my own French palate, trained by years of *foie gras* and abstruse concepts, finds difficult to savour. There is no repression in *Mille Plateaux*, no over-coding of the flow of desire, no restriction on the *délire* which, deep down, language always is.

So the question of enjoyment must be settled first. 'Le plaisir du texte', to use Barthes's phrase, runs high in *Anti-Oedipus* and *Mille Plateaux*. Barthes found that the three unlikely partners, Sade, Fourier, and Loyola had two things in common: a taste for nomenclature (for combination and syntax), and a style, the 'volume' (to use Barthes's metaphor) of *écriture*.[25] Perhaps Deleuze and Guattari should be added to the list. They like enumerating elements ('one and one and one and one': the beginning of all Nonsense), but they also *write*. Schizo-analysis is, if it is anything, a writing machine, a style.

But pleasure is not sufficient. Will the text last? Will it still be read in fifteen years' time? And is schizo-analysis likely to develop into a branch of psychiatry? The answer to the first two questions is, I think, positive; to the last, negative. This is due to the ambiguities of Deleuze and Guattari's involvement with psychoanalysis. After all, rejection does not prevent incorporation. This is clear from the case of the psychoanalytic concept of 'investment' or cathexis. Robert Castel says that Freud had two 'lines' on the question of cathexis. Sometimes he places it in a social structure; but elsewhere, he reduces institutions to forms of psychic cathexis, and explains social organizations in terms of psychological conflict. The second direction leads to a dead-end; but the first shows the importance of individual investment in social and political structures. Deleuze and Guattari have taken more from Freud than they think. They obviously believe in collective desire and social-historical *délire*; but they also adopt the second line, albeit in a less crude form. They interpret history from the point of view of desire, and therefore miss the social *qua* social. The non-metaphors of machine, flow and coding end up having a reductive effect: desire eats society away, like the worm which devoured Schreber's lungs.

So we are back with the problem of metaphor. The rejection of metaphor (that 'hysteria of signs', *Mille Plateaux*, p. 147) changes our conception of language. The problematic of lack and excess, of origin and repetition has given way to another – that of the literal production of *délire*: abundance, not lack, flight and 'devenir', not origin. Perhaps this is the real reason why *Anti-Oedipus* and *Mille Plateaux* deserve to survive: they give the first positive account of *délire* as constitutive of language.

The main point is that Deleuze and Guattari have abandoned the point of view of representation, which governs psychoanalysis. Although they are anything but orthodox, they are Marxist at least in adopting the point of view of production. This is what gives strength to their critique of fantasies, of ideology, and of the generalizations and reductions of all interpretations.

But the result is full of ambiguities, and these are perhaps more interesting than the achievements. There are at least three major ones. The first is Deleuze and Guattari's insistence on singularities: individual arrangements of desire rather than reductive generalizations; particular historical situations rather than global class analysis. But even when they assert the value of singularities, they are bound to use general concepts, such as fascism. Even if schizo-analysis makes no claim to be a science in the ordinary sense of the term, it has to conform to certain general rules, and the rule which forbids recourse to general rules of interpretation is itself a general rule of interpretation. A familiar paradox. You can enjoy or repeat the patient's individual delirium; but if you want to understand its production, you will need to go to another logical level, that of general concepts. In the end, you will not escape interpretation.

The second ambiguity concerns Deleuze and Guattari's attitude to history. Their critique of the unhistorical concepts used by Freud (*the* unconscious, *the* family: the multiplication of definite articles indicates that we are moving from culture to nature, from historical analysis to myth) is a powerful one. But, like the Althusserian conception of ideology, their own critique ultimately falls back on unhistorical concepts: like ideology, fascism is both historical and unhistorical. Nomadic tribes, we are told, forever fight the State, and their war-machine eventually captures it. Which tribe? and which desert? The price for such sweeping generalities is high: the disappearance of concrete historical analysis. Deleuze and Guattari manage to outdo the dogmatic Marxists on their own slippery ground, and their periodization is even more problematic.

The third ambiguity is a more general version of the first. I have noted that the logic of Deleuze and Guattari's texts is one of inclusion, not separation. Yet, even in *Mille Plateaux*, they proceed through conceptual dichotomies. Even if these do not exclude, even if boundaries are crossed, they still work through contrasts: paranoia vs schizophrenia, molar vs molecular. Deleuze and Guattari may admire Artaud, but they do not succeed in reproducing his style – or at least they always preserve the distinction between philosophy and *délire*, practice and reflection. They follow lines of flight, but they implicitly respect certain boundaries (although, as we have seen, *Mille Plateaux* is distinctly less 'paranoid' than *Anti-Oedipus*).

These ambiguities are all present in Deleuze and Guattari's conception of language. There are two aspects to this. The conception of language developed in *Anti-Oedipus* revolves around a critique of what Lacan calls the symbolic: the dialectic of excess and lack, rules of syntax, the laws of language. They opt for *parole* against *langue*, style against grammar, dialects or idiolects against standard languages, pragmatics against syntax: the individual, or what they call the 'minor' against the general; the material (speech acts are material in so far as they are acts) against the abstract. This is the mentality of the professional smuggler: give me a frontier, and I shall cross it; give me a rule, and I shall break it. But, as we saw in Chapter 2, the crossing of a linguistic frontier is an ambiguous act, since it acknowledges the rule which it breaks. Smugglers would be lost without frontiers and prohibitions: they are merely the shadows of customs officials. A minor language exists only because a major one oppresses it. You cannot escape from the symbolic any more than you can from interpretation: rejection is only a form of Freudian denial.

The return of the denied can be observed in the development from *Anti-Oedipus* to *Mille Plateaux*. In the former Deleuze and Guattari broke with one tenet of the tradition we have explored: the centrality of language. Language is put in its place, semiosis ceases to be a necessary filter on our perception of the external world. But semiotics pervades *Mille Plateaux*. Everything becomes a matter of signs again. There is no direct relationship to the external world, no direct speech, only the indirect repetition of an already uttered discourse. It is true that this is no mere return to a view of language as a mediation between ourselves and the world. Deleuze and Guattari's emphasis on pragmatics means that there *is* a direct connection between ourselves and the world, our praxis, our acts (language, instead of being an ideal abstract system, is made up of speech-acts and slogans – propositions endowed with material force). It is rather that there is no direct reference, no direct relationship between language and the extralinguistic. Instead of being a series of propositions referring to the world, a text is an unstable mixture of discourses, a locus for tensions and contradictions. The concept of 'minority' developed in *Kafka* turns out to be central.

These last two pages are an instance of paranoia: they express my resistance to the schizophrenic lines of flight in Deleuze and Guattari, my attempt to triangulate, interpret and reduce their work. But, of course, resistance implies fascination: the grandeur of Deleuze and Guattari, and the ultimate answer to my question ('will their work last?'; not 'what does it mean?' but 'what effect does it produce?') is that they compel the readers to cross the frontiers of their own thought, if only for a while, and to consider their own discourse without the comfort and protection of ready-made ideas.

Notes

1 Deleuze and Guattari, *Kafka* (Paris: Minuit 1975), p. 40.
2 G. Lakoff and M. Johnson, *Metaphors we live by* (Chicago: University of Chicago Press 1980).
3 cf. Deleuze and Guattari, *Mille Plateaux*, pp. 464–8.
4 The first chapter was published independently as *Rhizome* (1976).
5 G. Bateson, *Steps to an Ecology of Mind* (Paladin 1973), p. 85. Bateson uses the term 'plateau of intensity' to describe the interactive behaviour of the Balinese mother and her child: she sexually teases her child but curbs the intensity of the child's reaction. Balinese society is described as being in a 'steady' (as opposed to a 'schismogenetic') state, where tendencies towards competitive behaviour are discouraged. In this context 'plateau of intensity' is contrasted with 'climax' ('in general the lack of climax is characteristic for Balinese music, drama, and other art forms'). Bateson is an obvious influence on Deleuze and Guattari: in his work one finds the link between anthropology and psychiatry which is crucial to their position. After

one has read Bateson, who talks of flows of intensity and applies Von Neumann and Morgenstern's theory of games to primitive societies, Deleuze and Guattari seem less eccentric.

6 A. Stéphane, *L'Univers contestationnaire* (Paris: Payot 1969).

7 One can see here the influence of Franz Fanon, the West Indian psychiatrist who joined the Algerian liberation movement.

8 W. Reich, *The Mass Psychology of Fascism* (Pelican 1975; first published 1933).

9 This expression seems to be self-contradictory. But Deleuze and Guattari contest the implicit reduction of semiotics to written or spoken language: they wish to extend the boundaries of the study of language, in order to include gestures, dancing, etc. See the last paragraph of the section 'A critique of linguistics' in this chapter.

10 The extent to which the terms can be opposed in the psychiatric tradition is debatable (in the French psychiatric tradition, they usually are). Psychiatric terms have a long and complex history. There is no doubt that Deleuze and Guattari are *forcing* the terms into an opposition: but this is their (philosophical) privilege.

11 I. Wallerstein, *The Modern World System* (New York 1974).

12 Frank Kermode's *The Sense of an Ending* (New York: Oxford University Press 1966) studies the tradition of the apocalypse in religion and literature.

13 In this respect, *Anti-Oedipus* is conventional. It has a starting point (ch. 1: 'Desiring-Machines'); it proceeds in an orderly fashion with its critique of Freud and Marx (chs 2 and 3); and it ends when the positive goal has been reached (ch. 4: 'Introduction to schizo-analysis'). This structure is abandoned in *Mille Plateaux*: a thousand plateaux, a series of independent chapters, not progressing towards any goal (the 'conclusion' is just a summary of the main themes in the guise of a systematic index of notions), and which can be read in any order. *Mille Plateaux* no longer has an ending or a beginning; as Kermode would put it, quoting Sir Philip Sydney, it stays 'in the middest'.

14 One might add that it is, third, the product of a tradition, scarcely mentioned by Deleuze and Guattari. For beneath the obvious allusion to Marx, another kind of machine is referred to, found in the 'mechanistic' tradition which produced Descartes's 'animaux-machines', the eighteenth-century metaphor of the world as one large clock (wound up once and for all by God) and the taste for automata (from Vaucanson to Frankenstein). The climax was probably reached in La Mettrie's *L'Homme-Machine*. It is interesting to note that in this tradition, too, 'the machine' is not a metaphor: animals for Descartes or man for La Mettrie were, literally, machines.

15 This type of situation is common in fantastic tales. cf., for instance, J. Meade Falkner's *The Lost Stradivarius*.

16 The origin of this maxim is in Marx's *1844 Manuscripts*, third manuscript, 'Private property and communism'.

17 One would find a rich crop of mythical versions of the body without organs in medieval and Renaissance grotesques. The world map in Hereford cathedral represents strange creatures on the southern ridge of the world, men without mouths, skiapods who have only one foot which they use as an umbrella, etc. . . . Borges's *Book of Imaginary Beings* is about bodies striving to do without organs.

18 Desire differs from need in that it cannot attain fulfilment: it is an ever-renewed failure, a constant yearning and disappointment, a hesitation. But there are two ways of conceiving this. We have encountered the first in the psychoanalytic tradition: it is a failure of repetition, of striving after a lost primary object; desire is an attempt to retrace one's steps, to fill a necessary

195

lack, to make the impossible real. But desire can also be conceived as a forward movement, a flight towards an object which always eludes our grasp, the attempt, never successful but never frustrating, to reach the unattainable by exploring the paths of the possible. Deleuze and Guattari oppose the psychoanalytic tradition because they hold to the second conception of desire: it is certainly more joyous, and probably more liberating.

19 Based on a novel by Joseph Kessel.

20 The Lacanian concept of 'the real' belongs to the age-old tradition of negative theology: the 'real' is conceived negatively, as what is neither imaginary nor symbolic, as the impossible, the missing primary object, death. Deleuze and Guattari reject this, and all other theology: *Anti-Oedipus* is a pagan celebration of the positivity of reality and desire.

21 cf. *Dialogues*, p. 164: 'Broadly speaking, you can tell a Marxist from the way he defines a society through its contradictions, particularly class contradictions. We, on the other hand, state that in a society everything takes flight, that a society is defined through its lines of flight.'

22 This whole operation consists in reversing the course of metaphors, and taking them literally. Thus, the 'social pyramid' becomes a concrete shape, projected on to the map (a geographic and social inscription: roads, canals, administrative boundaries), and on to the king's body, with the well-known legal and political consequences: the king has two bodies, he can never die, etc. (see E. Kantorowicz, *The King's Two Bodies* (Princeton, NJ: Princeton University Press 1957)). The fictions of Deleuze and Guattari may sound a little wild: but no more so than the legal fictions which are a particular source of pride in the English legal system.

23 'Yet more difficult', because they are not the first to make the point, which has always been part of the Marxist critique of psychoanalysis. But in contemporary French culture, where psychoanalysis tends to play a dominant role, the forceful reiteration of a fifty-year-old criticism can have important philosophical effects.

24 The idea of a semiotics of faces is not as strange as it appears at first sight. At least, Deleuze and Guattari are not the only ones to propound it: Chomsky has predicted (*Rules and Representations* (Blackwell 1980), p. 248) the development of a 'universal grammar of faces'.

25 Roland Barthes, *Sade, Fourier, Loyola* (Paris: Seuil 1971) (English translation, by R. Miller (Jonathan Cape 1977)).

Further reading

1 The main works of Gilles Deleuze and Felix Guattari are *L'Anti-Oedipe* (Paris: Minuit 1972) (page numbers in this chapter refer to this edition). English translation by R. Hurley, M. Seem and H. R. Lane, *Anti-Oedipus* (New York 1977; The Athlone Press 1985); *Kafka* (Paris: Minuit 1975); and *Mille Plateaux* (Paris: Minuit 1980). The first chapter of *Mille Plateaux* was published independently as *Rhizome* (Paris: Minuit 1976). In addition, Guattari, during the same period, published *La Révolution Moléculaire* (1st edn, Paris: Editions Recherches 1977; 2nd, revised edn, Paris: UGE 1980; English translation, *Molecular Revolution*, Penguin 1984); and *L'Inconscient Machinique* (Paris: Editions Recherches 1979). While Deleuze's publications are *Francis Bacon: Logique de la sensation*, 2 vols (Paris: Editions de la Différence 1981); *Superpositions*, in collaboration with Carmelo Bene (Paris: Minuit 1979); and *Image-Mouvement* (Paris: Minuit 1983), the first text of the post-Guattari period, in which he goes back to Bergson. I have also used two shorter texts: G. Deleuze and F. Guattari, *Politique et Psychanalyse* (Paris: Des mots perdus 1977), on the critique of interpretation; and F. Guattari, 'Machine et Structure', *Change*, **12** (1972), pp. 49–59, on the critique

of the notion of structure (the article was written in 1969). The second part of Deleuze's *Entretiens* with Claire Parnet (cf. Chapter 3) deals with the *Anti-Oedipus* period.

2 The secondary literature on Deleuze and Guattari is limited. Apart from some of the items mentioned above, Chapter 3, the most important publication is *Critique*, **306** (Paris 1972), which contains two reviews of *Anti-Oedipus*; 'Capitalisme energumène', by Jean-François Lyotard; and 'Système du délire' by René Girard. One may also consult *Les Chemins de l'Anti-Oedipe* (Toulouse: Privat 1974); *Esprit*, **12** (Paris 1972); and *Sémiotexte*, **2** no. 3 (1977): all three publications are devoted to *Anti-Oedipus*.

3 Deleuze and Guattari's reading is encyclopaedic, and it is impossible to trace all their sources and inspirations. Here are some of the most important. On interpretation, they draw on the French tradition of political critique of psychoanalysis (R. Castel, *Le Psychanalysme* (Paris: Maspero 1973); cf. the work of F. Fanon, for instance, *Les Damnés de la Terre* (Paris: Maspero 1966) – English translation, *The Wretched of the Earth* (Penguin 1969)). They also refer to the Anglo-Saxon antipsychiatric tradition, especially to David Cooper (cf., for instance, *The Language of Madness* (Allen Lane 1978)) and to the work of Gregory Bateson (*Steps to an Ecology of Mind* (Paladin 1973)). On politics, and especially on Fascism, their point of reference is obviously Wilhelm Reich, *The Mass Psychology of Fascism* (Penguin 1975). On language, they draw on the Anglo-Saxon tradition of pragmatics and discourse analysis (cf., for instance, J. R. Ross, 'On decarative sentences', in R. A. Jacobs and P. S. Rosenbaum, *Readings in English Transformational Grammar* (Waltam, Mass.: Glinn and Co. 1970); cf. also William Labov, *Language and the Inner City* (Philadelphia: University of Pennsylvania Press 1972), and *Sociolinguistic Patterns* (Blackwell 1980)). They also use two other types of texts, the European structuralism of Louis Hjelmslev (*Prolegomena to a theory of speech* (Baltimore: Indiana University Press 1953)), and Marxist linguistics, notably V. V. Vološinov, *Marxism and the philosophy of language* (New York: Seminar Press 1973) (for a French work in the same tradition, cf. P. Bourdieu, *Ce que parler veut dire* (Paris: Fayard 1982)).

Conclusion

I have attempted to show that the notion of *délire* has been central to two distinct but related traditions at work in contemporary French philosophy. The first, which was considered in Chapters 2 and 4, uses linguistic and psychoanalytic concepts; whereas the second, expounded in Chapters 3 and 5, is based on the rereading of certain texts of classical philosophy (the Stoics, for instance), and draws on the findings of psychiatry and political economy.

The first tradition is centred on the concepts of language and the subject. It conceives language as a system, a set of rules (but rules of a particular kind, some of which are unconscious), and also as a set of frontiers, which are crossed in various other types of discourse, such as *délire*. The subject, a structure without a centre, is the embodiment of the constraints of the linguistic system – constraints which are suspended in *délire*, as a result of which the subject dissolves. The second tradition reverses this point of view. It deals with flows of energy (*libido*), not constraints; with machines, not structures; with the emergence of sense out of nonsense, not with rules and frontiers; with the production of meaning, not with its reduction by interpretation. For this tradition, the important question is not 'what does this mean?' but 'what is it used for and how does it work?'

In the first tradition, the function of *délire* is negative: it is a symptom of the dissolution of linguistic order. Hopefully, it is only a temporary aberration of discourse, and the analyst's task is to tame it. Interpretation is a form of cure. In the second tradition, the function of *délire* is positive. It is the substratum of all discourse, a necessary stage in the emergence of meaning, and one with which every speaker has to come to terms. These two versions are called by Deleuze and Guattari the paranoid and the schizophrenic forms of *délire*. Frontiers are opposed to lines of flight, the point of view of separation (between what is relevant and what is not: the necessary first step in the construction of a system) to the point of view of inclusion (where nothing is irrelevant as long as it works). In the first version, *délire* is an object of scientific study, treated by the analyst with the requisite distance; in the second, there is no such distance, and *délire* is necessarily reflexive, invading the theory that seeks to account for it.

From these two traditions, it is possible to extract two main theses on *délire*. The first tradition holds the weaker thesis, that *délire* as symptom is important because of the light it casts on the workings of ordinary language. Studying *délire* enables us to become conscious of the limits of structural linguistics, but also, conversely, of its value. For the special case of *délire* shows that the founding dichotomies of linguistics permit only a partial account of language. Thus, *délire* blurs the distinction between *langue* and *parole* (behind the delirious speech, there appears to be no fixed and stable system of *langue*); it is an instance of the domination of the signifier over the signified (and consequently the signs it uses are unstable); it casts doubt on the distinction between the literal and the metaphorical uses of words. The other Saussure is in fact an anti-Saussure. Or he would be, if this attack on the concepts of linguistics did not smack of Freudian denial. For *délire* remains a special case, whose crossing of frontiers enables the analyst to plot them more accurately.

The second tradition proposes a much stronger thesis. *Délire* is present in every utterance, as an element of possession, and also of creativity. All texts are in some way delirious, and consciousness, the control of the subject over his own utterances, represses a deeper *délire*. The advice is let yourself go. Do your own thing, scream your own screams. You must forget frontiers if you want to break new ground. Don't be a smuggler, the days of Jamaica Inn are past, be an astronaut or a Saharan nomad. In other words, take risks and go against the grain of common sense. This thesis offers no objective assessment of a state of affairs; it is rather a call for action, a *mot d'ordre* as Deleuze and Guattari would say. It does not purport to study or describe *délire* but to practise it. Or rather, it blurs the distinction between theory and practice: the theory of *délire* must itself be delirious. This type of reflexivity applies to *Capitalisme et Schizophrénie*. It also applies to this book.

It is time to settle the question of reflexivity. I have expressed the hope that this book will not be entirely delirious. I must show now in what way it is. For if the stronger thesis is correct, there is an inescapable element of *délire* in any use of language – and it must be particularly important in a book on *délire*. In the light of the weaker thesis I might describe a few symptoms; in the light of the stronger, I must admit an element of compulsion.

The symptoms are mild enough. They can be found in the difficulties, perhaps even the impossibility of the task. I have been writing a book, not in my native language, about untranslatable concepts, and dealing with theories that protect themselves from critical intrusion with a barrier of stylistic obscurity or conceptual intricacy. The first obstacle should not be exaggerated. Writing in a foreign language is common enough, perhaps even not a symptom at all: the relations of dominance between English and French have changed, and gone are the days when 'le chevalier Hamilton' and William Beckford preferred to tell their tales in French. But the other two obstacles have proved more serious. The very easiness of the translation of most of the concepts involved shows the impossibility of cultural acclimatization: *énonciation*? 'enunciation'! *déterritorialisation*? 'deterritorialization'! It is not only the words that refuse to cross the Channel, it is also, perhaps, the subject matter. And even if we cast aside the problem of translation, the theories I have dealt with – this is part of their fascination – do not invite easy acquaintance. The difficulty of Lacan's style is deliberate, and Deleuze's peculiar talent for *fuite en avant* makes him difficult to follow. (There is a considerable difference between this style of philosophy and the easy conversational style which is one of the main charms of some Anglo-Saxon philosophers, Austin for instance.) Attempting to bridge the cultural gap, and to enter by force into well-protected theories is a mild symptom of *délire*. The impossibility of the task, Lacan would say, makes it more real.

So far, the term '*délire*' has been misused; the symptoms are too mild. But there is also an element of compulsion in each of them. My interest in *délire* started when I read Wolfson's first book. As I write this conclusion, I have to acknowledge that – without being aware of it when I started – I have placed myself in Wolfson's position: in writing a text in a foreign language, I must, like him, be settling accounts with my mother tongue. That I have chosen to write a book of philosophy rather than memoirs of my nervous illness indicates only that my form of *délire* is paranoid rather than schizophrenic. There was also compulsion in my desire to translate the untranslatable, to bridge the cultural gap – at best a hazardous undertaking, which requires the irresponsibility of *délire*. To use the customary metaphor, I dwell in two cultures, and this book is an attempt to bring them together. Surely there is at least a modicum of *délire* in writing in English a book about theories so typically French that some of the main currents of Anglo-Saxon philosophy would dismiss them as nonsense, in the technical sense. (But the Deleuzian tradition, as we have seen, considers nonsense as one of its main fields of study.) And, finally, there was also an element of compulsion, or possession, in setting out to write a book largely concerned with the philosophy of Gilles Deleuze. In doing this I fall under the curse he has placed on all disciples. Since he refuses to be a master, I, as a potential disciple, find myself in a double-bind. But the compulsion runs deeper: the main reason why I have written about Deleuze is perhaps an urge to shake off the fascination he holds for me, or, in the approved fashion of Harold Bloom, to get his system out of mine.

Perhaps a more serious point is also at stake here, concerning reflexivity. When I attempted to appraise Deleuze's philosophy, I pointed out some characteristics of his way of writing philosophy which more generally belong to the French style of philosophizing. (They were his refusal to be confined within the habitual boundaries of philosophy; his constant retracing of steps and rereading of older texts; and his systematic misprision of these texts.) I think these characteristics mark an awareness of the element of *délire* that is present, according to the stronger thesis, in every utterance. A Wittgensteinian would perhaps describe this as a form of disease: the wheels revolve, but the machinery is out of order; language is deranged and nothing is produced. A French way of describing the same situation could go like this: the wheels revolve, there is even a certain amount of free-wheeling, for the machinery has taken over, and works of its own accord. Language is delirious, and much is produced; not clarifications, but concepts. The process involves many risks (not least those of *délire* as mere symptom) but the reward is considerable: the machine works, and philosophical effects occur.

This book is no exception to the reflexive *délire* that pervades French philosophy. If the Anglo-Saxon reader still finds it unpalatable, I can only make the answer the March Hare gave the Mad Hatter when accused by him of having spoilt his watch by filling the case with butter: 'it was the *best* butter which I used'.

Index